TOUCH IN VIRTUAL ENVIRONMENTS

Haptics and the Design of Interactive Systems

ISBN 0-13-065097-8

IMSC Press Multimedia Series

Integrated Media Systems Center

ANDREW TESCHER, Series Editor, *Compression Science Corporation*

Advisory Editors

LEONARDO CHIARIGLIONE, *CSELT*
TARIQ S. DURRANI, *University of Strathclyde*
JEFF GRALNICK, *E-splosion Consulting, LLC*
CHRYSOSTOMOS L. "MAX" NIKIAS, *University of Southern California*
ADAM C. POWELL III, *The Freedom Forum*

▶ Desktop Digital Video Production

    Frederic Jones

▶ Touch in Virtual Environments:
Haptics and the Design of Interactive Systems

    *Edited by Margaret L. McLaughlin,
João P. Hespanha, and Gaurav S. Sukhatme*

▶ The MPEG-4 Book

    Fernando Pereira and Touradj Ebrahimi

▶ Multimedia Fundamentals, Volume 1:
Media Coding and Content Analysis

    Ralf Steinmetz and Klara Nahrstedt

Integrated Media Systems Center

The Integrated Media Systems Center (IMSC), a National Science Foundation Engineering Research Center in the University of Southern California's School of Engineering, is a preeminent multimedia and Internet research center. IMSC seeks to develop integrated media systems that dramatically transform the way we work, communicate, learn, teach, and entertain. In an integrated media system, advanced media technologies combine, deliver, and transform information in the form of images, video, audio, animation, graphics, text, and haptics (touch-related technologies). IMSC Press, in partnership with Prentice Hall, publishes cutting-edge research on multimedia and Internet topics. IMSC Press is part of IMSC's educational outreach program.

TOUCH IN
VIRTUAL ENVIRONMENTS

Haptics and the Design of Interactive Systems

Margaret L. McLaughlin
João P. Hespanha
Gaurav S. Sukhatme
University of Southern California

Prentice Hall PTR
Upper Saddle River, NJ 07458
www.phptr.com

Library of Congress Cataloging-in-Publication Data
McLaughlin, Margaret L.
    Touch in virtual environments : haptics and the design of interactive systems / Margaret
  L. McLaughlin, João Hespanha, Gaurav Sukhatme.
    p. cm. — (Prentice Hall IMSC Press multimedia series)
    Includes bibliographic references and index.
    ISBN 0-13-065097-8
    1. Human-computer interaction. 2. Virtual reality. 3. Touch. I. Hesppanha, João II. Sukhatme, Gaurav. III.
  Title. IV. Series.

    QA76.9.H85 M42 2001
    006—dc21   2001036948

Editorial/Production Supervision: *Joan L. McNamara*
Acquisitions Editor: *Bernard Goodwin*
Editorial Assistant: *Michelle Vincenti*
Marketing Manager: *Dan DePasquale*
Manufacturing Manager: *Alexis R. Heydt-Long*
Cover Design: *Anthony Gemmellaro*
Cover Design Direction: *Jerry Votta*
Project Coordinator: *Anne R. Garcia*

© 2002 by Prentice Hall PTR
Prentice-Hall, Inc.
Upper Saddle River, New Jersey 07458

Cover image created by Immersion Corporation for the CyberGlove® product.

Prentice Hall books are widely used by corporations and government agencies for training, marketing, and resale.

The publisher offers discounts on this book when ordered in bulk quantities. For more information, contact:
Corporate Sales Department
Prentice Hall PTR
One Lake Street
Upper Saddle River, NJ 07458
Phone: 800-382-3419; Fax: 201-236-7141; Email (Internet): corpsales@prenhall.com

All product names mentioned herein are the trademarks of their respective owners.

Printed in the United States of America
10 9 8 7 6 5 4 3 2 1

ISBN: 0-13-065097-8 ✓

Pearson Education LTD.
Pearson Education Australia PTY, Limited
Pearson Education Singapore, Pte. Ltd
Pearson Education North Asia Ltd
Pearson Education Canada, Ltd.
Pearson Educación de Mexico, S.A. de C.V.
Pearson Education—Japan
Pearson Education Malaysia, Pte. Ltd

Contents

Preface

The *haptic* interface is becoming an increasingly important component of immersive systems. Haptics refers to the modality of touch and the sensation of shape and texture an observer feels when exploring a virtual object, such as a three-dimensional model of a tool, instrument, or art object. Researchers in the field are interested in developing, refining, and testing haptic devices and interfaces, and applying findings from psychological studies of human touch to the simulation of the tactile sense in virtual environments. *Touch in Virtual Environments: Haptics and the Design of Interactive Systems* is an outgrowth of a one-day conference on haptics held at the University of Southern California in February, 2001, sponsored by USC's Integrated Media Systems Center, a National Science Foundation Engineering Research Center, the Annenberg School for Communication at USC, and the IEEE Control Systems Society. Many of the chapters were first presented as papers at that venue. The contributors to this volume, who represent a variety of academic disciplines and institutional affiliations, are researchers who can fairly be said to be working at the cutting edge of engineering science, in an area that is just beginning to have an impact in the design of immersive systems.

In Chapters 1–8 of this book, the contributors ponder questions about the *haptic interface*, such as: How can current state-of-the-art haptic displays be improved via better sensing? What are the software tools and models needed to facilitate multi-user tactile exploration of shared virtual environments? How can we optimize low-level force control for haptic devices? What algorithms and techniques are needed to convey the feel of deformable objects? How do we capture users' exploration with haptic devices? How do we compress haptic exploration data so that it becomes possible to store or transmit long interactive sessions? In Chapters 9–12, the contributors consider the impact of the unpredictable, and highly variable, "human-in-the-loop." They examine questions like the following: How can we make haptic displays more usable for blind and visually impaired users? What are the differences between perceiving texture with the bare skin and with a probe, and how do factors like probe size and speed contribute? What can we learn about human thresholds for detecting small haptic effects that will be useful for the design of hand-held devices? To what extent do vision, sound, and haptics complement or interfere with one another in multimodal interactive systems?

In addition to exploring basic research issues in haptics such as acquisition of models, contact detection, force feedback, compression, capture, collaboration, and human factors, the contributors to *Touch in Virtual Environments* describe in detail several promising applications. A primary application area for haptics has been in surgical simulation and medical training. Haptics has also been incorporated into scientific visualization, providing an intuitive interface to complex displays of biological and geoscientific data. In some projects haptic displays have been used as alternative input devices for painting, sculpting and computer-assisted design. There have also been instances of the application of haptics to military training and simulation, providing an accurate source of orientation information in land, sea, and aerospace environments. In Chapters 13–15 the reader will find accounts of applications to telesurgery and surgical simulation, sign language recognition, and museum display.

Many persons contributed to the success of the "*Touch in Virtual Environments*" conference from which this volume emerged. In particular we would like to thank IMSC's visionary leader, Max Nikias, now Dean of USC's School of Engineering, for his encouragement and the substantial investment of time and resources that he has made in USC's program of haptics research. Thanks also are due to Geoffrey Cowan, Dean of the USC Annenberg School, and Patti Riley, Director of the School of Communication, for their continuing support of the kind of interdisciplinary collaboration needed to make haptics a human-centered engineering science. We are also grateful to Linda Wright, IMSC's Events Coordinator, for her outstanding efforts in creating a hospitable environment for our haptics conference, and to the Annenberg School's Rad Probst and Geoff Baum and IMSC's Lisette Garcia-Miller, Gloria Halfacre, Rick Keir, Sue Lewis, Issac Maya, Regina Morton, Nichole Phillips, Sandy Sawchuk, Seth Scafani, Ann Spurgeon, Allan Weber, Cheryl Weinberger, and our students Minoo Akbarian, Rajiv Garg, and Weirong Zhu for their generous gift of time and toil in helping to make the event a success. We would like to thank Andy Tescher, of compression|SCIENCE, Inc., Chair of IMSC's Scientific Advisory Board and Editor of IMSC Press, and Bernard Goodwin of Prentice Hall for their encouragement throughout this process. Finally, we extend our appreciation to the contributors for the many hours of thought-provoking discussion they have provided for us, and, we hope, for you as the reader.

Margaret L. McLaughlin, João Hespanha, and Gaurav Sukhatme
Los Angeles, California
October 2001

Introduction to Haptics

Margaret L. McLaughlin, João P. Hespanha, and Gaurav S. Sukhatme

Haptics refers to the modality of touch and associated sensory feedback. Researchers working in the area are concerned with the development, testing, and refinement of tactile and force feedback devices and supporting software that permit users to sense ("feel") and manipulate three-dimensional virtual objects with respect to such features as shape, weight, surface textures, and temperature. In addition to basic psychophysical research on human haptics, and issues in machine haptics such as collision detection, force feedback, and haptic data compression, work is being done in application areas such as surgical simulation, medical training, scientific visualization, and assistive technology for the blind and visually impaired.

How can a device emulate the sense of touch? Let us consider one of the devices from SensAble Technologies. The 3 DOF (degrees-of-freedom) PHANToM is a small robot arm with three revolute joints, each connected to a computer-controlled electric DC motor. The tip of the device is attached to a stylus that is held by the user. By sending appropriate voltages to the motors, it is possible to exert up to 1.5 pounds of force at the tip of the stylus, in any direction.

The basic principle behind haptic rendering is simple: Every millisecond or so, the computer that controls the PHANToM reads the joint encoders to determine the precise position of the stylus. It then compares this position to those of the virtual objects the user is trying to touch. If the user is away from all the virtual objects, a zero voltage is sent to the motors and the user is free to move the stylus (as if exploring empty space). However, if the system detects a collision between the stylus and one of the virtual objects, it drives the motors so as to exert on the user's hand (through the stylus) a force along the exterior normal to the surface being penetrated. In practice, the user is prevented from penetrating the virtual object *just as if the stylus collided with a real object that transmits a reaction to the user's hand.* Different haptic devices—such as Immersion Corporation's CyberGrasp—operate under the same principle but with different mechanical actuation systems for force generation.

Although the basic principles behind haptics are simple, there are significant technical challenges, such as the construction of the physical devices (cf. Chapter 4), real-time collision detection (cf. Chapters 2 and 5), simulation of complex mechanical systems for precise computation of the reaction forces (cf. Chapter 2), and force control (cf. Chapters 3 and 5). Below we provide an overview of haptics research; we consider *haptic devices*, *applications*, *haptic rendering*, and *human factors* issues.

HAPTIC DEVICES

Researchers have been interested in the potential of force feedback devices such as stylus-based masters like SensAble's PHANToM (Salisbury, Brock, Massie, Swarup, & Zilles, 1995; Salisbury & Massie, 1994) as alternative or supplemental input devices to the mouse, keyboard, or joystick. As discussed above, the PHANToM is a small, desk-grounded robot that permits simulation of single fingertip contact with virtual objects through a thimble or stylus. It tracks the *x, y,* and *z* Cartesian coordinates and pitch, roll, and yaw of the virtual probe as it moves about a three-dimensional workspace, and its actuators communicate forces back to the user's fingertips as it detects collisions with virtual objects, simulating the sense of touch. The CyberGrasp, from Immersion Corporation, is an exoskeletal device that fits over a 22 DOF CyberGlove, providing force feedback. The CyberGrasp is used in conjunction with a position tracker to measure the position and orientation of the forearm in three-dimensional space. (A newly released model of the CyberGrasp is self-contained and does not require an external tracker.) Similar to the CyberGrasp is the Rutgers Master II (Burdea, 1996; Gomez, 1998; Langrana, Burdea, Ladeiji, & Dinsmore, 1997), which has an actuator platform mounted on the palm that gives force feedback to four fingers. Position tracking is done by the Polhmeus Fastrak.

Alternative approaches to haptic sensing have employed vibrotactile display, which applies multiple small force vectors to the fingertip. For example, Ikei, Wakamatsu, and Fukuda (1997) used photographs of objects and a contact pin array to transmit tactile sensations of the surface of objects. Each pin in the array vibrates commensurate with the local intensity (brightness) of the surface area, with image intensity roughly correlated with the height of texture protrusions. There is currently a joint effort underway at MIT and Carnegie Mellon (Srinivasan, 2001) to explore the incorporation of microelectromechanical systems (MEMS) actuator arrays into haptic devices and wearables. Researchers at the University of Wisconsin are experimenting with tactile strips containing an array of sensors that can be attached to various kinds of force-feedback devices (Tyler, 2001). Howe (1994) notes that vibrations are particularly helpful in certain kinds of sensing tasks, such as assessing surface roughness or detecting system events (for example, contact and slip in manipulation control).

Researchers at the Fraunhofer Institute for Computer Graphics in Darmstadt have developed a glove-like device they call the ThermoPad, a haptic temperature display based on Peltier elements and simple heat transfer models. They are able to simulate not only the "environmental" temperature but also the sensation of heat or cold one experiences when grasping or colliding with an object. At the University of Tsukuba in Japan, Iwata, Yano, and Hashimoto (1997) are using the HapticMaster, a 6 DOF device with a ball grip that can be replaced by various real tools for surgical simulations and other specialized applications. A novel type of haptic display is the Haptic Screen (Iwata, Yano, and Hashimoto, 1997), a device with a rubberized elastic surface with actuators, each with force sensors, underneath. The surface of the Haptic Screen can be deformed with the naked hand. An electromagnetic interface couples the ISU Force Reflecting Exoskeleton (Luecke & Chai, 1997), developed at Iowa State University, to the operator's two fingers, eliminating the burdensome heaviness usually associated with exoskeletal devices. Researchers at the University of California, Berkeley (Chapter 4, this volume) developed a high performance 3 DOF hand-scale haptic interface. Their device exhibits high stiffness due to a 10-link design with three closed kinematic loops and a direct-drive mechanical system that avoids transmission elements.

Finally, there is considerable interest in 2D haptic devices. For example, Pai and Reissell at the University of British Columbia have used the Pantograph 2D haptic interface, a two-DOF force-feedback planar device with a handle the user moves like a mouse, to feel the edges of shapes in images (Pai & Reissell, 1997). A new 2D haptic mouse from Immersion Corporation is based on optical technology and is free-moving rather than tethered to a base. Other 2D devices, like the Moose, Sidewinder, and the Wingman mouse, are described below in the section on "Assistive Technology for the Blind and Visually Impaired."

REPRESENTATIVE APPLICATIONS OF HAPTICS

Surgical Simulation and Medical Training

A primary application area for haptics has been in surgical simulation and medical training. Langrana, Burdea, Ladeiji, and Dinsmore (1997) used the Rutgers Master II haptic device in a training simulation for palpation of subsurface liver tumors. They modeled tumors as comparatively harder spheres within larger and softer spheres. Realistic reaction forces were returned to the user as the virtual hand encountered the "tumors," and the graphical display showed corresponding tissue deformation produced by the palpation. Finite Element Analysis was used to calculate the reaction forces corresponding to deformation from experimentally obtained force/deflection curves. Researchers at the Universidade Catolica de Brasilia-Brasil (D'Aulignac & Balaniuk, 1999) have produced a physical simulation system providing graphic and haptic interfaces for an echographic examination of the human thigh, using a spring damper model defined from experimental data. Machaco, Moraes and Zuffo (2000) have used haptics in an immersive simulator of bone marrow harvest for transplant. Andrew Mor of the Robotics Institute at Carnegie Mellon (Mor, 1998) employed the PHANToM in conjunction with a 2 DOF planar device in an arthroscopic surgery simulation. The new device generates a moment measured about the tip of a surgical tool, thus providing more realistic training for the kinds of unintentional contacts with ligaments and fibrous membranes that an inexperienced resident might encounter. At Stanford, Balaniuk and Costa (2000) have developed a method to simulate fluid-filled objects suitable for interactive deformation by "cutting," "suturing," and so on. At MIT, De and Srinivasan (1998) have developed models and algorithms for reducing the computational load required to generate visual rendering of organ motion and deformation and the communication of forces back to the user resulting from tool-tissue contact. They model soft tissue as thin-walled membranes filled with fluid. Force-displacement response is comparable to that obtained in *in vivo* experiments. At Berkeley, Sastry and his colleagues (Chapter 13, this volume) are engaged in a joint project with the surgery department of the University of California at San Francisco and the Endorobotics Corporation to build dexterous robots for use inside laparoscopic and endoscopic cannulas, as well as tactile sensing and teletactile display devices and masters for surgical teleoperation (2001). Aviles and Ranta of Novint Technologies have developed the Virtual Reality Dental Training System dental simulator (Aviles & Ranta, 1999). They employ a PHANToM with four tips that mimic dental instruments; they can be used to explore simulated materials like hard tooth enamel or dentin. Giess, Evers, and Meinzer (1998) integrated haptic volume rendering with the PHANToM into the presurgical process of classifying liver parenchyma, vessel trees, and tumors. Surgeons at the Pennsylvania State University School of Medicine, in collaboration with Cambridge-based Boston Dynamics, used two PHANToMs in a training simulation in which residents passed simulated needles through blood vessels, allowing them to collect baseline data on the surgical skill of new trainees. Iwata, Yano, and Hashimoto (1998) report the development of a surgical simulator with a "free form tissue" which can be "cut" like real tissue. There are few accounts of any systematic testing and evaluation of the simulators described above. Gruener (1998), in one of the few research reports with hard data, expresses reservations about the potential of haptics in medical applications; he found that subjects in a telementoring session did not profit from the addition of force feedback to remote ultrasound diagnosis.

Museum Display

Although it is not yet commonplace, a few museums are exploring methods for 3D digitization of priceless artifacts and objects from their sculpture and decorative arts collections, making the images available via CD-ROM or in-house kiosks. For example, the Canadian Museum of Civilization collaborated with Ontario-based Hymarc to use the latter's ColorScan 3D laser camera to create three-dimensional models of objects from the museum's collection (Canarie, Inc., 1998; Shulman, 1998). A similar partnership was formed between the Smithsonian Institution and Synthonic Technologies, a Los Angeles-area company. At Florida State University, the Department of Classics has worked with a team to digitize Etruscan artifacts using the RealScan 3D imaging system from Real 3D (Orlando, Florida), and art historians from Temple University have collaborated with researchers from the Watson Research Laboratory's visual and geometric computing group to create a model of Michaelangelo's *Pieta*, using the Virtuoso shape camera from Visual Interface (Shulman, 1998).

Few museums have yet explored the potential of haptics to allow visitors access to three-dimensional museum objects such as sculpture, bronzes, or examples from the decorative arts. The "hands-off" policies that museums must impose limit appreciation of three-dimensional objects, where full comprehension and understanding rely on the sense of touch as well as vision. Haptic interfaces can allow fuller appreciation of three-dimensional objects without jeopardizing conservation standards, giving museums, research institutes, and other conservators of priceless objects a way to provide the public with a vehicle for object exploration in a modality that could not otherwise be permitted (McLaughlin, Goldberg, Ellison, & Lucas, 1999). At the University of Southern California, researchers at the Integrated Media Systems Center (IMSC) have digitized daguerreotype cases from the collection of the Seaver Center for Western Culture at the Natural History Museum of Los Angeles County and made them available at a PHANToM-equipped kiosk alongside an exhibition of the "real" objects (see Chapter 15, this volume). Bergamasco, Jannson and colleagues (Jansson, 2001) are undertaking a "Museum of Pure Form"; their group will acquire selected sculptures from the collections of partner museums in a network of European cultural institutions to create a digital database of works of art for haptic exploration.

Haptics raises the prospect of offering museum visitors not only the opportunity to examine and manipulate digitized three-dimensional art objects visually, but also to interact remotely, in real time, with museum staff members to engage in joint tactile exploration of the works of art such that someone from the museum's curatorial staff can interact with a student in a remote classroom and together they can jointly examine an ancient pot or bronze figure, note its interesting contours and textures, and consider such questions as "What is the mark at the base of the pot?" or "Why does this side have such jagged edges?" (Hespanha, Sukhatme, McLaughlin, Akbarian, Garg, & Zhu, 2000; McLaughlin, Sukhatme, Hespanha, Shahabi, Ortega, & Medioni, 2000; Sukhatme, Hespanha, McLaughlin, Shahabi, & Ortega, 2000).

Painting, Sculpting, and CAD

There have been a few projects in which haptic displays are used as alternative input devices for painting, sculpting, and computer-assisted design (CAD). Dillon and colleagues (Dillon, Moody, Bartlett, Scully, Morgan, & James, 2000) are developing a "fabric language" to analyze the tactile properties of fabrics as an information resource for haptic fabric sensing. At CERTEC, the Center of Rehabilitation Engineering in Lund, Sweden, Sjostrom (Sjostrom, 1997) and his colleagues have created a painting application in which the PHANToM can be used by the visually impaired; line thickness varies with the user's force on the fingertip thimble and colors are discriminated by their tactual profile. At Dartmouth, Henle and Donald (1999) developed an application in which animations are treated as palpable vector fields that can be edited by manipulation with the PHANToM. Marcy, Temkin, Gorman, and Krummel (1998) have developed the Tactile Max, a PHANToM plug-in for 3D Studio Max. *Dynasculpt,* a prototype from Interval Research Corporation (Snibbe, Anderson, & Verplank, 1998) permits sculpting in three dimensions by attaching a virtual mass to the PHANToM position and constructing a ribbon through the path of the mass through the 3D space. Gutierrez, Barbero, Aizpitarte, Carrillo, and Eguidazu (1998) have integrated the PHANToM into DATum, a geometric modeler. Objects can be touched, moved, or grasped (with two PHANToMs), and the assembly/disassembly of mechanical objects can be simulated.

Visualization

Haptics has also been incorporated into scientific visualization. Durbeck, Macias, Weinstein, Johnson, and Hollerbach (1998) have interfaced SCIrun, a computation software steering system, to the PHANToM. Both haptics and graphics displays are directed by the movement of the PHANToM stylus through haptically rendered data volumes. Similar systems have been developed for geoscientific applications (e.g., the Haptic Workbench, Veldkamp, Truner, Gunn, and Stevenson, 1998). Green and Salisbury (1998) have produced a convincing soil simulation in which they have varied parameters such as soil properties, plow blade geometry, and angle of attack. Researchers at West Virginia University (Van Scoy, Baker, Gingold, Martino, & Burton, 1999) have applied haptics to mobility training. They designed an application in which a real city block and its buildings could be explored with the PHANToM, using models of the buildings created in CANOMA from digital photographs of the scene from the streets. At Interactive Simulations, a San Diego-based company, researchers have added a haptic feedback component to *Sculpt,* a program for analyzing chemical and biological molecular structures, which will permit analysis of molecular conformational flexibility and interactive docking. At the University of North Carolina, Chapel Hill (Chapter 5, this volume), 6 DOF PHANToMs have been used for haptic rendering of high-dimensional scientific datasets, including three-dimensional force fields and tetrahedralized human head volume datasets. We consider further applications of haptics to visualization below, in the section "Assistive Technology for the Blind and Visually Impaired."

Military Applications

Haptics has also been used in aerospace and military training and simulations. There are a number of circumstances in a military context in which haptics can provide a useful substitute information source; that is, there are circumstances in which the modality of touch could convey information that for one reason or another is not available, not reliably communicated, nor even best apprehended through the modalities of sound and vision. In some cases, combatants may have their view blocked or may not be able to divert attention from a display to attend to other information sources. Battlefield conditions, such as the presence of artillery fire or smoke, might make it difficult to hear or see. Conditions might necessitate that communications be inaudible (Transdimension, 2000). For certain applications, for example where terrain or texture information needs to be conveyed, haptics may be the most efficient communication channel. In circumstances like those described above, haptics is an *alternative* modality to sound and vision that can be exploited to provide low-bandwidth situation information, commands, and threat warning (Transdimension, 2000). In other circumstances haptics could function as a *supplemental* information source to sound or vision. For example, users can be alerted haptically to interesting portions of a military simulation, learning quickly and intuitively about objects, their motions, what persons may interact with them, and so on.

At the Army's National Automotive Center, the SimTLC (Simulation Throughout the Life Cycle) program has used VR techniques to test military ground vehicles under simulated battlefield conditions. One of the applications has been a simulation of a distributed environment where workers at remote locations can collaborate in reconfiguring a single vehicle chassis with different weapons components, using instrumented force-feedback gloves to manipulate the three-dimensional components (National Automotive Center, 1999). The SIRE simulator (Synthesized Immersion Research Environment) at the Air Force Research Laboratory, Wright-Patterson Air Force Base, incorporated data gloves and tactile displays into its program of development and testing of crew station technologies (Wright-Patterson Air Force Base, 1997). Using tasks such as mechanical assembly, researchers at NASA-Ames have been conducting psychophysical studies of the effects of adding a 3 DOF force-feedback manipulandum to a visual display, noting that control and system dynamics have received ample research attention but that the human factors underlying successful haptic display in simulated environments remain to be identified (Ellis & Adelstein, n.d.). The Naval Aerospace Medical Research Laboratory has developed a "Tactile Situation Awareness System" for providing accurate orientation information in land, sea, and aerospace environments. One application of the system is to alleviate problems related to the spatial disorientation that occurs when a pilot incorrectly perceives the attitude, altitude, or motion of his aircraft; some of this error may be attributable to momentary distraction, reduced visibility, or an increased workload. Because the system (a vibrotactile transducer) can be attached to a portable sensor, it can also be used in such applications as extravehicular space exploration activity or Special Forces operations. Among the benefits claimed for integration of haptics with audio and visual displays are increased situation awareness, the ability to track targets and information sources spatially, and silent communication under conditions where sound is not possible or desirable (e.g., hostile environments) (Naval Aerospace Medical Research Laboratory, 2000).

Interaction Techniques

An obvious application of haptics is to the user interface, in particular its repertoire of *interaction techniques*, loosely considered that set of procedures by which basic tasks, such as opening and closing windows, scrolling, and selecting from a menu, are performed (Kirkpatrick & Douglas, 1999). Indeed, interaction techniques have been a popular application area for 2D haptic mice like the Wingman and I-Feel, which work with the Windows interface to add force feedback to windows, scroll bars, and the like. For some of these force-feedback mice, shapes, textures, and other properties of objects (spring, damping) can be "rendered" with Javascript and the objects delivered for exploration with the haptic mice via standard Web pages. Haptics offers a natural user interface based on the human gestural system. The resistance and friction provided by stylus-based force feedback adds an intuitive feel to such everyday tasks as dragging, sliding levers, and depressing buttons. There are more complex operations, such as concatenating or editing, for which a grasping metaphor may be appropriate. Here the whole-hand force feedback provided by glove-based devices could convey the feeling of stacking or juxtaposing several objects or of plucking an unwanted element from a single object. The inclusion of palpable physics in virtual environments, such as the constraints imposed by walls or the effect of altered gravity on weight, may enhance the success of a user's interaction with the environment (Adelstein & Ellis, 2000).

Sometimes too much freedom to move is inefficient and has users going down wrong paths and making unnecessary errors that system designers could help them avoid by the appropriate use of built-in force constraints that encourage or require the user to do things in the "right" way (Hutchins & Gunn, 1999). Haptics can also be used to constrain the user's interaction with screen elements, for example, by steering him or her away from unproductive areas for the performance of specific tasks, or making it more difficult to trigger procedures accidentally by increasing the stiffness of the controls.

Assistive Technology for the Blind and Visually Impaired

Most haptic systems still rely heavily on a combined visual/haptic interface. This dual modality is very forgiving in terms of the quality of the haptic rendering. This is because ordinarily the user is able to see the object being touched and naturally persuades herself that the force feedback coming from the haptic device closely matches the visual input. However, in most current haptic interfaces, the quality of haptic rendering is actually poor and, if the user closes her eyes, she will only be able to distinguish between very simple shapes (such as balls, cubes, etc.).

To date there has been a modest amount of work on the use of machine haptics for the blind and visually impaired. Among the two-dimensional haptic devices potentially useful in this context, the most recent are the Moose, the Wingman, the I-Feel, and the Sidewinder. The Moose, a 2D haptic interface developed at Stanford (O'Modhrain & Gillespie, 1998), reinterprets a Windows screen with force feedback such that icons, scroll bars, and other screen elements like the edges of windows are rendered haptically, providing an alternative to the conventional graphical user interface (GUI). For example, drag-and-drop operations are realized by increasing or decreasing the apparent mass of the Moose's manipulandum. Although not designed specifically with blind users in mind, the Logitech Wingman, developed by Immersion Corporation and formerly known as the "FEELit" mouse, similarly renders the Windows screen haptically in two dimensions and works with the Web as well, allowing the user to "snap to" hyperlinks or feel the "texture" of a textile using a "FeeltheWeb" ActiveX control programmed through Javascript. (The Wingman mouse is now no longer commercially available). Swedish researchers have experimented, with mixed results, with two-dimensional haptic devices like the Microsoft Sidewinder joystick in games devised for the visually impaired, such as "Labyrinth," in which users negotiate a maze using force feedback (Johansson & Linde, 1998, 1999).

Among the three-dimensional haptic devices, Immersion's Impulse Engine 3000 has been shown to be an effective display system for blind users. Colwell et al. (1998) had blind and sighted subjects make magnitude estimations of the roughness of virtual textures using the Impulse Engine and found that the blind subjects were more discriminating with respect to the roughness of texture and had different mental maps of the location of the haptic probe relative to the virtual object than sighted users. The researchers found, however, that for complex virtual objects, such as models of sofas and chairs, haptic information was simply not sufficient to produce recognition and had to be supplemented with information from other sources for all users.

Most of the recent work in 3D haptics for the blind has tended to focus on SensAble's PHANToM. At CERTEC, the Center of Rehabilitation Engineering in Lund, Sweden, in addition to Sjöstrom's painting application, described earlier (Sjöstrom, 1997), a program has been developed for "feeling" mathematical curves and surfaces, and a variant of the game "Battleship" that uses force feedback to communicate the different sensations of the "water surface" as bombs are dropped and opponents are sunk. The game is one of the few that can also be enjoyed by deaf-blind children. Blind but hearing children may play "The Memory Game," a variation on "Concentration" based on sound-pair buttons that disappear tactually when a match is made (Rassmuss-Gröhn & Sjöstrom, 1998).

Jansson and his colleagues at Uppsala University in Sweden have been at the forefront of research on haptics for the blind (Jannson, 1998; Jansson & Billberger, 1999; Jansson, Faenger, Konig, & Billberger, 1998). Representative of this work is an experiment reported in Jansson and Billberger (1999), in which blindfolded subjects were evaluated for speed and accuracy in identifying virtual objects (cubes, spheres, cylinders, and cones) with the PHANToM and corresponding physical models of the virtual objects by hand exploration. Jansson

Jansson and Billberger found that both speed and accuracy in shape identification were significantly poorer for the virtual objects. Speed in particular was affected by virtue of the fact that the exploratory procedures most natural to shape identification, grasping and manipulating with both hands, could not be emulated by the single-point contact of the PHANToM tip. They also noted that subject performance was not affected by the type of PHANToM interface (thimble versus stylus). However, shape recognition of virtual objects with the PHANToM was significantly influenced by the size of the object, with larger objects being more readily identified. The authors noted that shape identification with the PHANToM is a considerably more difficult task than texture recognition, in that in the case of the latter a single lateral sweep of the tip in one direction may be sufficient, but more complex procedures are required to apprehend shape. In Chapter 9 of this volume Jansson reports on his work with nonrealistic haptic rendering and with the method of successive presentation of increasingly complex scenes for haptic perception when visual guidance is unavailable.

Multivis (Multimodal Visualization for Blind People) is a project currently being undertaken at the University of Glasgow, which will utilize force feedback, 3D sound rendering, braille, and speech input and output to provide blind users access to complex visual displays. Yu, Ramloll, and Brewster (2000) have developed a multimodal approach to providing blind users access to complex graphical data such as line graphs and bar charts. Among their techniques are the use of "haptic gridlines" to help users locate data values on the graphs. Different lines are distinguished by applying two levels of surface friction to them ("sticky" or "slippery"). Because these features have not been found to be uniformly helpful to blind users, a toggle feature was added so that the gridlines and surface friction could be turned on and off. Subjects in their studies had to use the PHANToM to estimate the x and y coordinates of the minimum and maximum points on two lines. Both blind and sighted subjects were effective at distinguishing lines by their surface friction. Gridlines, however, were sometimes confused with the other lines, and counting the gridlines from right and left margins was a tedious process prone to error. The authors recommended, based on their observations, that lines on a graph should be modeled as grooved rather than raised ("engraving" rather than "embossing"), as the PHANToM tip "slips off" the raised surface of the line.

Ramloll, Yu, and their colleagues (2000) note that previous work on alternatives to graphical visualization indicates that for blind persons, pitch is an effective indicator of the location of a point with respect to an axis. Spatial audio is used to assist the user in tasks such as detecting the current location of the PHANToM tip relative to the origin of a curve (Ramloll, Yu, et al., 2000). Pitches corresponding to the coordinates of the axes can be played in rapid succession to give an "overview" picture of the shape of the curve. Such global information is useful in gaining a quick overall orientation to the graph that purely local information can provide only slowly, over time. Ramloll et al. also recommend a guided haptic overview of the borders, axes, and curves—for example, at intersections of axes, applying a force in the current direction of motion along a curve to make sure that the user does not go off in the wrong direction.

Other researchers working in the area of joint haptic-sonification techniques for visualization for the blind include Grabowski and Barner (Grabowski, 1999; Grabowski & Barner, 1998). In this work, auditory feedback—physically modeled impact sound—is integrated with the PHANToM interface. For instance, sound and haptics are integrated such that a virtual object will produce an appropriate sound when struck. The sound varies depending on such factors as the energy of the impact, its location, and the user's distance from the object (Grabowski, 1999).

ISSUES IN HAPTIC RENDERING

Acquisition of Models

There are several commercial 3D digitizing cameras available for acquiring models of objects, such as the ColorScan and the Virtuoso shape cameras mentioned earlier. The latter uses six digital cameras, five black and white cameras for capturing shape information and one color camera that acquires texture information that is layered onto the triangle mesh. At USC's IMSC one of the approaches to the digitization process begins with models acquired from photographs, using a semiautomatic system to infer complex 3-D shapes from photographs (Chen & Medioni, 1997, 1999, 2001). Images are used as the rendering primitives and multiple input pictures are allowed, taken from viewpoints with different position, orientation, and camera focal length. The direct output of the IMSC program is volumetric but is converted to a surface representation for the purpose of graphic rendering. The reconstructed surfaces are quite large, on the order of 40 MB. They are decimated with a modified version of a program for surface simplification using quadric error metrics written by Garland and Heckbert (1997). The LightScribe system (formerly known as the 3Scan system) incorporates stereo vision techniques developed at IMSC, and the process of matching points between images has been fully automated. Other comparable approaches to digitizing museum objects (e.g., Synthonics) use an older version of shape-from-stereo technology that requires the cameras to be calibrated whenever the focal length or relative position of the two cameras is changed.

Volumetric data is used extensively in medical imaging and scientific visualization. Currently the GHOST SDK, which is the development toolkit for the PHANToM, construes the haptic environment as scenes composed of geometric primitives. Huang, Qu, and Kaufman of SUNY-Stony Brook have developed a new interface that supports volume rendering, based on volumetric objects, with haptic interaction. The APSIL library (Huang, Qu, & Kaufman, 1998) is an extension of GHOST. The Stony Brook group has developed successful demonstrations of volume rendering with haptic interaction from Computer Tomography data of a lobster, a human brain, and a human head, simulating stiffness, friction, and texture solely from the volume voxel density. The development of the new interface may facilitate working directly with the volumetric representations of the objects obtained through view synthesis methods.

The surface texture of an object can be displacement mapped with thousands of tiny polygons (Srinivasan & Basdogan, 1997), although the computational demand is such that force discontinuities can occur. More commonly, a "texture field" can be constructed from 2D image data. For example, as described above, Ikei, Wakamatsu, and Fukuda (1997) created textures from images converted to grayscale, then enhanced them to heighten brightness and contrast, such that the level and distribution of intensity corresponds to variations in the height of texture protrusions and retractions.

Surface texture may also be rendered haptically through techniques like force perturbation, where the direction and magnitude of the force vector is altered using the local gradient of the texture field to simulate effects such as coarseness (Srinivasan & Basdogan, 1997). Synthetic textures, such as wood, sandpaper, cobblestone, rubber, and plastic, may also be created using mathematical functions for the height field (Anderson, 1996; Basdogan, Ho, & Srinivasan, 1997). The ENCHANTER environment (Jansson, Faenger, Konig, & Billberger, 1998) has a texture mapper which can render sinusoidal, triangular, and rectangular textures, as well as textures provided by other programs, for any haptic object provided by the GHOST SDK.

In many applications of haptics, it is desirable to be able to explore and manipulate deformable objects as well as rigid-body objects like vases and teapots. One area that IMSC researchers are beginning to explore is the development of reliable vision-based control systems for robotic applications such as the acquisition of images for 3D modeling. Two topics that have been identified as crucial for the development of such systems for robotic applications (e.g., 3D and 4D modeling for haptics) are the development of self-calibrating control algorithms (Hager, Chang, & Morse, 1995) and the use of single-camera image acquisition systems in feedback control. One can use images of an object taken from multiple viewpoints to construct a 3D model of the object to be used for haptics. To automate the procedure of collecting the multiple views, one needs to have a camera mounted on a computer-controlled robot arm. This is particularly important for constructing 4D models of objects whose shape is evolving (e.g., a work of art as it is being produced). From a controls perspective the research problem is to build algorithms to position the camera. The desired position can be specified directly in terms of its Cartesian coordinates or indirectly in terms of desired locations of parts of the object in the image. The latter falls in the area of vision-based control and is much more interesting, because the use of vision in the feedback loop allows for great accuracy with not very precise, therefore relatively inexpensive, robotic manipulators.

Latency

The realism of haptic rendering can be adversely affected by slow update rates, as can occur in the case of the extreme computation time required by real-time rendering of deformable objects, or the delays induced by network congestion and bandwidth limitations in distributed applications.

Floyd (1999) deals with the issue of computational latency and haptic fidelity in bit-mapped virtual environments. In traditional systems with some latency there is a lack of fidelity if, say, the user penetrates a virtual object and the lag is such that there is no immediate feedback of force to indicate that a collision has occurred and that penetration is not possible. Floyd proposes that the server inform the haptic client when the user has penetrated a surface in the environment, and where that contact occurred. The client uses this information to offset the coordinate system the user is operating in so that instead of having significantly penetrated the surface, the user is just within it, computes an appropriate force response, and caches the constraint implicit in the existence of that surface so that forces to impede further progress in that direction are computed on the client alone.

Mark and his colleagues (Mark, Randolph, Finch, van Verth, & Taylor, 1996) have proposed a number of solutions to recurring problems in haptics, such as improving the update rate for forces communicated back to the user. They propose the use of intermediate representation of force through a "plane and probe" method: A local planar approximation to the user's hand location is computed when the probe or haptic tool penetrates the plane, and the force is updated at approximately 1 kHz by the force server, while the application recomputes the position of the plane and updates it at approximately 20 kHz. Balaniuk (1999) has proposed a buffer model to transmit information to the PHANToM at the necessary rate. The buffer can also be used to implement a proxy-based calculation of the haptic forces.

Networked virtual reality (VR) applications may require that force and positional data be transmitted over a communication link between computers where significant and unpredictable delays are the norm, resulting in instability in the haptic system. The potential for significant harm to the user exists in such circumstances due to the forces that the haptic devices can generate. Buttolo, Oboe, Hannaford, and McNeely (1996) note that the addition of force feedback to multiuser environments demands low latency and high collision detection sampling rates. Local area networks (LANs), because of their low communication delay, may be conducive to applications in which users can touch each other, but for wide area networks, or any environment where the demands above cannot be met, Buttolo et al. propose a "one-user-at-a-time" architecture. While some latency can be tolerated in "static" applications with a single user and no effect of the user's action on the 3D object, in collaborative environments where users make modifications to the environment it is important to make sure that any alterations from individual clients are coordinated through the server. In effect the server can queue the users so that only one can modify the object at a time and can lock the object until the new information is uploaded to the server and incorporated into the "official" version of the virtual environment. Then and only then can the next user make a modification. Delay can be tolerated under these conditions because the haptic rendering is done on a local copy of the virtual environment at each user's station.

Hespanha, McLaughlin, and Sukhatme (Chapter 8, this volume) note that latency is a critical factor that governs whether two users can truly share a common haptic experience. They propose an algorithm where the nature of the interaction between two hosts is decided dynamically based on the measured network latency between them. Users on hosts that are near each other (low communication latency) are dynamically added to fast local groups. If the communication latency is high, users are allowed a slower form of interaction where they can touch and feel objects but cannot exert forces on them. Users within a fast local group experience true haptic collaboration since the system is able to resolve the interaction forces between them quickly enough to meet stability criteria.

Fukuda and Matsumoto (Chapter 7, this volume) have also addressed the issue of the impact of network delay on collaborative haptic environments. They conducted a study of a multiuser environment with force feedback. They found that the performance of the PHAN-ToM is sensitive to network delay, and that their SCES (Sharing Contact Entity's State) solution demonstrated good performance, as compared to taking no countermeasure against delay. Other approaches for dealing with random time delays, including Transmission Line Modeling and Haptic Dead Reckoning, are considered in Wilson et al. (1999).

Contact Detection

A fundamental problem in haptics is to detect contact between the virtual objects and the haptic device (a mouse, a PHANToM, a glove, etc.). Once this contact is reliably detected, a force corresponding to the interaction physics is generated and rendered using the probe. This process usually runs in a tight servo loop within a haptic rendering system. Lin et al. (1998, 1999) have proposed an extensible framework for contact detection that deconstructs the workspace into regions and at runtime identifies the region(s) of potential contacts. The algorithm takes advantage of temporal and spatial coherence by caching the contact geometry from the immediately prior step to perform incremental computations. Mascarenhas et al. (Chapter 5, this volume) report on a recent application of this system to the visualization of polygonal and scientific datasets. The contact detection problem is well studied in computer graphics. The reader is referred to Held (1995) and to Lin and Gottschalk (1998) for a survey.

Another technique for contact detection is to generate the so-called surface contact point (SCP), which is the closest point on the surface to the actual tip of the probe. The force generation can then happen as though the probe were physically at this location rather than within the object. Existing methods in the literature generate the SCP by using the notion of a god-object (Zilles & Salisbury, 1995), which forces the SCP to lie on the surface of the virtual object. A technique which finesses contact point detection using a voxel-based approach to 6 DOF haptic rendering is described in McNeely et al. (1999). The authors use a short-range force field to repel the manipulated object in order to maintain a minimum separation distance between the (static) environment and the manipulated object. At USC's IMSC, the authors are developing algorithms for SCP generation that use information from the current contact detection cycle and *past* information from the contact history to predict the next SCP effectively. As a first step, we are experimenting with a well-known linear predictor, the Kalman Filter, by building on our prior results in applying similar techniques to the problem of robot localization (Roumeliotis, Sukhatme, & Bekey, 1999).

Force Feedback

Two requirements drive the force feedback research in haptics: high fidelity rendering and stability. It turns out that these two goals are somewhat conflicting because high fidelity haptic rendering generally calls for high force-feedback gains that often lead to self-induced oscillations and instability.

Inspired by electrical networks, Adams and Hannaford (1999) regard the haptic interface as a two-port system terminated on one side by the human operator and on the other side by the virtual environment (cf. Figure 1-1). The energy exchange between the human operator and the haptic interface is characterized by a force F_h and velocity v_h, whereas the exchange between the interface and the simulated virtual environment is characterized by a force F_e and velocity v_e. For ideal rendering, the haptic interface should be transparent (in the sense that $F_h = F_e$ and $v_h = v_e$), but stability requirements generally force the designer of the haptic interface to introduce some haptic distortion.

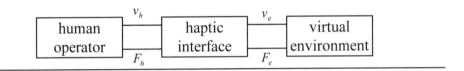

Figure 1-1: Two-port framework for haptic interfaces.

It is generally assumed that a human operator interacting with a haptic interface behaves passively (Hogan, 1989) in the sense that he or she does not introduce energy in the system. Since most mechanical virtual environments are also passive, the stability of the overall system could be guaranteed by simply designing the interface to be passive. However, as observed by Colgate, Grafing, Stanley, and Schenkel (1993), time-sampling can destroy the natural passivity of a virtual environment. In fact, these authors showed that the smaller the sampling rate, the more energy can be "generated" by a virtual wall.

Several approaches have been proposed to deal with this difficulty. Colgate and Schenkel (1997) determined conditions on the simplest virtual environment (the virtual wall) that guarantee the stability of the haptic interface for any passive human operator. These conditions reflect the fact that the amount of energy generated by a time-discretized virtual wall depends on the sampling rate. They also involve the virtual wall's stiffness and damping coefficient, posing constraints on the range of stiffness/damping parameters that can be rendered. This range is referred to by Colgate and Brown (1994) as the *z*-width of the haptic interface and is an important measure of its performance.

Adams and Hannaford (1999) followed a distinct approach by advocating the introduction of virtual coupling in the haptic interface so as to guarantee the stability of the system *for any continuous-time passive virtual environment*, even if its discrete-time version is no longer passive. The virtual coupling can be designed to provide sufficient energy dissipation to guarantee the stability of the overall system for any passive virtual environment. This approach decouples the haptic interface control problem from the design of the virtual environment. Miller, Colgate, and Freeman (1999) extended this work to virtual environments that are not necessarily passive. The drawback of virtual coupling is that it introduces haptic distortion (because the haptic interface is no longer transparent). Hannaford, Ryu, and Kim (Chapter 3, this volume) present a new method to control instability that depends on the time domain definition of passivity. They define the "Passivity Observer," and the "Passivity Controller," and show how they can be applied to haptic interface design in place of fixed-parameter virtual couplings. This approach minimizes haptic distortion.

The work described above assumes that the human operator is passive, but poses no other constraints on her behavior. This can lead to small z-width, significant haptic distortion, or both. Tsai and Colgate (1995) tried to overcome this by modeling the human as a more general discrete-time linear time-invariant system. They derive conditions for stability that directly exclude the possibility of periodic oscillations for a virtual environment consisting of a virtual wall. Gillespie and Cutkosky (1996) address the same issue by modeling the human as a second order continuous-time system. They conclude that to make the approach practical, online estimation of the human mechanical model is needed, because the model's parameters change from operator to operator and, even with the same operator, from posture to posture. The use of multiple-model supervisory control (Anderson et al., 1999; Hespanha et al., 2001; Morse, 1996) to estimate online the operator's dynamics promises to bring significant advantages to the field, because it is characterized by very fast adaptation to sudden changes in the process or the control objectives. Such changes are expected in haptics due to the unpredictability of the human-in-the-loop. In fact, it is shown in Hajian and Howe (1995) that changes in the parameters of human limb dynamics become noticeable over periods of time larger than 20 ms.

Although most of the work referenced above focuses on simple prototypical virtual environments, a few researchers developed systems capable of handling very complex ones. Ruspini and Khatib (Chapter 2, this volume) are among these, having developed a general framework for the dynamic simulation and haptic exploration of complex interaction between generalized articulated virtual mechanical systems. Their simulation tool permits direct "hands-on" interaction with the virtual environment through the haptic interface.

Capture, Storage, and Retrieval of Haptic Data

One of the newest areas in haptics is the search for optimal methods for the description, storage, and retrieval of moving-sensor data of the type generated by haptic devices. With such techniques we can capture the hand or finger movement of an expert performing a skilled movement and "play it back," so that a novice can retrace the expert's path, with realistic touch sensation; further, we can calculate the correlation between the two exploratory paths as time series and determine if they are significantly different, which would indicate a need for further training. The INSITE system (Faisal, Shahabi, McLaughlin, & Betz, 1999) is capable of providing instantaneous comparison of two users with respect to duration, speed, acceleration, and thumb and finger forces. Techniques for recording and playing back raw haptic data (Shahabi, Ghoting, Kaghazian, McLaughlin, & Shanbhag, forthcoming; Shahabi, Kolahdouzan, Barish, Zimmermann, Yao, & Fu, 2001) have been developed for the

PHANToM and CyberGrasp. Captured data include movement in three dimensions, orientation, and force (contact between the probe and objects in the virtual environment). Shahabi and colleagues address haptic data at a higher level of abstraction in Chapter 14, in which they describe their efforts to understand the semantics of hand actions (see also Eisenstein, Ghandeharizadeh, Huang, Shahabi, Shanbhag, & Zimmermann, 2001).

Haptic Data Compression

Haptic data compression and evaluation of the perceptual impact of lossy compression of haptic data are further examples of uncharted waters in haptics research (see Ortega, this volume, Chapter 6). Data about the user's interaction with objects in the virtual environment must be continually refreshed if they are manipulated or deformed by user input. If data are too bulky relative to available bandwidth and computational resources, there will be improper registration between what the user sees on screen and what he "feels." Ortega's work begins by analyzing data obtained experimentally from the PHANToM and the CyberGrasp, exploring compression techniques, starting with simple approaches (similar to those used in speech coding) and continuing with methods that are more specific to the haptic data. One of two lossy methods to compress the data may be employed: One approach is to use a lower sampling rate; the other is to note small changes during movement. For example, for certain grasp motions not all of the fingers are involved. Further, during the approaching and departing phases tracker data may be more useful than the CyberGrasp data. Vector coding may prove to be more appropriate to encode the time evolution of a multifeatured set of data such as that provided by the CyberGrasp. For cases where the user employs the haptic device to manipulate a static object, compression techniques that rely on knowledge of the object may be more useful than the coding of an arbitrary trajectory in three-dimensional space.

Haptic Collaboration

The many potential applications in industry, the military, and entertainment for force feedback in multiuser environments, where two or more users orient to and manipulate the same objects, have led to work such as that of Buttolo and his colleagues (Buttolo, Oboe, & Hannaford, 1997; Buttolo, Hewitt, Oboe, & Hannaford, 1997; Buttolo, Oboe, Hannaford, & McNally, 1996), who as noted above remind us that adding haptics to multiuser environments creates additional demand for frequent position sampling for collision detection and fast update.

It is also reasonable to assume that in multiuser environments, there may be a heterogenous assortment of haptic devices with which users interact with the system. One of our primary concerns thus would be to ensure proper registration of the disparate devices with the 3D environment and with each other. Of potential use in this regard is work by Iwata, Yano, and Hashimoto (1997) on LHX (Library for Haptics), which is modular software that can support a variety of different haptic displays. LHX allows a variety of mechanical configurations, supports easy construction of haptic user interfaces, allows networked applications in virtual spaces, and includes a visual display interface. The chapter by Hespanha, McLaughlin, and Sukhatme (Chapter 8, this volume) proposes an architecture for distributed haptic collaboration with heterogeneous devices.

There have only been a few studies of cooperation/collaboration between users of haptic devices. In a study by Basdogan, Ho and their colleagues (Basdogan, Ho, Slater, & Srinavasan, 1998; Ho, Basdogan, Slater, Durlach, & Srinivasan, 1998), partners at remote locations were assigned three cooperative tasks requiring joint manipulation of 3D virtual objects, such as moving a ring back and forth along a wire while minimizing contact with the wire. Experiments were conducted with visual feedback only, and with both visual and haptic feedback. Both performance and feelings of togetherness were enhanced in the dual modality condition. Performance was best when visual feedback alone was followed by the addition of haptic feedback rather than vice versa. Durlach and Slater (n.d.) note that factors that contribute to a sense of copresence include being able to observe the effect on the environment of actions by one's interlocutors, and being able to work collaboratively with copresent others to alter the environment. Point of view (egocentric vs. exocentric) with respect to avatars may also influence the sense of copresence. Touching, even virtual touching, is believed to contribute to the sense of copresence because of its associations with closeness and intimacy.

HUMAN FACTORS

Human Haptics

The behavior of the human haptic system has been the subject of far more systematic study than has machine haptics. There are several haptically important dimensions of object recognition, including texture, hardness, shape, and thermal conductivity (Klatzky, Lederman, & Reed, 1987). Most researchers report that subjects are able to discriminate textures and to a lesser extent shapes using the haptic sense only. For example, Ballesteros, Manga, and Reales (1997) reported a moderate level of accuracy for single-finger haptic detection of raised-line shapes, with asymmetric shapes being more readily discriminated. Hatwell (1995) found that recall of texture information coded haptically was successful when memorization was intentional, but not when it was incidental, indicating that haptic information processing may be effortful for subjects.

Available evidence indicates that haptic information processing in adults involves construal of a stimulus object, such as a texture sample, as coordinates on a set of *underlying perceptual dimensions*, like "hard-soft" or "rough-smooth." Developmental studies by Berger and Hatwell (1993, 1995) have shown that in discriminating texture samples varying with respect to the density and hardness dimensions, older subjects were less likely than younger ones to make global assessments of the stimuli and more likely to invoke the separate dimensions as judgment criteria. Hughes and Jansson (1994) note that texture gradients, like textures, can be multidimensional and suggest candidate dimensions such as variations in the size, height, and shape of elements. Hollins, Faldowski, Rao, and Young (1993) passed samples of 17 textures over the fingertips of subjects whose view of the samples was restricted. The subjects sorted the texture samples into categories based on similarity, and then rated the samples against a series of scales measuring well-established perceptual dimensions such as roughness and hardness, and several other less-well studied potential dimensions such as "slippery-sticky." Co-occurrence data from the sorting task were converted to dissimilarities and submitted to a multidimensional scaling analysis. The researchers reported that there were two clear, orthogonal perceptual dimensions, "rough-smooth" and "soft-hard," underlying the classification of samples and speculated about a possible third dimension, "springiness."

Hughes and Jansson (1994) lament the inadequacy of embossed maps and other devices intended to communicate information through the sense of touch, a puzzling state of affairs insomuch as perception by active touch (purposeful motion of the skin surface relative to the surface of some distal object) appears to be comparatively accurate, and even more accurate than vision in apprehending certain properties such as smoothness (Hughes & Jansson, p. 302). The authors note in their critical review of the literature on active-passive equivalence that active and passive touch (as when a texture is presented to the surface of the fingers, see Hollins et al., 1993) have repeatedly been demonstrated by Lederman and her colleagues (Lederman, 1985; Lederman, Thorne, & Jones, 1986; Loomis & Lederman, 1986) to be functionally equivalent, in that touch modality does not seem to account for a significant proportion of the variation in judgments of such basic dimensions as roughness, even though the two types of touch may lead to different sorts of attributions (respectively, about the texture object and about the cutaneous sensing surface) and motor information should clearly be useful in assessing the size and distribution of surface protrusions and retractions. Active and passive touch are more likely to be equivalent in certain types of perceptual tasks; active touch should be less relevant to judgments of "hardness" than it is to assessments of "springiness." Such findings should be of interest to those working with machine haptics, as most of the application development in this field involves using the displays under conditions of active rather than passive touch.

Some researchers have reported that shape and texture recognition improve with the addition of vision, although there is not uniform agreement as to the extent of the similarity between haptic and visual information processing. Balakrishnan, Klatzky, and Loomis (1989), although reporting that length-distortion effects (attributing greater distances between two points as a path between them becomes more winding) were less pronounced under visual path tracing than had been found in previous experiments using haptic exploration, nonetheless concluded that the encoding processes are similar in the two domains. Klatzky, Lederman, and Reed (1987), however, concluded after a series of experiments that the encoding pathways are fundamentally different in the haptic and visual systems, such that the visual system is more oriented to the discrimination of shape and the haptic system to substance. Heller's work (1982) suggests that the addition of visual information about "where the hand is" (as opposed to what the surface texture looks like) is the critical contributory factor in any improved performance arising from bimodal information acquisition.

Work reported by Lederman, Thorne, and Jones (1986) indicates that the dominance of one system over the other in texture discrimination tasks is a function of the dimension of judgment being employed. In making judgments of *density*, the visual system tends to dominate, while the haptic system is most salient when subjects are asked to discriminate textures on the basis of *roughness*.

Lederman, Klatzky, Hamilton, and Ramsay (1999) studied the psychophysical effects of haptic exploration speed and mode of touch on the perceived roughness of metal objects when subjects used a rigid probe, not unlike the PHANToM stylus (see also Klatzky and Lederman, Chapter 10, this volume). In earlier work, Klatzky and Lederman found that subjects wielding rigid stick-like probes were less effective at discriminating surface textures than with the bare finger. In a finding that points to the importance of tactile arrays to haptic perception, the authors noted that when a subject is actively exploring an object with the bare finger, speed appears to have very little impact on roughness judgments, because subjects may have used kinesthetic feedback about their hand movements; however, when a rigid probe is used, people should become more reliant on vibrotactile feedback, since the degree of displacement of fingertip skin no longer is commensurate with the geometry of the surface texture.

Machine Haptics

Psychophysical studies of machine haptics are now beginning to accumulate. Experiments performed by von der Heyde and Hager-Ross (1998) have produced classic perceptual errors in the haptic domain: For instance, subjects who haptically sorted cylinders by weight made systematic errors consistent with the classical size-weight illusion. Experiments by Jansson, Faenger, Konig, and Billberger (1998) on shape sensing with blindfolded sighted observers were described above. Ernst and Banks (2001) reported that although vision usually "captures" haptics, in certain circumstances information communicated haptically (via two PHANToMs) assumes greater importance. They found that when noise is added to visual data, the haptic sense is invoked to a greater degree. Ernst and Banks concluded that the extent of capture by a particular sense modality is a function of the statistical reliability of the corresponding sensory input.

Kirkpatrick and Douglas (1999) argue that if the haptic interface does not support certain exploratory procedures, such as enclosing an object in the case of the single-point PHANToM tip, then the quick grasping of shape that enclosure provides will have to be done by techniques that the interface does support, such as tracing the contour of the virtual object. Obviously, this is slower than enclosing. The extent to which the haptic interface supports or fails to support exploratory processes contributes to its usability. Kirkpatrick and Douglas evaluated the PHANToM interface's support for the task of shape determining, comparing and contrasting its usability in three modes: vision only; haptics only; and haptics and vision combined, in a non-stereoscopic display. When broad exploration is required for quick object recognition, haptics alone is not likely to be very useful when the user is limited to a single finger whose explorations must be recalled and integrated to form an overall impression of shape. Vision alone may fail to provide adequate depth cues (e.g., the curved shape of a teapot). Kirkpatrick and Douglas assert that the effect of haptics and vision is not additive and that the combination of them would provide a result exceeding what an additive model might predict.

Kirkpatrick and Douglas (1999) also report that among the factors that influence the speed of haptic recognition of objects are the number of different object attributes that can be perceived simultaneously and the number of fingers that are employed. This work suggests that object exploration with devices like the PHANToM, which offer kinesthetic but not cutaneous feedback, will yield suboptimal results with respect both to exploration speed and accuracy when compared to the bare hand. It further suggests that speed and accuracy may improve with additional finger receptors.

With the advent of handheld devices and the possibility of the incorporation of haptics into such devices, it is becoming increasingly important to determine just how small a haptic effect can be perceived. Dosher, Lee, and Hannaford (Chapter 12, this volume) report that users can detect haptic effects whose maximum force is about half the measured Coulomb friction level of the device and about one-third the measured static friction level. They note that their results can be expected to vary by device and that it remains to be seen whether or not a measurable effect is necessarily one that can help users accomplish their tasks.

Srinivasan and Basdogan (1997) note the importance of other modalities in haptic perception (e.g., sounds of collision with objects, etc.). They report that with respect to object deformation, visual sensing dominates over proprioception and leads to severe misjudgments of object stiffness if the graphic display is intentionally skewed (Srinavasan, Beauregard, & Brock, 1996). Sound appears to be a less important perceptual mediator than vision. In an unpublished study by Hou and Srinivasan, reported in Srinivasan and Basdogan (1997), subjects navigating through a maze were found to prefer large visual-haptic ratios and small haptic workspaces. Best results were achieved in the dual-modality condition, followed by haptic only and then vision only. It is apparent that the relative contribution of visual and haptic perception will vary as a function of task, but it is also apparent, as Srinivasan and Basdogan conclude, that the inadequacies of force-feedback display (e.g., limitations of stiffness) can be overcome with appropriate use of other modalities. In Chapter 11 Jeong and Jacobson consider the question of how effective haptic and auditory displays are when combined, whether or not they interfere with one another, and how a user's previous experience with a modality affects the success of the integration and the efficacy of the multimodal display.

REFERENCES

Adams, R. J., & Hannaford, B. (1999). Stable haptic interaction with virtual environments. *IEEE Transactions on Robotics and Automation, 15*(3), 465–474.

Adelstein, B. D., & Ellis, S. R. (2000). *Human and system performance in haptic virtual environments*. Retrieved from vision.arc.nasa.gov:80/IHH/highlights/H%26S%20performance.html.

Aloliwi, B., & Khalil, H. K. (1998). Robust control of nonlinear systems with unmodeled dynamics. *Proceedings of the 37th IEEE Conference on Decision and Control* (pp. 2872–2873). Piscataway, NJ: IEEE Customer Service.

Anderson, B. D. O., Brinsmead, T. S., de Bruyne, F., Hespanha, J. P., Liberzon, D., & Morse, A. S. (2000). Multiple model adaptive control. I. Finite controller coverings. *International Journal of Robust and Nonlinear Control, 10*(11–12), 909–929.

Anderson, T. (1996). A virtual universe utilizing haptic display. In J. K. Salisbury & M. A. Srinivasan (Eds.), *Proceedings of the First PHANToM User's Group Workshop*. AI Technical Report no. 1596 and RLE Technical Report no. 612. Cambridge, MA: MIT.

Aviles, W., & Ranta, J. (1999). A brief presentation on the VRDTS—Virtual Reality Dental Training System. In J. K. Salisbury & M. A. Srinivasan (Eds.), *Proceedings of the Fourth PHANToM User's Group Workshop*. AI Lab Technical Report No. 1675 and RLE Technical Report No. 633. Cambridge, MA: MIT.

Balakrishnan, J. D., Klatzky, R. L., & Loomis, J. M (1989). Length distortion of temporally extended visual displays: Similarity to haptic spatial perception. *Perception & Psychophysics, 46*(4), 387–394.

Balaniuk, R. (1999). Using fast local modeling to buffer haptic data. In J. K. Salisbury & M. A. Srinivasan (Eds.), *Proceedings of the Fourth PHANToM User's Group Workshop*. AI Lab Technical Report No. 1675 and RLE Technical Report No. 633. Cambridge, MA: MIT.

Balaniuk, R., & Costa, I. F. (2000). An approach for physically based soft tissue simulation suitable for haptic interaction. *Preprints of the Fifth Annual PHANToM Users Group Workshop*. Aspen, CO: Given Institute.

Ballesteros, S., Manga, D., & Reales, J. (1997). Haptic discrimination of bilateral symmetry in 2-dimensional and 3-dimensional unfamiliar displays. *Perception and Psychophysics, 59*(1), 37–50.

Basdogan, C., Ho, C-H., Slater, M., & Srinavasan, M. A. (1998). The role of haptic communication in shared virtual environments. In J. K. Salisbury & M. A. Srinivasan (Eds.), *Proceedings of the Third PHANToM Users Group Workshop, PUG98*. AI Technical Report no. 1643 and RLE Technical Report no. 624. Cambridge, MA: MIT.

Basdogan, C., Ho, C-H., & Srinivasan, M. A. (1997). A ray-based haptic rendering technique for displaying shape and texture of 3-D objects in virtual environments. *Proceedings of the ASME Dynamic Systems and Control Division*, Dallas, TX.

Berger, C., & Hatwell, Y. (1993). Dimensional and overall similarity classifications in haptics: A developmental study. *Cognitive Development, 8*(4), 495–516.

Berger, C., & Hatwell, Y. (1995). Development of dimensional vs. global processing in haptics: The perceptual and decisional determinants of classification skills. *British Journal of Developmental Psychology, 13*(2), 143–162.

Brown, J. M., & Colgate, J. E. (1994). Physics-based approach to haptic display. In *Proceedings of the ISMRC 94: International Symposium on Measurement and Control in Robotics, Topical Workshop on Virtual Reality* (pp. 101–106). Los Alamitos, CA: IEEE.

Burdea, G. C. (1996). *Force and touch feedback for VR.* New York: John Wiley & Sons.

Buttolo, P., Hewitt, J., Oboe, R., & Hannaford, B. (1995). Force feedback in virtual and shared environments. *Proceedings of the IEEE International Conference on System, Man and Cybernetics*, Vancouver, BC.

Buttolo, P., Oboe, R., & Hannaford, B. (1997). Architectures for shared haptic virtual environments. *Computers and Graphics, 21*(4), 421–429.

Buttolo, P., Oboe, R., Hannaford, B., & McNeely, B. (1996). *Force feedback in shared virtual simulations.* Paper presented at MICAD, France.

Canarie, Inc. (1998). *Rivers of light: The Ca*net II experiments.* Brochure.

Carignan, C. R., & Cleary, K. R. (2000). Closed-loop force control for haptic simulation of virtual environments. *Haptics-e, The Electronic Journal of Haptics Research*, 1(2).

Çavusoglu, C., & Sastry. S. (2001). Haptic interfaces to real and virtual surgical environments. In M. L. McLaughlin, J. P. Hespanha, & G. S. Sukhatme (Eds.), *Touch in Virtual Environments*. IMSC Series in Multimedia. New York: Prentice Hall.

Chen, Q., & Medioni, G., (1997, October). *Image synthesis from a sparse set of views.* Paper presented at IEEE Visualization '97, Phoenix, AZ.

Chen, Q., & Medioni., G. (1999). *A semiautomatic system to infer complex 3-D shapes from photographs.* Paper presented at the IEEE Conference on Multimedia Computing and Systems (ICMCS'99), Florence, Italy.

Chen, G., & Medioni, G. (2001). Building human face models from two images. *Journal of VLSI Signal Processing, 27*(1/2).

Chung, R., Adelstein, B. D., & Kazerooni, H. (2001). Hardware for improved haptic interface performance. In M. L. McLaughlin, J. P. Hespanha, & G. S. Sukhatme (Eds.), *Touch in Virtual Environments*. IMSC Series in Multimedia. New York: Prentice Hall.

Colgate, J. E., Grafing, P., Stanley, M. C., & Schenkel, G. (1993). Implementation of stiff virtual walls in force-reflecting interfaces. In *Proceedings of the IEEE Virtual Reality Annual International Symposium* (pp. 202–208). Piscataway, NJ: IEEE Service Center

Colgate, J. E., & Brown, J. M. (1994). Factors affecting the z-width of a haptic display. In *Proceedings of the 1994 IEEE International Conference on Robotics and Automation* (pp. 3205 -3210). Piscataway, NJ: IEEE Service Center

Colgate, J. E., & Schenkel, G. (1997). Passivity of a class of sampled-data systems: Application to haptic interfaces. *Journal of Robotic Systems, 14*(1), 37–47.

D'Aulignac, D., & Balaniuk, R. (1999). Providing reliable virtual, echographic exam of the human thigh. In J. K. Salisbury & M. A. Srinivasan (Eds.), *Proceedings of the Fourth PHANToM User's Group Workshop*. AI Lab Technical Report No. 1675 and RLE Technical Report No. 633. Cambridge, MA: MIT.

De, S., & Srinivasan, M. A. (1998). Rapid rendering of "tool-tissue" interactions in surgical simulations: Thin walled membrane models. In J. K. Salisbury & M. A. Srinivasan (Eds.), *Proceedings of the Third PHANToM Users Group, PUG98*. AI Technical Report no. 1643 and RLE Technical Report no. 624. Cambridge, MA: MIT.

Dijkstra, E. W. (1965). Solution of a problem in concurrent programming control. *Communications of the ACM, 8*(9), 569.

Dillon, P., Moody, W., Bartlett, R., Scully, P., Morgan, R., & James, C. (2000). *Sensing the fabric.* Paper presented at the Workshop on Haptic Human-Computer Interaction, Glasgow. Retrieved from www.dcs.gla.ac.uk/~stephen/workshops/haptic/papers/dillon.pdf.

Dosher, J., Lee, G., & Hannaford, B. (2001). Detection thresholds for small haptic effects. In M. L. McLaughlin, J. P. Hespanha, & G. S. Sukhatme (Eds.), *Touch in Virtual Environments*. IMSC Series in Multimedia. New York: Prentice Hall.

Durbeck, L. J. K., Macias, N. J., Weinstein, M., Johnson, C. R., & Hollerbach, J. M. (1998). SCIRun haptic display for scientific visualization. In J. K. Salisbury & M. A. Srinivasan (Eds.), *Proceedings of the Third PHANToM Users Group, PUG98*. AI Technical Report no. 1643 and RLE Technical Report no. 624. Cambridge, MA: MIT.

Durlach, N., & Slater, M. (n.d.). *Presence in shared virtual environments and virtual togetherness.* Retrieved from http://www.cs.ucl.ac.uk/staff/m.slater/BTWorkshop/durlach.html.

Eisenstein, J., Ghandeharizadeh, S., Huang, L., Shahabi, C., Shanbhag, G., & Zimmermann, R. (2001, May). *Analysis of clustering techniques to detect hand signs.* Paper presented at the International Symposium on Intelligent Multimedia, Video and Speech Processing, Hong Kong.

Ellis, S. R., & Adelstein, B. D. (n.d.). *Performance in haptic virtual environments with visual supplement.* http://human-factors.arc.nasa.gov/ihh/spatial/research/adsp_haptic_summary.html.

Ernst, M. O., & Banks, M. S. (2001, February). *Does vision always dominate haptics?* Paper presented at the Touch in Virtual Environments Conference, University of Southern California.

Faisal, A., Shahabi, C., McLaughlin, M., &. Betz, F. (1999). InSite: A generic paradigm for interpreting user-Web space interaction. *Proceedings of the ACM CIKM'99 2nd Workshop on Web Information and Data Management (WIDM'99),* Kansas City, MO.

Floyd, J. (1999). *Haptic interaction with three-dimensional bitmapped environments.* Unpublished Master's Thesis, Massachusetts Institute of Technology.

Fukuda, I., & Matsumoto, S. (2001). A robust system for haptic collaboration over the network. In M. L. McLaughlin, J. P. Hespanha, & G. S. Sukhatme (Eds.), *Touch in Virtual Environments*. IMSC Series in Multimedia. New York: Prentice Hall.

Garland, M., & Heckbert, P. S. (1997). *Surface simplification using quadric error metrics.* Paper presented at the annual meeting of SIGGRAPH.

Giess, C., Evers, H., & Meinzer, H-P. (1998). Haptic volume rendering in different scenarios of surgical planning. In J. K. Salisbury & M. A. Srinivasan (Eds.), *Proceedings of the Third PHANToM User's Group, PUG98.* AI Technical Report no. 1643 and RLE Technical Report no. 624. Cambridge, MA: MIT. Retrieved from www.sensable.com/community/98papers/3%20giess-pug98.fm.pdf.

Gillespie, B., & Cutkosky, M. (1996). Stable user-specific rendering of the virtual wall. In *Proceedings of the ASME International Mechanical Engineering Conference and Exposition*, Vol. 58, 397–406.

Gomez, D. H. (1998). *A dextrous hand master with force feedback for virtual reality.* Unpublished Ph.D. dissertation, Rutgers, The State University of New Jersey.

Grabowski, N. (1999). Structurally-derived sounds in a haptic rendering system. In J. K. Salisbury & M. A. Srinivasan (Eds.), *Proceedings of the Fourth PHANToM User's Group Workshop.* AI Lab Technical Report No. 1675 and RLE Technical Report No. 633. Cambridge, MA: MIT.

Grabowski, N. A., & Barner, K. E. (1998). *Data visualisation methods for the blind using force feedback and sonfication.* Paper presented at the SPIE Conference on Telemanipulator and Telepresence Technologies V, Boston, MA.

Green, D. F., & Salisbury, J. K. (1997). Texture sensing and simulation using the PHANToM: Towards remote sensing of soil properties. In J. K. Salisbury and M. A. Srinivasan (Eds.), *Proceedings of the Second PHANToM User's Group Workshop.* AI Technical Report no. 1617 and RLE Technical Report no. 618, MIT, Reading, MA.

Gruener, G. (1998). *Telementoring using haptic communication.* Unpublished Ph.D. dissertation, University of Colorado.

Gutierrez, T., Barbero, J. L., Aizpitarte, M., Carillo, A. R., & Eguidazu, A. (1998). Assembly simulation through virtual prototypes. In J. K. Salisbury & M. A. Srinivasan (Eds.), Proceedings of the Third PHANToM User's Group, PUG98. AI Technical Report no. 1643 and RLE Technical Report no. 624. Cambridge, MA: MIT. Retrieved from www.sensable.com/community/98papers/12%20gutpug98.pdf.

Hager, G. D., Chang, W-C., & Morse, A. S. (1995). Robot hand-eye coordination based on stereo vision. *IEEE Control Systems Magazine, 15*, 30–39.

Hajian, A. Z., & Howe, R. D. (1995). Identification of the mechanical impedance at the human finger tip. *ASME Journal of Biomechanical Engineering, 119*(1), 109-114.

Hannaford, B., Ryu, J-H., & Kim, Y. (2001). Stable control of haptics. In M. L. McLaughlin, J. P. Hespanha, & G. S. Sukhatme (Eds.), *Touch in Virtual Environments.* IMSC Series in Multimedia. New York: Prentice Hall.

Hatwell, Y. (1995). Children's memory for location and object properties in vision and haptics: Automatic or attentional processing? *Cahiers de Psychologie Cognitive/Current Psychology of Cognition, 14*(1), 47-71.

Held, M., Klosowski, J. T., & Mitchell, J. S. B. (1995). Evaluation of collision detection methods for virtual reality fly-throughs. In C. Gold and J. Robert (Eds.), *Proceedings of the 7th Canadian Conference on Computational Geometry*, Université Laval.

Heller, M. A. (1982). Visual and tactual texture perception: Intersensory cooperation. *Perception & Psychophysics, 31*, 339–344.

Henle, F., & Donald, B. (1999). Haptics for animation motion control. In J. K. Salisbury & M. A. Srinivasan (Eds.), *Proceedings of the Fourth PHANToM User's Group Workshop.* AI Lab Technical Report No. 1675 and RLE Technical Report No. 633. Cambridge, MA: MIT.

Hespanha, J. P., Liberzon, D., Morse, A. S., Anderson, B. D. O., Brinsmead, T. S., & de Bruyne, F. (2001). Multiple model adaptive control, part 2: Switching. *International Journal of Robust and Nonlinear Control Special Issue on Hybrid Systems in Control, 11*(5), 479–496.

Hespanha, J. P., McLaughlin, M. L., & Sukhatme, G. S. (2001). Haptic collaboration over the Internet. In M. L. McLaughlin, J. P. Hespanha, & G. S. Sukhatme (Eds.), *Touch in virtual environments.* IMSC Series in Multimedia. New York: Prentice Hall.

Hespanha, J., Sukhatme, G., McLaughlin, M., Akbarian, M., Garg, R., & Zhu, W. (2000). Hetereogeneous haptic collaboration over the Internet. *Preprints of the Fifth PHANToM User's Group Workshop*, Aspen, CO.

Ho, C., Basdogan, C., Slater, M., Durlach, N., & Srinivasan, M. A. (1998). *An experiment on the influence of haptic communication on the sense of being together.* Paper presented at the British Telecom Workshop on Presence in Shared Virtual Environments, Ipswitch. Retrieved from www.cs.ucl. ac.uk/staff/m.slater/BTWorkshop/touchexp.html.

Hogan, N. (1989). Controlling impedance at the man/machine interface. In *Proceedings of the IEEE International Conference on Robotics and Automation*, Vol. 3, 1626–1631. Scottsdale, AZ.

Hollins, M., Faldowski, R., Rao, S., & F. Young (1993). Perceptual dimensions of tactile surface texture: A multidimensional scaling analysis. *Perception and Psychophysics, 54*, 697–705.

Howe, R. D. (1994). Tactile sensing and control of robotic manipulation. *Journal of Advanced Robotics, 8*(3), 245–261.

Huang, C., Qu, H., & Kaufman, A. E. (1998). Volume rendering with haptic interaction. In J. K. Salisbury & M. A. Srinivasan (Eds.), Proceedings of the Third PHANToM Users Group, PUG98. AI Technical Report no. 1643 and RLE Technical Report no. 624. Cambridge, MA: MIT. Retrieved from www sensable.com/community/98papers/2%20cwhuang-pug98.pdf.

Hughes, B., & Jannson, G. (1994). Texture perception via active touch. Special Issue: Perception-movement, information and dynamics. *Human Movement Science, 13*(3–4), 301–333.

Hutchins, M., & Gunn, C. (1999). A haptics constraints class library. In J. K. Salisbury & M. A. Srinivasan (Eds.), *Proceedings of the Fourth PHANToM User's Group Workshop*. AI Lab Technical Report No. 1675 and RLE Technical Report No. 633. Cambridge, MA: MIT.

Ikei, Y., Wakamatsu, K., & Fukuda, S. (1997). *Texture presentation by vibratory tactile display*. Paper presented at the Virtual Reality Annual International Symposium, Albuquerque, NM.

Iwata, H., Yano, H., & Hashimoto, W. (1997). LHX: An integrated software tool for haptic interface. *Computers and Graphics*, *21*(4), 413–420.

Jansson, G. (1998). Can a haptic force feedback display provide visually impaired people with useful information about texture roughness and 3D form of virtual objects? In P. Sharkey, D. Rose, & J.-I. Lindstrom (Eds.), *Proceedings of the 2nd European Conference on Disability, Virtual Reality, and Associated Technologies* (pp. 105–111). Reading, UK.

Jansson, G. (2001). Perceiving complex virtual scenes with a PHANToM without visual guidance. In M. L. McLaughlin, J. P. Hespanha, & G. S. Sukhatme (Eds.), *Touch in Virtual Environments*. IMSC Series in Multimedia. New York: Prentice Hall.

Jansson, G. (2001, June 1). *Personal communication*.

Jansson, G., & Billberger, K. (1999). The PHANToM used without visual guidance. In Proceedings of the First PHANToM Users Research Symposium (PURS'99).

Jansson, G., Faenger, J., Konig, H., & Billberger, K. (1998). Visually impaired persons' use of the PHANToM for information about texture and 3D form of virtual objects. In J. K. Salisbury & M. A. Srinivasan (Eds.), *Proceedings of the Third PHANToM User's Group, PUG98*. AI Technical Report no. 1643 and RLE Technical Report no. 624. Cambridge, MA: MIT.

Jeong, W., & Jacobson, D. (2001). Haptic and auditory display for multimodal information systems. In M. L. McLaughlin, J. P. Hespanha, & G. S. Sukhatme (Eds.), *Touch in Virtual Environments*. IMSC Series in Multimedia. New York: Prentice Hall.

Johansson, A. J., & Linde, J. (1998). *Using simple force feedback mechanisms to visualize structures by haptics*. Paper presented at the Second Swedish Symposium of MultiModal Communications.

Johansson, A. J., & Linde, J. (1999). *Using simple force feedback mechanisms as haptic visualization tools*. Paper presented at the 16th IEEE Instrumentation and Measurement Technology Conference.

Kirkpatrick, A., & Douglas, S. (1999). Evaluating haptic interfaces in terms of interaction techniques. In J. K. Salisbury & M. A. Srinivasan (Eds.), *Proceedings of the Fourth PHANToM Users Group Workshop*. AI Lab Technical Report No. 1675 and RLE Technical Report No. 633. Cambridge, MA: MIT.

Klatzky, R., & Lederman, S. (2001). Perceiving texture through a probe. In M. L. McLaughlin, J. P. Hespanha, & G. S. Sukhatme (Eds.), *Touch in Virtual Environments*. IMSC Series in Multimedia New York: Prentice Hall.

Klatzky, R. L., Lederman, S. J., & Reed, C. (1987). There's more to touch than meets the eye: The salience of object attributes for haptics with and without vision. *Journal of Experimental Psychology: General, 116*(4), 356–369.

Lamport, L. (1997). Concurrent reading and writing. *Communications of the ACM, 20*(11), 806–811.

Langrana, N., Burdea, G., Ladeiji, J., & Dinsmore, M. (1997). Human performance using virtual reality tumor palpation simulation. *Computers and Graphics, 21*(4), 451–458.

Lazzari, M., McLaughlin, M. L., Jaskowiak, J., Wong, W. L., & Akbarian, M. (2001). A haptic exhibition of daguerreotype cases for USC's Fisher Gallery. In M. L. McLaughlin, J. P. Hespanha, & G. S. Sukhatme (Eds.), *Touch in Virtual Environments*. IMSC Series in Multimedia. New York: Prentice Hall.

Lederman, S. J. (1985). Tactual roughness perception in humans: A psychological assessment of the role of vibration. In I. Darian-Smith & A. Goodwin (Eds.) *Hand function and the neocortex* (pp. 77–92). Berlin: Springer-Verlag.

Lederman, S. L., Thorne, G., & Jones, B. (1986). Perception of texture by vision and touch: Multidimensionality of sensory integration. *Journal of Experimental Social Psychology: Human Perception & Performance, 12*(2), 169-180.

Lin, M. C., Gregory, A., Ehmann, S., Gottschalk, S., & Taylor, R. (1999). Contact determination for real-time haptic interaction in 3D modeling, editing, and painting. In J. K. Salisbury & M. A. Srinivasan (Eds.), *Proceedings of the Fourth PHANToM User's Group Workshop*. AI Lab Technical Report No. 1675 and RLE Technical Report No. 633. Cambridge, MA: MIT.

Lin, M. C., & Gottschalk, S. (1998). *Collision detection between geometric models: A survey*. Technical report. University of North Carolina.

Loomis, J. M., & Lederman, S. J. (1986). Tactual perception. In K. Boff, L. Kaufman, & J. Thomas, (Eds.), *Handbook of human perception and performance*, Vol. II, 31-1-31-41. New York: John Wiley and Sons.

Luecke, G. R, & Chaim, Y. H. (1997). Contact sensation in the synthetic environment using the ISU force reflecting exoskeleton. In *Proceedings of the Virtual Reality Annual International Symposium (VRAIS '97)* (pp. 192–198). Albuquerque, NM.

Machado, L. S., Moraes, R. M., & Zuffo, M. K. (2000). Fuzzy rule-based evaluation for a haptic and stereo simulator for bone marrow harvest for transplant. *Preprints of the Fifth Annual PHANToM Users Group Workshop*. Aspen, CO: Given Institute.

Marcy, G., Temkin, B., Gorman, P. J., & Krummel, T. M. (1998). Tactile Max: A haptic interface for 3D Studio Max. In *Proceedings of the Third PHANToM User's Group, PUG98*. AI Technical Report no. 1643 and RLE Technical Report no. 624. Cambridge, MA: MIT.

Mark, W. R., Randolph, S. C., Finch, M., van Verth, J. & Taylor, II, R. M. (1996). Adding force feedback to graphics systems: Issues and solutions. In *Computer Graphics Proceedings, Annual Conference Series, ACM SIGGRAPH* (pp. 447–452).

Mascarenhas, A., Ehmann, S., Gregory, A., Lin, M. C., & Manocha, D. (2001). Six degrees-of-freedom haptic visualization. In M. L. McLaughlin, J. P. Hespanha, & G. S. Sukhatme (Eds.), *Touch in Virtual Environments*. IMSC Series in Multimedia. New York: Prentice Hall.

Massie, T. (1998). A tangible goal for 3D modeling. *IEEE Computer Graphics and Applications, 18* (3), 62–65.

Massie, T. H., & Salisbury, J. K. (1994). The PHANToM haptic interface: A device for probing virtual objects. In *Proceedings of the ASME Winter Annual Meeting, Symposium on Haptic Interfaces for Virtual Environment and Teleoperator Systems*, Chicago, IL.

McLaughlin, M. L., Goldberg, S. G., Ellison, N. B., & Lucas, J. (1999). Measuring Internet audiences: Patrons of an online art museum. In S. Jones (Ed.), *Doing Internet research* (pp. 163–178). Newbury Park, CA: Sage Publications.

McLaughlin, M. L., Sukhatme, G., Hespanha, J., Shahabi, C., Ortega, A., & Medioni, G. (2000). The haptic museum. *Proceedings of the EVA 2000 Conference on Electronic Imaging and the Visual Arts*, Florence, Italy.

McNeely, W. A., Puterbaugh, K. D., & Troy, J. J. (1999). Six degree-of-freedom haptic rendering using voxel sampling. In *Computer Graphics Proceedings, Annual Conference Series, ACM SIGGRAPH* (pp. 401–408).

Miller, B. E., Colgate, J. E., & Freeman, R. A. (1999). Passive implementation for a class of static nonlinear environments in haptic display. In *Proceedings of the IEEE International Conference on Robotics and Automation*, Vol. 4 (pp. 2937–2942).

Mor, A. B. (1998). 5 DOF force feedback using the 3 DOF PHANToM and a 2 DOF device. *Proceedings of the Third PHANToM Users Group, PUG98*. AI Technical Report no. 1643 and RLE Technical Report no. 624. Cambridge, MA: MIT.

Morse, A. S. (1996). Supervisory control of families of linear set-point controllers. Part 1: Exact matching. *IEEE Transactions on Automatic Control*, 41, 1413–1431.

National Automotive Center (1999). *By fighting computer wars today, U.S. Army soldiers will help design better weapons for any real war in the future.* Retrieved from www.tacom.army.mil/tardec/nac/newsletter/compwars.htm.

Naval Aerospace Medical Research Laboratory (2000). *Accurate orientation information through a tactile sensory pathway in aerospace, land, and sea environments.* Retrieved from www.namrl.navy.mil/accel/tsas/body.htm.

O'Modhrain, M. S., & Gillespie, B. (1999). The Moose: A haptic user interface for blind persons. Retrieved from archimedes.stanford.edu/videotap/moose.html.

Ortega, A. (2001). Haptic data compression. In M. L. McLaughlin, J. P. Hespanha, & G. S. Sukhatme (Eds.), *Touch in virtual environments*. IMSC Series in Multimedia. New York: Prentice Hall.

Pai, D. K., & Reissell, L. M. (1997). Haptic interaction with multiresolution image curves. *Computers and Graphics*, *21*(4), 405–411.

Ramloll, R., Yu, W., Brewster, S., Riedel, B., Burton, M, & Dimigen, G. (2000*). Constructing sonified haptic line graphs for the blind student: First steps*. Paper presented at ASSETS 2000. Retrieved from www.dcs.gla.ac.uk/~rayu/Publications/Assets2000.pdf.

Rassmuss-Gröhn, K., & Sjöstrom, C. (1998). *Using a force feedback device to present graphical information to people with visual disabilities.* Paper presented at the Second Swedish Symposium on Multimodal Communication, Lund, Sweden. Retrieved from www.certec.lth.se/doc/usinga/.

Roumeliotis, S. I., Sukhatme, G. S., & Bekey, G. A. (1999). Smoother based 3-D attitude estimation for mobile robot localization. In *Proceedings of the 1999 IEEE International Conference on Robotics and Automation*, Detroit, MI.

Ruspini, D., & Khatib., O. (2001). Simulation with contact for haptic interaction. In M. L. McLaughlin, J. P. Hespanha, & G. S. Sukhatme (Eds.), *Touch in Virtual Environments*. IMSC Series in Multimedia. New York: Prentice Hall.

Salisbury, K., Brock, D., Massie, T., Swarup, N., & Zilles, C. (1995) Haptic rendering: Programming touch interaction with virtual objects. In *Proceedings of the 1995 Symposium on Interactive 3D Graphics* (pp. 123–130).

Shahabi, C., Ghoting, A., Kaghazian, L., McLaughlin, M., & Shanbhag, G. (forthcoming). Analysis of haptic data for sign language recognition. *Proceedings of the First International Conference on Universal Access in Human-Computer Interaction (UAHCI),* New Orleans, LA. Hillsdale, NJ: Lawrence Erlbaum.

Shahabi, C., Ghoting, A., Kaghazian, L., McLaughlin, M., & Shanhag, G. (2001). Recognition of sign language utilizing two alternative representations of haptic data. In M. L. McLaughlin, J. P. Hespanha, & G. S. Sukhatme (Eds.), *Touch in Virtual Environments*. IMSC Series in Multimedia. New York: Prentice Hall.

Shahabi, C., Kolahdouzan, M., Barish, G., Zimmermann, R., Yao, D., & Fu, L. (2001, June). *Alternative techniques for the efficient acquisition of haptic data.* Paper presented at the meeting of ACM SIGMETRICS/Performance 2001, Cambridge, MA.

Shulman, S. (1998). Digital antiquities. *Computer Graphics World, 21*(11), 34–38.

Sjöstrom, C. (1997). The Phantasticon: The PHANToM for disabled children. Center of Rehabilitation Engineering Research, Lund University. Retrieved from www.certec.lth.se/.

Snibbe, S., Anderson, S., & Verplank, B. (1998). Springs and constraints for 3D drawing, In J. K. Salisbury & M. A. Srinivasan (Eds.), Proceedings of the Third PHANToM Users Group Workshop, PUG98. AI Technical Report no. 1643 and RLE Technical Report no. 624. Cambridge, MA: MIT. Retrieved from www.sensable.com/community/98papers/13%20springs98.pdf.

Srinivasan, M. (2001, February). *Haptic research in the MIT Touch Lab*. Paper presented at the Touch in Virtual Environments Conference, University of Southern California.

Srinivasan, M., & Basdogan, C. (1997). Haptics in virtual environments: Taxonomy, research status, and challenges. *Computers and Graphics, 21*(4), 393–404.

Srinivasan, M. A., Beauregard, G. L., & Brock, D. L. (1996). The impact of visual information on haptic perception of stiffness in virtual environments. *Proceedings of the ASME Dynamic Systems and Control Division*, Atlanta, GA.

Sukhatme, G., Hespanha, J., McLaughlin, M., Shahabi, C. & Ortega, A, (2000). Touch in immersive environments. *Proceedings of the EVA 2000 Conference on Electronic Imaging and the Visual Arts*, Edinburgh, Scotland.

Transdimension (2000). *Motivations for military applications of tactile interface.* Retrieved from www.transdimension.com/tactile3.htm.

Tsai, J. C., & Colgate, J. E. (1995). Stability of discrete time systems with unilateral nonlinearities. *Proceedings of the ASME International Mechanical Engineering Conference and Exposition.*

Tyler, M. (2001, February 23). *Personal communication.*

Veldkamp, P., Turner, G., Gunn, C., & Stevenson, D. (1998). Incorporating haptics into mining industry applications. *Proceedings of the Third PHANToM User's Group, PUG98.* AI Technical Report no. 1643 and RLE Technical Report no. 624. Cambridge, MA: MIT.

Way, T. P., & Barner, K. E. (1997). Automatic visual to tactile translation, Part I: Human factors, Access methods and image manipulation. *IEEE Transactions on Rehabilitation Engineering, 5*, 81– 94.

Wilson, J. P, Kline-Schoder, R., Kenton, M. A., & Hogan, N. (1999). Algorithms for network-based force feedback. In J. K. Salisbury & M. A. Srinivasan (Eds.), *Proceedings of the Fourth PHANToM User's Group Workshop.* AI Lab Technical Report No. 1675 and RLE Technical Report No. 633. Cambridge, MA: MIT.

Wright-Patterson Air Force Base (1997). (PAM #97-091) Synthesized Immersion Research Environment (SIRE). Retrieved from www.wpafb.af.mil/ascpa/factshts/scitech/sire97.htm.

Yu, W., Ramloll, R., & Brewster, S. (2000). *Haptics graphs for blind computer users.* Paper presented at the Haptic Human-Computer Interaction Workshop, University of Glasgow.

Zilles, C. B., & Salisbury, J. K. (1995). A constraint-based God-object method for haptic display. *Proceedings of the IEEE/RSJ International. Conference on Intelligent Robots and Systems (*pp. 146–151). Pittsburgh, PA

Simulation with Contact for Haptic Interaction

Diego Ruspini and Oussama Khatib

In recent years, there have been many efforts to simulate physical environments accurately in both robotics and computer graphics. A physically accurate simulation can be used to obtain insight into the real-world behavior of a robotic, manufacturing, space, or other dynamic environment. Haptics is one area where the need to find the dynamic motions of a virtual environment rapidly is particularly important.

In haptics, a force-reflecting mechanical device is used to apply forces to a user (typically through the user's finger or hand), and thus create the illusion of physical contact with a real physical environment. To deliver a convincing and intuitive sense of presence, the motions of the virtual model must behave realistically as they are influenced by the forces applied by the user. In this way the user can easily obtain information about an object's size, shape, effective mass, and stiffness, as well as many other internal and external object properties. In this paper we discuss our effort to develop a general purpose dynamic virtual environment allowing direct "hands-on" interaction through a haptic interface.

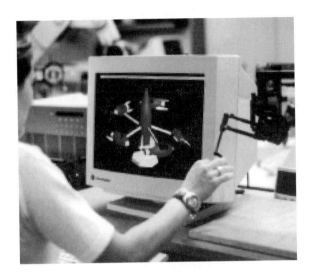

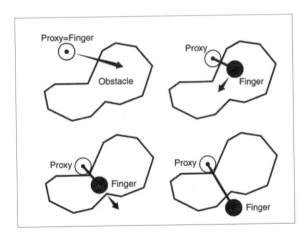

Figure 2-1(a)(b): A user haptically interacting with a dynamic virtual environment (a). The virtual proxy moves to locally minimize the distance to the user's finger position subject to the constraints in the environment (b).

HAPTIC RENDERING

Early haptic rendering systems modeled surface contacts by generating a repulsive force proportional to the amount of penetration into an obstacle. While these penalty-based methods worked well to model simple obstacles, such as planes or spheres, a number of difficulties were encountered when trying to extend these models to display more complex environments. An alternative is to look not at the penetration of the user's finger into the object at all, but instead to constrain the motions of a substitute virtual object. In the method we proposed (Ruspini, Kolarov, & Khatib, 1996), a representative object, a "proxy," substitutes in the virtual environment for the physical finger or probe. The "virtual proxy" can be viewed as if connected to the user's real finger by a stiff spring. As the user moves his/her finger in the workspace of the haptic device, he/she may pass into or through one or more of the virtual obstacles. The proxy, however, is stopped by the obstacles and quickly moves to a position that minimizes its distance to the user's finger position. The haptic device is used to generate the forces of the virtual spring that appear to the user as the constraint forces caused by contact with a real environment. This approach is similar to the method for the "god-object" first proposed by Zilles and Salisbury (1994) but does not require a priori knowledge of the surface topology. An example of the system can be seen in Figure 2-1(a)(b).

DYNAMIC MOTION MODELS

In the system described previously (Ruspini et al., 1996), only interactions between a simple representative object were considered. Interobject interactions were not modeled. Considerable work in modeling interactions between multiple simple rigid bodies has been conducted (Baraff, 1989, 1994; Mirtich, 1994). Most of these systems, however, are too slow for interactive simulation and cannot model articulated linkages efficiently.

Take, for example, the modeling of a articulated manipulator shown in Figure 2-2(a)(b). The robot modeled has a total of 26 degrees of freedom (DOF). If each link is modeled as a separate 6 DOF object, the entire system has an effective total of 156 DOF. At each step in the simulation not only must the simulator integrate the equations of motion for this large system but it must also find five internal forces that constrain each joint ($5 \times 26 = 130$ total).

While for simple linkages it has been shown that this constraint equation can be solved in $O(n)$ time (the constraint matrix is banded) (Baraff, 1996), the amount of unnecessary computation is still huge. In addition, small errors caused during the integration of the 156 DOF system can add up and cause one or more of the original internal constraints to be violated. Specifying the appropriate motion for each link to correct these errors can be problematic.

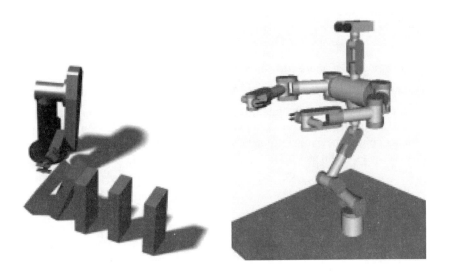

Figure 2-2(a)(b): An interactive dynamic environment.

Efficiency can be improved by modeling only the true degrees of freedom of the system and avoid solving for the internal constraints of the system. The configuration of an n-DOF object can be described by q, a set of n independent generalized coordinates. The equation of motion for the system can be described by

$$\ddot{q} = A^{-1}(q)\left[\Gamma - b(q,\dot{q}) - g(q)\right]$$ (2.1)

where $A(q)^{-1}$ designates the inverse kinetic energy matrix, $b(q,\dot{q})$ the centrifugal and Coriolis force vector, $g(q)$ the gravity force vector, and Γ the generalized torque vector of the object. Several methods of computing the inverse equation of motion for a set of rigid bodies have been proposed (Featherstone, 1987).

When two or more objects exist in an environment their configuration vectors can be combined into a new configuration vector $q = \begin{bmatrix} q_1^T & q_2^T & q_3^T & q_l^T \end{bmatrix}^T$ where l is the number of independent objects in the environment and q_i is the configuration vector for the ith object. Because the equations for a set of objects have the same form as equations for a single object, the entire system can be treated as a single n degrees-of-freedom body where n is the sum of the degrees of freedom of each object.

When contact or collision occurs between objects or links in the system, a constraint exists and one or more of the terms in q is no longer independent. In this case a set of constraint forces or impulses must be applied to prevent interpenetrations between the primitives.

CONTACT SPACE

Given two bodies, A and B, in collision there exists a set of points c_a on body A and c_b on body B such that at collision time $t, c_a(t) = c_b(t)$. If the objects in the world are modeled as being constructed from the union of convex polyhedra, the contact region between two bodies will be defined by a set of convex polygons. In this situation it is sufficient to consider contact only at the extremal-points of the contact region created by the intersection of the contact surfaces (Palmer, 1987).

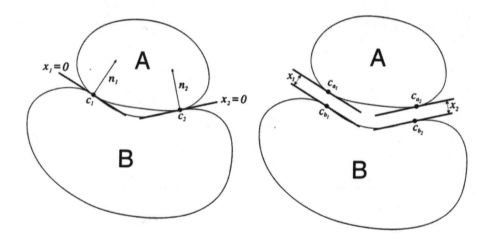

Figure 2-3: Contact space parameter $x_\oplus = \begin{bmatrix} x_1 & x_2 \end{bmatrix}^T$ locally describe the motion at the contact normal to the surface.

Given this polygonal contact region assumption, only a finite number of contact points need to be considered. We shall define c_{a_i} as the ith contact point attached to body A. In addition for each contact point a unit normal n_i perpendicular to the contact region is defined. This information can be used to define a set of contact parameters x_i that describe the relative distance between contact point c_{a_i} and c_{b_i} in the direction perpendicular to the contact surface:

$$x_i = n_i^T \left(c_{a_i} - c_{b_i} \right) \tag{2.2}$$

for $1 \le i \le m$. These "contact" parameters form a space that describes the motion of the bodies during contact and collision. An example of this space is illustrated in Figure 2-3. For clarity, this space is shown when the objects are separating; in reality the space is only defined in the immediate neighborhood around the time of contact.

The contact space parameters will in general not be independent. Consider when a four-legged rigid table rests on a flat surface. The position of any one of the legs can be inferred by knowing the positions of the other three. Additionally, because of the rigidity condition, at most three forces at the contact points are required to prevent the table from penetrating the floor. The force on one of the legs will be zero.

We will therefore define two sets of contact space parameters, x and $x_\oplus$. The vector $x_\oplus$ consists of the full "augmented" set of contact space parameters (one per contact point). A subset of the contact parameters $x \subseteq x_\oplus$ contains only the "active" contact points of the entire contact space. A contact point is "active" if the force or impulse applied at the contact point is nonzero. Which parameters belong to the "active" subset is for now unknown, but will be identified later.

We will associate a matrix S such that $x = Sx_\oplus$ that selects the members of $x_\oplus$ that belong to x. Given these spaces we can define other parameters for velocity $v_\oplus = \dot{x}_\oplus$, acceleration $a_\oplus = \ddot{x}_\oplus$, forces $f_\oplus = Sf$, and impulses $p_\oplus = Sp$.

At the time of contact/collision t, $x_\oplus = \vec{0}$ and a Jacobian $v_\oplus = J_\oplus \dot{q}$ can be found (Ruspini & Khatib, 1999). In addition it is possible to define the augmented operational (contact) inertia matrix:

$$\Lambda_\oplus^{-1} = J_\oplus A^{-1} J_\oplus^T. \tag{2.3}$$

This matrix is very similar to the operational space inertia matrix used in robotic control (Khatib, 1987). The matrix $\Lambda_\oplus$ represents the effective mass seen at all the contact points and characterizes the dynamic relationships between the contact points. The inverse active contact space inertia matrix

$$\Lambda^{-1} = S\Lambda_\oplus^{-1} S^T \tag{2.4}$$

being composed from a set of independent contact parameters is positive definite and hence invertible.

Impulse Force Resolution

If two or more bodies in the system are colliding, then some elements of $v_\oplus$ are negative. In a system of rigid bodies an impulse must be applied to prevent the interpenetration of objects. While the nature of the deformations that occur during a real collision is quite complex, several analytical methods have been proposed to compute the needed impulse forces.

Here we will examine one of the most common models for rigid body collision/contact. This framework, however, is sufficiently general to allow other contact models to be used.

Collision Model

A common empirical model is to require that for each active contact point, the velocity after the collision must be $-\varepsilon$ times the relative velocity of the contact point prior to the collision, where ε is a known coefficient of restitution. This constraint can be written as:

$$v^+ = -\varepsilon v^-, \tag{2.5}$$

where v^-, v^+ is the relative velocity vector of the contacts before and after the collision.

The above constraint only describes the behavior of the active contact points. At these the impulse force must be greater then zero,

$$p > \vec{0}. \tag{2.6}$$

Lastly, an additional constraint is required to constrain the motion at all the contact points.

$$v_\oplus^+ \geq -\varepsilon v_\oplus^-. \tag{2.7}$$

The active contact points satisfy this constraint by default. The constraint requires that if a contact force is inactive (contact impulse force is zero), then the relative velocity at the contact point must be at least as large as it would be if the point were active. The zero impulse force requirement on the nonactive contact points can be achieved by defining

$$p_\oplus = S^T p \tag{2.8}$$

Equations (2.5–2.8) describe the nature of the collision, but are not in a form where the unknown impulse forces p can be solved for directly. We can rewrite the constraints, however, so that the solution no longer depends on any unknown quantities.

Finding the Impulse Constraint Equations

The unknown impulse forces and the contact space velocities are related by the expression:

$$p \stackrel{def}{=} \Lambda \Delta v, \tag{2.9}$$

where $\Delta v = v^+ - v^-$ is the change in contact space velocity caused by the collision. Combining equations 2.9 and 2.5 we can rewrite constraint equation 2.5 as:

$$\Lambda^{-1}p + (1+\varepsilon)v^- = \vec{0}. \tag{2.10}$$

Observing that in equation 2.7 each row of the left hand side is strictly positive even if nonactive points are considered and that $p > 0$, we can obtain a new form of the constraint by multiplying each side of equation 2.10 by p^T:

$$p^T\left(\Lambda^{-1}p + (1+\varepsilon)v^-\right) = 0. \tag{2.11}$$

The above expression is still defined in the unknown space of the active contacts, but by noting that $v^- = Sv_\oplus^-$ and using the definition of Λ^{-1} (equation 2.4), we obtain

$$p^T S\left(\Lambda_\oplus^{-1}S^T p + (1+\varepsilon)v_\oplus^-\right) = 0. \tag{2.12}$$

Finally, using our definition of $p_\oplus$ from equation 2.8 and noting that $v_\oplus = J_\oplus \dot{q}^-$ we obtain an expression for constraint equation 2.5 that is in a form that does not depend on any unknown parameters except $p_\oplus$:

$$p_\oplus^T\left(\Lambda_\oplus^{-1}p_\oplus + (1+\varepsilon)J_\oplus q^-\right) = 0. \tag{2.13}$$

Equation 2.5 is only valid if constraint equation 2.7 is also satisfied. Equation 2.7 places an inequality constraint on all the contact points, not just the points in the active set. Only the active contact points, where the impulse forces are positive, alter the motion of the system. The change in contact space velocities caused by the active contacts can be found to be:

$$\Delta v_\oplus = J_\oplus A^{-1}J^T p. \tag{2.14}$$

Rewriting equation 2.7 using equation 2.14, we obtain:

$$\Lambda_\oplus^{-1}p_\oplus \geq -(1+\varepsilon)J_\oplus q^-. \tag{2.15}$$

We can now write all the constraint equations, 2.13, 2.6, and 2.15, in a form suitable for finding the unknown impulse vector $p_\oplus$:

Impulse Constraint Equations

$$\boxed{\begin{aligned} p_\oplus^T\Lambda_\oplus^{-1}p_\oplus + (1+\varepsilon)p_\oplus^T J_\oplus q^- &= 0, \\ p_\oplus &\geq 0, \\ \Lambda_\oplus^{-1}p_\oplus &\geq -(1+\varepsilon)J_\oplus q^-. \end{aligned}} \tag{2.16}$$

Given that $\Lambda_{\oplus}^{-1}$ is positive semidefinite such a system can be solved using a quadratic programming package as described by Gill, Hammarling, Murray, Saunders, and Wright (1996). In addition it should be noted that these constraints have the same form as the linear complementary problem (LCP) solved by Baraff (1994) for simple rigid-body simulation. As can now be seen, the constraints described above form the same set of constraints for generalized articulated body systems as was derived for simple rigid bodies previously (Baraff, 1989, 1994).

Once a solution of the augmented contact space impulse vector $p_{\oplus}$ has been found the vector of active contact parameters and the selection matrix S can easily be computed. The non-zero terms of $p_{\oplus}$ form the active set of contact points p. The post-collision-in-configuration space velocities $\dot{q}^{+}$ created by a contact space impulse p is given by

$$\dot{q}^{+} = \dot{q}^{-} + \Delta\dot{q} = \dot{q}^{-} + A^{-1}J^{T}p \qquad (2.17)$$

and the integration of the equations of motion continued from this updated state.

Collision Analysis

The largest benefit of describing the constraint equations in contact space is that the interaction between groups of dynamic systems can be described easily without having to examine the complex equations of motion of each individual system. As such, a collision model can be developed with the same ease as if one were considering interaction only between simple bodies.

Further insight into the nature of the collision constraints can be found by explicitly inverting the inverse active contact space inertia matrix Λ^{-1}. While not strictly required for the purpose of simulation, it provides additional understanding about the constraint equations. Given Λ the vector of contact space impulses p can be expressed from equation 2.1 as:

$$p = -(1+\varepsilon)\Lambda J\dot{q}^{-}. \qquad (2.18)$$

Inserting p into equation 17, a linear expression for $\dot{q}^{+}$ from $\dot{q}^{-}$ is obtained:

$$\dot{q}^{+} = \left[I - (1+\varepsilon)\overline{J}J\right]\dot{q}^{-}, \qquad (2.19)$$

where $\overline{J} = A^{-1}J^{T}\Lambda$ is the dynamically consistent generalized inverse of J. This is the unique generalized inverse of J that is consistent with the natural dynamics of the system (Khatib, 1988, 1990; Russakow, 1995).

Separating the ε term, we obtain

$$\dot{q}^{+} = \overline{J}\left(-\varepsilon J\dot{q}^{-}\right) + \left[I - \overline{J}J\right]\dot{q}^{-}. \qquad (2.20)$$

The matrix $\left| I - \bar{J}J \right|$ is the basis of the null space of the contact space. The contact space velocities are not affected by velocity vectors mapped through this space. Lastly, by noting that $-\varepsilon J\dot{q}^- = -\varepsilon v^- = v^+$ we see that

$$\dot{q}^+ = \bar{J}v^+ + \left[I - \bar{J}J \right]\dot{q}^-. \tag{2.21}$$

In this expression we can clearly see the effect of the collision constraints on the simulated system. The configuration space velocity after the collision is made up of two components:

- The configuration space velocities that realize the desired empirical restitution velocity v^+ with the minimum change in the kinetic energy of the system.

- The prior configuration space velocities q^- mapped through the contact space null space $\left| I - \bar{J}J \right|$ eliminating any motion that would affect the velocities in the contact space.

Equation 2.21 is similar in form to the expression for the cartesian space control of redundant mechanisms (Khatib, 1990). Such a connection with control is natural since the constraint equations are in effect commanding an operational space velocity in the contact space while allowing motions in the redundant (unconstrained) directions to continue unmodified.

CONTACT FORCE RESOLUTION

As was the case for computing collision impulse forces, contact forces can be computed in a similar manner. For brevity we will only highlight the derivation that follows closely the work done in the previous section. A resting or sliding contact occurs when $v_{\oplus} = 0$ and no penetration exists. If a negative acceleration ($a < 0$) exists at any of the contact parameters, however, objects in the environment may immediately begin to penetrate. To prevent this from occurring, a contact force f must be applied at the contact points in order to prevent penetration.

As was the case for collision, we can establish three constraints required to prevent penetration

$$\begin{aligned} a &= \vec{0}, \\ a_{\oplus} &\geq \vec{0}, \\ f &> 0. \end{aligned} \tag{2.22}$$

As in the situation with collision, we will establish a selection matrix S_c that will be used to select the contact points that belong to the active set. Note that this set can be and is often different than the set of contacts active during collision.

From equation 2.1 we can obtain an expression for the active contact space acceleration

$$a = JA^{-1}[\Gamma - b - g] + \dot{J}\dot{q}. \qquad (2.23)$$

Breaking the generalized torque vector Γ into actuator torques Γ_{joint} and external forces $\Gamma_{ext} = J^T f$ we obtain a general expression for the contact space accelerations in terms of f

$$a = JA^{-1}J^T f + JA^{-1}[\Gamma_{joint} - b - g] + \dot{J}\dot{q}. \qquad (2.24)$$

Now expanding $J = S_c J_\oplus$ and following a similar line of action as we did for collision we can obtain a similar set of constraints:

Resting/Sliding Contact Constraint Equations

$$f_\oplus^T \left(\Lambda_\oplus^{-1} f_\oplus + a_{\oplus(free)} \right) = 0,$$
$$f_\oplus \geq 0, \qquad (2.25)$$
$$\Lambda_\oplus^{-1} f_\oplus \geq -a_{\oplus(free)},$$

where $a_{\oplus(free)} = J_\oplus A^{-1}[\Gamma_{joint} - b - g] + \dot{J}_\oplus \dot{q}$ represents the contact space acceleration that would occur if no contact existed. As is the case with collision, these constraints form a LCP system and can be solved by using a quadratic programming package like Gill et al. (1996) or as was done by Baraff (1994).

Once the unknown augmented contact spaces forces $f_\oplus$ have been found the active forces f and selection matrix S_c can be obtained trivially. The configuration space acceleration $\ddot{q}$ that results from the application of the contact space forces is

$$\ddot{q} = A^{-1}(q)\left[\Gamma_{joint} + J^T f - b(q,\dot{q}) - g(q)\right]. \qquad (2.26)$$

COMBINING HAPTIC AND DYNAMIC ENVIRONMENTS

Haptic interaction can be combined with dynamic simulation to allow rich, intuitive interactions with virtual environments. Attaching the virtual proxy to a virtual object allows it to be used as a virtual tool that is no longer restricted to a simple point or sphere. Its shape and movement can be selected as appropriate for a given task. The constraints affixing the virtual proxy to the virtual tool may restrict all or only a few of the degrees of freedom of the virtual tool. This may be needed if the number of degrees of freedom of the haptic device is less then that of the virtual tool.

Figure 2-4(a): A frame of an animation showing the dynamic interaction of multiple articulated/rigid bodies.

This framework has been used as the basis for the development of a dynamic haptic simulation system. Figure 2-4(a)(b) illustrates some of the environments that have been modeled with this system. Other environments, including construction and underwater environments, have also been modeled (Lee, Ruspini, & Khatib, 1994).

Figure 2-4(a) is one frame from an animation consisting of two puma560 manipulators (6 DOF each) on which a rain of large blocks is allowed to fall. A total of 366 DOF are modeled. Figure 2-4(b) depicts a similar environment where two puma560 manipulators and two rigid-bodies (16 DOF) are modeled. Direct haptic interaction is permitted via a 3 DOF PHANToM haptic manipulator. The user is allowed to push and attach himself/herself to any of the objects in the environment and feel the force and impact created by their interaction.

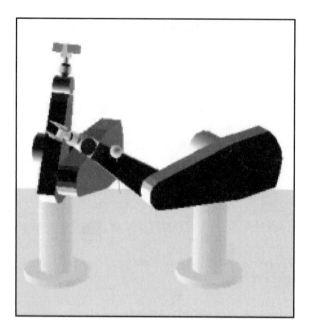

Figure 2-4(b): A frame from an animation in which direct haptic interaction is permitted
between the user and the objects in the environment.

CONCLUSION

We have presented a framework for haptic interaction with complex articulated multibody systems. The use of generalized contact space parameters allows the interactions between arbitrarily complex models to be efficiently represented. Impact and contact forces
between the bodies can then be efficiently solved to prevent penetration between all the objects in the environment. In the future we hope to apply this technology to model realistic
real-world environments that cannot be easily modeled with traditional physical mock-ups.

REFERENCES

Baraff, D. (1994). Fast contact force computation for nonpenetrating rigid bodies. *Proceedings of SIGGRAPH '94* (pp. 23–34).

Baraff, D. (1996). Linear-time dynamics using Lagrange multipliers. *Proceedings of SIGGRAPH '96* (pp. 137–146).

Baraff, D. (1989). Analytical methods for dynamic simulation of non-penetrating rigid bodies. *Proceedings of SIGGRAPH '89. Computer Graphics, 23*, 223–232.

Featherstone, R. (1987). *Robot dynamics algorithms*. Boston/Dordrecht/Lancaster: Kluwer.

Gill, P., Hammarling, S., Murray, W., Saunders, M., & Wright, M. (1996). *User's guide to LLSOL*. Stanford University Technical Report, SOL 86-1.

Khatib, O. (1990). Reduced effective inertia in macro/mini-manipulator systems. *IEEE Journal of Robotics and Automation, 5*(1), 279–284.

Khatib, O. (1988). Object manipulation in a multi-effector robot system. *IEEE Journal of Robotics and Automation, 4*(1), 137–144.

Khatib, O. (1987). A unified approach to motion and force control of robot manipulators: The operational space formulation. *IEEE Journal of Robotics and Automation, 3*(1), 43–53.

Lee, P., Ruspini, D., & Khatib, O. (1994). Dynamic simulation of interactive robotic environment. *Proceedings of the IEEE International Conference on Robotics and Automation*, Vol. 1 (pp. 1147–1152).

Mirtich, B. (1994). Impulse-based dynamic simulation. *Proceedings of the Workshop on the Algorithmic Foundations of Robotics*.

Palmer, R. S. (1987). *Computational complexity of motion and stability of polygons*. Unpublished Ph.D. dissertation, Cornell University.

Ruspini, D., & Khatib, O. (1999). Collision/contact models for dynamic simulation and haptic interaction. *Proceedings of the Ninth International Symposium of Robotics Research (ISRR'99)*(pp. 185–195). Snowbird, Utah.

Ruspini, D., Kolarov, K., & Khatib, O. (1997). The haptic display of complex graphical environments. *Proceedings of SIGGRAPH '97* (pp. 345–352).

Ruspini, D., Kolarov, K., & Khatib, O. (1996, September). *Graphical and haptic manipulation of 3D objects*. In J. K. Salisbury & M. A. Srinivasan (Eds.), *Proceedings of the First PHANToM User's Group Workshop*. AI Technical Report no. 1596 and RLE Technical Report no. 612. Cambridge, MA: MIT.

Russakow, J., (1995). *Experiments in manipulation and assembly by two-arm, free-flying space robots*. Unpublished Ph.D. dissertation, Stanford University.

Zilles, C., & Salisbury, J. K. (1994). Constraint-based God-object method for haptic display. *ASME Haptic Interfaces for Virtual Environment and Teleoperator Systems, Dynamic Systems and Control*, Vol. 1 (pp. 146–150). Pittsburgh, PA.

Stable Control of Haptics

Blake Hannaford, Jee-Hwan Ryu, and Yoon Sang Kim

Humans interact with their surrounding environment through five sensory channels, popularly labeled "sight," "sound," "taste," "smell," and "touch." It is our sense of touch that provides us with much of the information necessary to modify and manipulate the world around us. The word haptic refers to something "of or relating to the sense of touch" (Hogan, 1985). It conveys information about physical properties such as inertia, friction, compliance, temperature, and roughness. This sense can be divided into two categories: the kinesthetic sense, through which we sense movement or force in muscles and joints; and the tactile sense, through which we sense shapes and textures. This chapter will focus on the stable control of devices and systems that support haptic interaction, especially relating to the use of kinesthetic sense in virtual environments.

OVERVIEW

History of Haptics

Figure 3-1(a): Excalibur, developed by the University of Washington and HTI.

Haptics research grew rapidly in the 1990s as researchers and corporations discovered more uses for force-feedback technology. Some representative examples and applications follow. One important catalyst in this frenzy of research was the development and commercialization of the PHANToM family of haptic displays (Massie & Salisbury, 1994). At the University of Washington, a small, portable desktop system, the Pen-Based Force Display (PBFD) (Buttolo & Hannaford, 1995), was developed for interaction with three degrees-of-freedom environments. Another compact master device, developed at IBM and Carnegie Mellon University for teleoperation, departs from more conventional designs by suspending the handle using magnetic levitation (Hollis, Salcudean, & Allan, 1991). Subsequent versions of the device have been used at the University of British Columbia as haptic interfaces to virtual environments (Salcudean & Vlaar, 1997; Salcudean, Wong, & Hollis, 1995). While small desktop manipulanda, such as those mentioned above, are useful for many applications, others demand a much larger workspace and higher force output. The University of Washington High-Bandwidth Force Display (HBFD) (Moreyra, 1996) and Excalibur (Adams, Moreyra, & Hannaford, 1999) (Figure 3-1(a)) by Haptic Technologies Incorporated (HTI) provide large workspace and high forces through direct drive motors and a novel steel cable transmission. In contrast to manipulanda that provide forces only to the user's hand or fingers, exoskeletal systems may generate sensations affecting an entire limb. One such device was developed at the Scuola Superiore Sant' Anna in Pisa, Italy (Bergamasco, 1994). The Sarcos Dexterous Arm Master is another exoskeleton-like system with contact points at the forearm and upper arm of the user; it is being used to provide force feedback in CAD applications (Maekawa & Hollerbach, 1998).

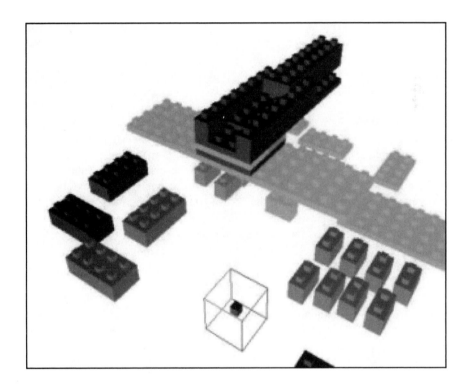

Figure 3-1(b): Virtual Lego™ blocks developed by University of Washington and HTI.

The early history of force-feedback technology, dominated by research applications, changed in 1996 when CH Products released the first consumer-level haptic display, the Force FX joystick. Microsoft entered the market in 1997 with the Sidewinder Force Feedback Pro joystick. By working with the Immersion Corporation to integrate force-feedback technology into the industry standard DirectX API, they gained rapid acceptance among programmers. Logitech joined the mix in 1998 with the WingMan Force joystick, a cable-driven device that raised the bar for fidelity in consumer haptic systems. The consumer market penetration of haptics continues with the arrival of numerous force-feedback steering wheels for use with racing simulators.

State-of-the-Art in Control of Haptics

Virtual environments of interest are always nonlinear and the dynamic properties of a human operator are always involved. These factors make it difficult to analyze haptic systems in terms of known parameters and linear control theory. One discipline that becomes more important with the rapid growth of haptics is control engineering. The control engineer is concerned with ensuring the haptic system—including the haptic display, the application software, and the human operator—remains stable while creating a compelling sense of haptic presence.

Early Research

Early efforts for control in haptics can be found in the adaptation of two-port network theory to the analysis of teleoperators and passivity criteria to design control gains for a master-slave manipulator (Anderson & Spong, 1989; Hannaford, 1989a, 1989b; Raju, Verghese, & Sheridan, 1989). In the mid-1980's, Neville Hogan discovered that while the neuromuscular system is internally complex, it exhibits externally simple, spring-like behavior (1986). The significance of this result is that the human arm can be assumed stable when coupled to any external system that is itself passive. Human arm impedance can therefore be considered as passive for the purposes of studying system stability.

Modern Research

Faster and cheaper computer growth has enabled haptic feedback with increasingly complex virtual reality simulations, but the stability of haptic feedback now depends on the intricate interactions taking place in the virtual world, adding complex geometry to the factors affecting stabilty. In 1995, Colgate, Stanley, and Brown proposed the introduction of a "virtual coupling" between the haptic display and the virtual environment to eliminate this problem (Colgate, Stanley, & Brown, 1995). J. Michael Brown explored conditions under which the virtual coupling parameters guaranteed a passive interface to the human operator. He developed design criteria for an arbitrary discrete-time passive environment (Brown & Colgate, 1997) and for a nonpassive virtual mass simulation (Brown & Colgate, 1998). Zilles and Salisbury from the MIT Artificial Intelligence Laboratory presented their own technique for stable haptic rendering of complex virtual objects (Zilles & Salisbury, 1995). Their approach was to servo the haptic display to an artificial "god-object" which conformed to the virtual environment. MIT's god-object was actually a special case of Northwestern's virtual coupling for point contact with a static virtual environment. The above-mentioned two works were complementary in the sense that Northwestern provided a strong theoretical basis while MIT demonstrated a relatively sophisticated application of the approach.

The virtual coupling promotes stability by placing an upper limit on the mechanical impedance that can be displayed to the operator. The virtual coupling also inherently distorts the haptic properties built into the virtual environment, reducing environment stiffness and damping in most cases. We thus seek a method of guaranteeing stability that minimizes the distortion imposed on the environment. While important, the virtual coupling idea considered only one class of haptic displays, "impedance displays," which measure motion and display force. A second class, "admittance displays," which measure force and display motion, was not considered.

Recent Research

The major problem with using passivity for design of haptic interaction systems is that it is overly conservative. Adams et al. derived a method of virtual coupling design from two-port network theory that applied to all causality combinations and was less conservative than passivity-based design (Adams & Hannaford, 1999; Adams, Klowden, & Hannaford, 2000; Adams, Moreyra, & Hannaford, 1998). They were able to derive optimal virtual coupling parameters using a dynamic model of the haptic device as well as by satisfying Lewellyn's "absolute stability criterion," an inequality composed of terms in the two-port description of the combined haptic interface and virtual coupling system. This procedure guaranteed a stable and high performance virtual coupling as long as the virtual environment was passive. Miller, Colgate, and Freeman have derived another design procedure that extends the analysis to nonlinear environments and extracts a damping parameter to guarantee stable operation (Miller, Colgate, & Freeman, 1998a, 1998b, 2000).

We have recently proposed a new energy based method, the "Passivity Observer" (PO) and "Passivity Controller" (PC) (Hannaford & Ryu, 2001, in press; Kim & Hannaford, 2001), for reducing the performance compromise required for stable contact. This new method can be applied to haptics and bilateral teleoperators in place of fixed-parameter virtual couplings.

CONTROL OF HAPTICS USING TIME DOMAIN DEFINITION OF PASSIVITY

In this section we review passivity properties of networks and define our observer and controller. Force and velocity are the key variables that define the nature of haptic contact. First, we define the sign convention for all forces and velocities so that their product is positive when power enters the system port (Figure 3-2(a)(b)).

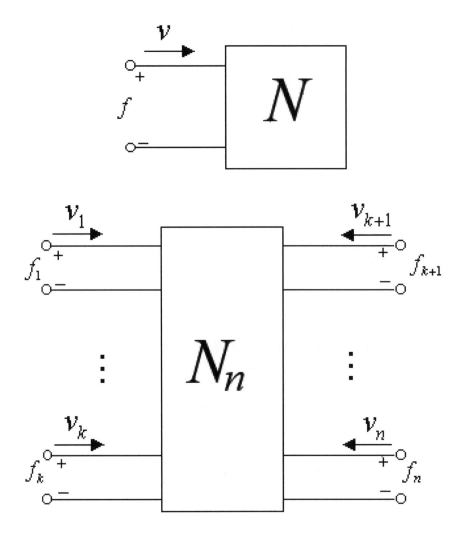

Figure 3-2(a)(b): One-port and M-port networks.

We also assume that the system has initial stored energy at $t = 0$ of $E(0)$. We then use the following widely known definition of passivity.

Definition 1: *The M-port network, N_M, with initial energy storage E(0), is passive if and only if,*

$$\int_0^t \left(f_1(\tau) v_1(\tau) + \cdots + f_M(\tau) v_M(\tau) \right) d\tau + E(0) \geq 0, \ \forall t \geq 0 \qquad (3.1)$$

for all admissible forces $(f_1; \ldots; f_M)$ and velocities $(v_1; \ldots; v_M)$. Equation 3.1 states that the energy applied to a passive network must exceed $-E(0)$ for all time (Adams & Hannaford, 1999; Desoer & Vidyasagar, 1975).

In haptic interface systems, the relevant forces and velocities can be measured by the computer and 3.1 can be computed in real time by appropriate software. This software is very simple in principle because at each time step, 3.1 can be evaluated with few mathematical operations.

Passivity Observer

The conjugate variables that define power flow in such a computer system are discrete-time values. Thus, we can easily "instrument" one or more blocks in the system with the following PO:

$$E_{obsv}(n) = (\sum_{k=1}^{n} [f_1(k)v_1(k) + \cdots + f_M(k)v_M(k)]) \times \Delta \text{T} \qquad (3.2)$$

where ΔT is a sampling time.

If $E_{obsv}(n) \geq 0$ for every n, this means the system dissipates energy. If there is an instance that $E_{obsv}(n) < 0$, this means the system generates energy and the amount of generated energy is $-E_{obsv}(n)$. When there are multiple interconnected elements, we might want to observe each one separately in order to determine which ones are active and which are passive. For any arbitrarily connected network system with P open ends, the amount of dissipation or generation of energy can be calculated using input and output values of the open-ended port(s), such as

$$E_{obsv}(n) = (\sum_{k=1}^{n} [f_1(k)v_1(k) + \cdots + f_P(k)v_P(k)]) \times \Delta \text{T} \qquad (3.3)$$

and if $E_{obsv}(n) \geq 0$ for every n, this system dissipates energy; else if there is a instance that $E_{obsv}(n) < 0$, this system generates energy and the amount of generated energy is $-E_{obsv}(n)$.

Passivity Controller

Consider a one-port system that may be active. Depending on operating conditions and the specifics of the one-port element's dynamics, the PO may or may not be negative at a particular time. However, if it is negative at any time, we know that the one-port may then be contributing to instability. Moreover, we know the exact amount of energy generated and we can design a time varying element to dissipate only the required amount of energy. We will call this element a "Passivity Controller" (PC).

The PC takes the form of a dissipative element in a series or parallel configuration (Figure 3-3(a)(b)). Both obey the constitutive equation

$$f = \alpha v \qquad (3.4)$$

Specifically, for the series connection (Figure 3- 3(a))

$$f_1 = f_2 + \alpha v$$ (3.5)

and for the parallel case (Figure 3-3(b))

$$v_2 = v_1 - \frac{f_1}{\alpha}$$ (3.6)

For a series PC with impedance causality, we compute α in real time as follows:

1) $v_1(n) = v_2(n)$

2) $f_2(n) = F_{VE}(v_2(n))$

where $F_{VE}()$ is the output of the virtual environment.

3) $E_{obsv}(n) = E_{obsv}(n-1) + (v_2(n)f_2(n) + \alpha(n-1)v_2(n-1)^2) \times \Delta T$

4)

$$\alpha(n) = \begin{cases} \dfrac{-E_{obsv}(n)}{\Delta T \, v_2(n)^2} & \text{if } E_{obsv}(n) < 0 \\ 0 & E_{obsv}(n) \geq 0 \end{cases}$$ (3.7)

5) $f_1(n) = f_2(n) + \alpha v_2(n) \rightarrow$ output

Note that ΔT can be canceled from equations 3.3 and 3.4 for brevity and to reduce computation. Thus, we can also express the PO as:

$$W(n) = \sum_{k=1}^{n} f_2(k)\, v_2(k) + \sum_{k=1}^{n-1} \alpha(k)\, v_2(k)^2$$ (3.8)

where $W(n) = 1/\Delta T \times E_{obsv}(n)$.

We can easily demonstrate that the system computed by 3.7 is passive:

$$\sum_{k=1}^{n} f_1(k)\, v_1(k) = \sum_{k=1}^{n} f_2(k)\, v_2(k) + \sum_{k=1}^{n-1} \alpha(k)\, v_2(k)^2 + \alpha(n)\, v_2(n)^2$$

$$= W(n) + \alpha(n)\, v(n)^2$$ (3.9)

using 3.7.

$$\sum_{k=1}^{n} f_1(k)v_1(k) \geq 0 \quad \forall n$$

We can similarly derive the case of admittance causality with a parallel PC (for more details, see Hannaford & Ryu, in press).

The dynamical properties of the device are altered when the operator interacts with a manipulandum. This variability in system behavior presents a significant challenge for control law design. We may have an application in which the load applied to the one-port can be counted on to dissipate energy; for example, the load may be

$$f_1 = \beta(-v_1)$$ (3.10)

In this case we may wish to replace zero on the RHS of equation 3.7 with a negative value such as

$$\hat{\beta} = \begin{cases} -\beta \sum_{k=1}^{n} v_1(k)^2 & \text{for impedance causality} \\ -\dfrac{1}{\beta} \sum_{k=1}^{n} f_1(k)^2 & \text{for admittance causality} \end{cases} \tag{3.11}$$

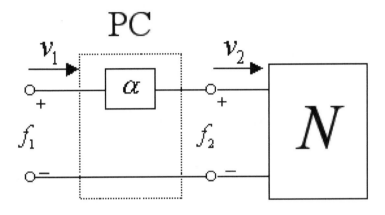

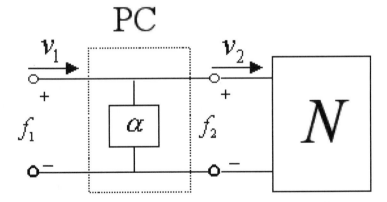

Figure 3-3(a)(b): Configuration of Passivity Controller for one-port networks. (a) Series or velocity-conserving Passivity Controller; (b) Parallel or force-conserving Passivity Controller.

IMPLEMENTATION ISSUE FOR STABLE HIGH PERFORMANCE CONTROL

The PC begins to operate when the PO detects active behavior from the system. This means that if the PO has a "build-up" of dissipated energy, then the PC does not work until all "built-up" energy is dissipated. For example, consider the case of a virtual environment that may interact extensively with a very dissipative object. In this case the PO will accumulate a large positive value. A second case occurs locally, when nonlinear behavior of the environment can cause dissipative behavior closely followed by active behavior. In both cases, if the energy accumulated in the PO can be reset to zero properly, then the faster stable contact can be achieved with smaller bounces. With this motivation we want to derive a heuristic rule, called "resetting" throughout this chapter, based on the detection of free motion state.

The rule is as follows.

*If $|f| \prec \varepsilon$ for τ sec, then Reset the **PO** to zero,*

where we call ε the force threshold, and τ the duration.

The idea is that this rule can detect free motion and that problems of active behavior do not persist from one contact state to the next. Thus it might be appropriate to reset the PO in between contacts with virtual surfaces.

Dissipation "Buildup"

Let us begin with three simulations (Figure 3-5(a)(b)(c)(d), Figure 3-6(a)(b)(c)(d), and Figure 3-7(a)(b)(c)(d)) illustrating the operation of the PO/PC. The basic haptic interface simulation (Figure 3-4) consists of the human operator (HO), the haptic interface (HI), the Passivity Controller (PC), and the virtual environment (VE). Note that the series passivity controller appears in Figure 3-4 to be connected in parallel, but this is an artifact of switching to block diagram notation for the connections between the HI, PC, and VE. The VE includes a spring constant of $k = 30$ kN/m and operates at a relatively slow sampling rate of 66.67 Hz (15 msec). The Passivity Observer (PO) is set up to monitor only the VE and PC. Without the PC, operation is highly unstable after the HO makes contact with the virtual environment (Figure 3-5, $t = 1.2$ sec). The only difference between Figure 3-6 and Figure 3-7 is whether or not the PO has zero initial value. Figure 3-6(d) shows the PC does not begin to operate until all the energy in the PO is dissipated ($t = 1.5$ sec). In contrast, with zero initial value (Figure 3-7), the PC begins to operate sooner after contact ($t = 1.2$ sec) and the contact transient is smaller (compare Figure 3-7(b) to Figure 3-6(b)).

Force Threshold and Duration

We experimented with the force threshold ε and duration τ to get values for correct detection of the free regime. A wide variety of values were studied and explored in the experiment. We expressed the force threshold as a fraction of the maximum force output of the device and the duration as multiples of the sampling time T (Table 3-1). In free motion, $f = 0$ by constraint of the virtual environment. When $10^{-7} \times F_{MAX}$ was chosen for the force threshold, and τ was $1 \times T$ or $100 \times T$, we found a very sluggish feeling in free motion: The resetting was continuous and the PC was operating all the time. Next, when a big value $(10^{-1} \times F_{MAX})$ was chosen as the force threshold with $\tau = 100 \times T$, we found no resetting even during the contact: The PC could not operate and instability was not prevented. Second, assume the extremely short case that the duration equals the sampling time $1 \times T$ sec, $\varepsilon = 10^{-1} \times F_{MAX}$. With such a short duration, resetting is being done when even a single noisy signal is less than the force threshold, as the PC operates too much. Finally, we determined $\varepsilon = 0.2$ N, $(10^{-3} \times F_{MAX})$ and $\tau = 0.01$ sec, $(10 \times T)$ were useful values for the resetting.

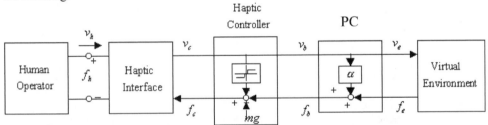

Figure 3-4: Basic haptic interface system.

Table 1: Guideline for Choosing the ε and τ .

	$10^{-7} \times F_{MAX}$	$10^{-3} \times F_{MAX}$	$10^{-1} \times F_{MAX}$
$1 \times T$	viscous feeling and PC on in free motion	no experiment	too much resetting
$10 \times T$	no experiment	good performance	no experiment
$100 \times T$	viscous feeling and PC on in free motion	no experiment	no resetting
$(T = 1\ msec, F_{MAX} = 200\,N)$			

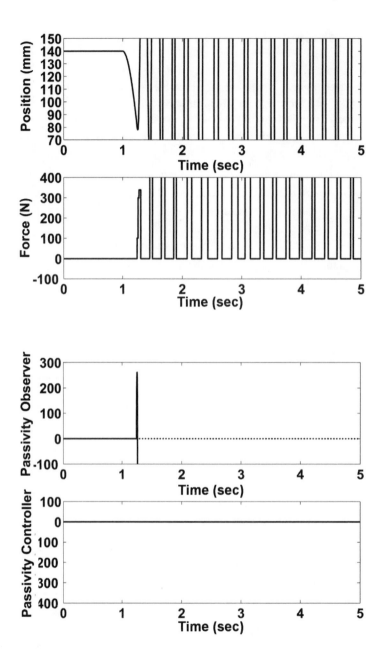

Figure 3-5(a)(b)(c)(d): Basic haptic simulation without PC.

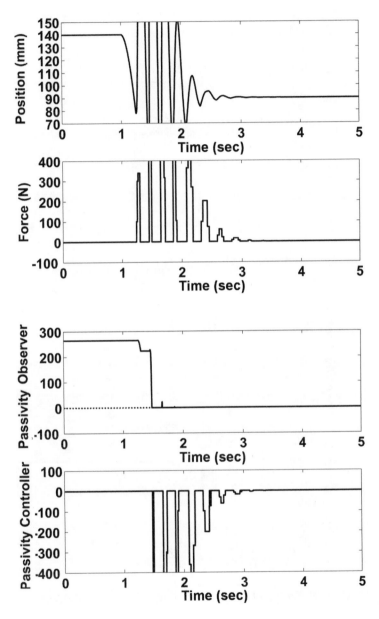

Figure 3-6(a)(b)(c)(d): Simulation with PC and a large initial value of PO.

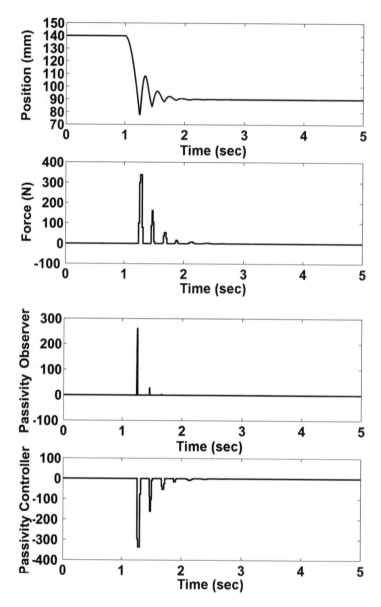

Figure 3-7(a)(b)(c)(d): Simulation with the PC and zero initial PO value.

EXPERIMENTAL RESULTS

In this section, the PO/PC is validated experimentally on actual hardware, our "Excalibur," three-axis, high force output haptic interface system in the laboratory (Adams, Moreyra, & Hannaford, 1999); (see Figure 3-1(a) and Figure 3-8). This system consists of the following elements: human operator (HO), Haptic Interface (HI), haptic controller (HC) with feed forward gravity compensation and friction compensation, the passivity controller (PC), and the virtual environment (VE). The system is entirely synchronous at 1000 Hz. The HI senses position in 0.008 mm increments, and can display 200 N force inside a 300 × 300 × 200 mm workspace. The virtual environment consists of virtual LEGO™ blocks (see Figure 3-1(b)). In the experiments, the PO accounted for energy flow in the HC, PC, and VE. The virtual object parameter had very high stiffness (k = 30 to 90 kN/m). The operator approached the object at about 200 mm/s.

Delayed Environment

One of the most challenging problems for further application of haptics is application to slow computing environments. These slow VEs are characteristic of complex simulations such as deformable objects for surgery or macromolecular dynamics. We modified the basic Excalibur system to artificially slow down the VE to a rate of 66.67 Hz. The output force value of the simulation was held constant for 15 samples and then replaced with the new force value based on its input 15 samples prior. Environment stiffness was set to 30 kN/m.

Without the PC, the result is a very unstable system (Figure 3-9(a)(b)(c)(d)). The sampling delay due to the slow VE is visible in the shape of the force pulses that are as high as 200 Newtons (Figure 3-9(b)). With the PC, the contact was stabilized within a single bounce (Figure 3-10(a)(b)(c)(d)). The contact force (Figure 3-10(b)) is limited to a single pulse that tapers exponentially during about one second. The PO (Figure 3-10(c)) consists of a single positive peak and is constrained to positive values. The passivity control output (Figure 3-10(d)) consists of a single large pulse, followed by a noise-like signal during the exponential decay of force ($t = 0.8$ sec $- t = 1.2$ sec). The noisy behavior of the passivity controller coincides with a period of low velocity (Figure 3-10(a), t = 0.8 sec $- t = 1.2$ sec).

Contact with High Stiffness

Unstable Operation and Behavior of PO

In the first experiment, without the PC, the contact was unstable, resulting in an oscillation observable as force pulses (Figure 3-11(b)); the PO (Figure 3-11(c)) was initially positive, but grew to more and more negative values with each contact. Note that the initial two bounces were passive, but after the third bounce the system gets active.

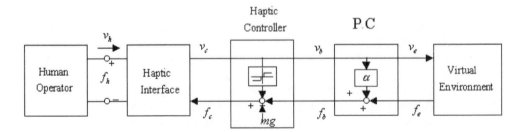

Figure 3-8: "Excalibur" three-axis, high force output haptic interface system.

Operation of the Basic PO/PC

In the second experiment, with the PC turned on, the operator approached the virtual object at the same velocity (Figure 3-12(a)), but a stable contact was achieved with about 13 bounces (Figure 3-12(b)). Again the first bounce can be seen to behave passively, but the subsequent bounces are smaller (Figure 3-12(c)). After eight bounces, the PC began to operate (Figure 3-12(d)) and eliminated the oscillation.

Resetting Operation

We added resetting to the experimental system under the conditions above. With the PC and resetting turned on, a stable contact is achieved with about eight bounces (Figure 3-13(b)). Compared to the case without resetting (Figure 3-12), the contact transient is shorter (8 vs. 13 bounces) because the PC operates about 200 msec sooner after the initial contact. Resetting helps the PC to operate exactly and immediately when the system becomes active without changing the stability, just proposed.

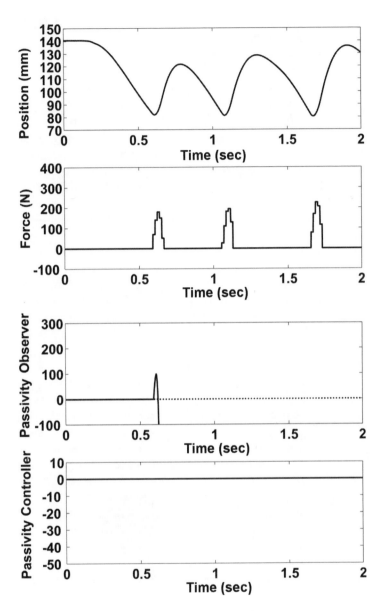

Figure 3-9(a)(b)(c)(d): Delayed environment without PC.

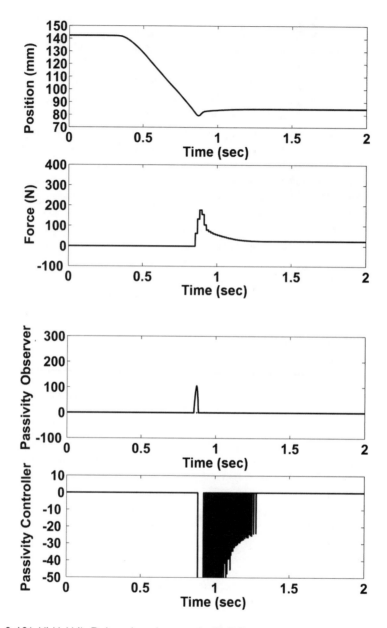

Figure 3-10(a)(b)(c)(d): Delayed environment with PC.

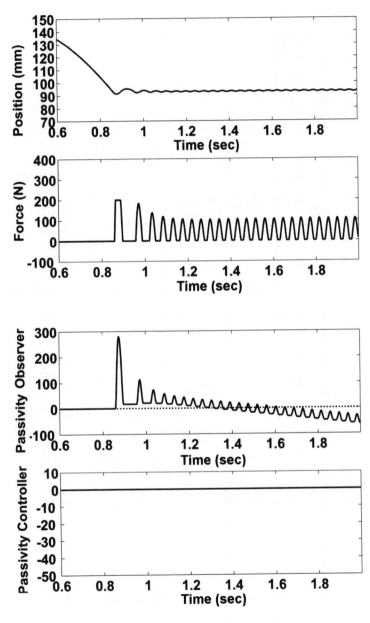

Figure 3-11(a)(b)(c)(d): Contact with high stiffness without PC.

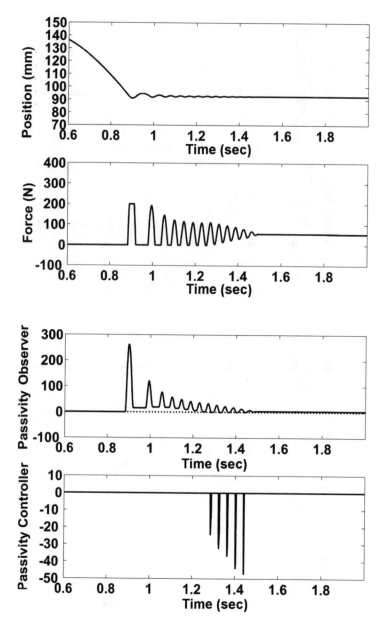

Figure 3-12(a)(b)(c)(d): Contact with high stiffness with only PC.

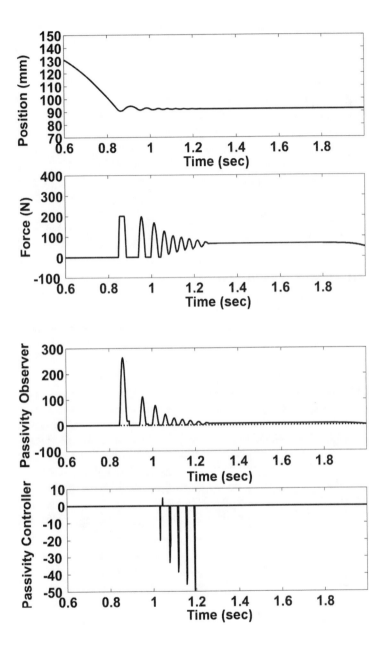

Figure 3-13(a)(b)(c)(d): Contact with high stiffness with both PC and resetting.

FUTURE RESEARCH CHALLENGES

Estimation of Human Factor

The existence of physical interaction between human and machine distinguishes haptic displays from other robotic manipulators. When the operator interacts with a manipulandum, the dynamical properties of the device are altered. This variability in system behavior presents a significant challenge for control law design. Identification of the dissipation constant (β in equation 3.11) for the human operator and haptic interface mechanism may allow the PC to operate with a different threshold and thus distort the virtual environment even less. We intend to study ways of automatically estimating this parameter during operation.

Hybrid Form of Passivity Control

Another issue will be implementation for the hybrid form of PC that includes both series and parallel dissipative elements and selects the most appropriate one for the operating conditions.

CONCLUSION

The advance of haptic technology is not likely to slow any time soon. The rapid evolution of the field leads one to speculate on where it will lead. What is the supreme vision for haptics? One answer is that the ultimate haptic system is one in which the user cannot distinguish between the virtual and the real. The subject might be made to experience a swim in the ocean or to climb a rocky cliff. Reflecting once again on the complexity of the human senses of touch and kinesthesia, the field still has a very long way to go with many exciting applications!

REFERENCES

Adams, R. J., & Hannaford, B. (1999). Stable haptic interaction with virtual environments. *IEEE Transactions on Robotics and Automatation, 15*(3), 465–474.

Adams, R. J., Klowden, D., & Hannaford, B. (2000). Stable haptic interaction using the Excalibur force display. *Proceedings of the IEEE International Conference on Robotics and Automation* (pp. 770–775).

Adams, R. J., Moreyra, M. R., & Hannaford, B. (1999). *Excalibur: A three axis force display.* Paper presented at the ASME Winter Annual Meeting Haptics Symposium.

Adams, R. J., Moreyra, M. R., & Hannaford, B. (1998). Stability and performance of haptic displays: Theory and experiments. *Proceedings of the ASME International Mechanical Engineering Congress and Exhibition* (pp. 227–34).

Anderson, R. J., & Spong, M. W. (1989). *Bilateral control of teleoperators with time delay.* IEEE Transactions on Automatic Control, *34*(5), 494–501.

Bergamasco, M., et al. (1994). An arm exoskeleton system for teleoperation and virtual environments applications. *Proceedings of the IEEE International Conference on Robotics and Automation* (pp. 1449–1454).

Brown, J. M., & Colgate, J. E. (1998). Minimum mass for haptic display simulations. *Proceedings of the ASME International Mechanical Engineering Congress and Exhibition* (pp. 249–256).

Brown, J. M., & Colgate, J. E. (1997). Passive implementation of multibody simulations for haptic display. *Proceedings of the ASME International Mechanical Engineering Congress and Exhibition* (pp. 85–92).

Buttolo, P., & Hannaford, B. (1995). Pen based force display for precision manipulation of virtual environments. *Proceedings of the IEEE Virtual Reality Annual International Symposium* (pp. 217–225).

Colgate, J. E., Stanley, M. C., & Brown, J. M. (1995). Issues in the haptic display of tool use. *Proceedings of the IEEE/RSJ International Conference on Intelligent Robots and Systems* (pp. 140–145).

Hannaford, B., & Ryu, J. H. (in press, a). Time domain passivity control of haptic interfaces. *Proceedings of the IEEE International Conference on Robotics and Automation.*

Hannaford, B., & Ryu, J. H. (in press, b). Time domain passivity control of haptic interfaces. *IEEE Transactions on Robotics and Automation.*

Hannaford, B. (1989a). A design framework for teleoperators with kinesthetic feedback. *IEEE Transactions on Robotics and Automation, 5*(4), 426–434.

Hannaford, B. (1989b). Stability and performance tradeoffs in bi-lateral tele-manipulation. *Proceedings of the IEEE International Conference on Robotics and Automation* (pp. 1764–1767).

Hogan, N. (1986). Multivariable mechanics of the neuromuscular system. *Proceedings of the IEEE Annual Conference of the Engineering in Medicine and Biology Society* (pp. 594–598).

Hogan, N. (1985). Impedance control: An approach to manipulation: Part I—theory. *Journal of Dynamic Systems, Measurement, and Control, 107*, 1–7.

Hollis, R. L., Salcudean, S. E., & Allan, A. P. (1991). A six-degree-of-freedom magnetically levitated variable compliance fine-motion wrist: Design, modeling, and control. *IEEE Transactions on Robotics and Automation, 7*(3), 320–332.

Kim, Y. S., & Hannaford, B. (in press). Some practical issues in time domain passivity control of haptic interfaces. *Proceedings of the IEEE/RSJ International Conference on Intelligent Robots and Systems.*

Maekawa, H., & Hollerbach, J. M. (1998). Haptic display for object grasping and manipulating in virtual environment. *Proceedings of the IEEE International Conference on Robotics and Automation* (pp. 2566–2573).

Massie, T. H., & Salisbury, J. K. (1994). The PHANToM haptic interface: A device for probing virtual objects. *Proceedings of the ASME International Mechanical Engineering Congress and Exhibition* (pp. 295–302).

Miller, B. E., Colgate, J. E., & Freeman, R. A. (2000). Environment delay in haptic systems. *Proceedings of the IEEE International Conference on Robotics and Automation* (pp. 2434–2439).

Miller, B. E., Colgate, J. E., & Freeman, R. A. (1999a). Passive implementation for a class of static nonlinear environments in haptic display. *Proceedings of the IEEE International Conference on Robotics and Automation* (pp. 2937–2942).

Miller, B. E., Colgate, J. E., & Freeman, R. A. (1999b). Computational delay and free mode environment design for haptic display. *Proceedings of the ASME Dynamic Systems Control Division* (pp. 259–236).

Moreyra, M. R. (1996). *Design of a planar high bandwidth force display with force sensing.* Unpublished M.S. thesis, University of Washington.

Raju, G. J., Verghese G. C., & Sheridan T. B. (1989). Design issues in 2-port network models of bilateral remote manipulation. *Proceedings of the IEEE International Conference on Robotics and Automation* (pp. 1316–1321).

Salcudean, S. E., & Vlaar, T. D. (1997). On the emulation of stiff walls and static friction with a magnetically levitated input/output device. *Transactions ASME, Journal of Dynamic Systems, Measurement, and Control, 119*(1), 127–132.

Salcudean, S. E., Wong, N. M., & Hollis, R. L. (1995). Design and control of a force-reflecting teleoperation system with magnetically levitated master and wrist. *IEEE Transactions on Robotics and Automation, 11*(6), 844–858.

Zilles, C. B., & Salisbury, J. K. (1995). A constraint-based God-object method for haptic display. *Proceedings of the IEEE/RSJ International. Conference on Intelligent Robots and Systems(*pp. 146–151). Pittsburgh, PA.

Hardware for Improved Haptic Performance

R. Chung, B. D. Adelstein, and H. Kazerooni

In order to couple the human user to computer-generated simulations, haptic interfaces not only comprise mechanical linkages but also sensors, actuators, and control systems. By acting together, these interface components must enable both the temporal and spatial resolution as well as the simulation dynamic range (Colgate & Brown, 1994; Hayward & Astley, 1995; Morrell & Salisbury, 1996) necessary for faithful haptic rendering.

Unlike the 30-60 Hz update rates deemed sufficient for visually presented VEs, haptic simulation places more stringent demands on temporal performance, with rates of 1 kHz typically cited as desirable for stable, responsive haptic interaction. To this end, especially as VE content and model dynamics grow more complex, it has been recognized that there is benefit to segregating the faster haptic from the slower visual aspects in multimodal simulation. This separation is seen in recent VE system architectures that employ multirate multiprocessing (or multithreading) within a single host computer (e.g., Ho, Basdogan, & Srinivasan, 1998) and in architectures that offload varying degrees of haptic control onto separate processor units (e.g., Gupta, Sheridan & Witney, 1997; Ho et al., 1998).

The work we report here centers on the design and implementation of "low-level" control hardware that is part of a compact Digital Signal Processor (DSP) based architecture developed for standalone local control of our previously introduced three degrees-of-freedom (3 DOF) hand-scale haptic interface (Adelstein et al., 1998) shown in Figure 4-1. At this stage, the DSP is responsible for "mid-level" functions such as servo-control of the interface's actuators, computation of kinematic transformations specific to the interface's linkage configuration (Adelstein et al., 1996), workspace boundary enforcement to prevent internal linkage interference and operation near linkage singularities, and active mass balance to compensate for linkage weight that would otherwise have to be supported by the human operator. The "low-level" hardware, implemented using a Field Programmable Gate Array (FPGA), is responsible for enhanced position resolution through angular encoder interpolation and smooth brushless motor torque control by sinusoidal commutation. Both of these enhancements are essential to the improvement of our interface's haptic dynamic range and simulation fidelity.

Figure 4-1: Hand-scale haptic interface.

RATIONALE

Our interest in DSP-based control was initiated by observations during efforts to use our 3 DOF haptic interfaces (Adelstein et al., 1996; Adelstein et al., 1998) for interaction with visually presented simulations created using EAI-Sense8's WorldToolKit (WTK) VE application programming interface (API). The WTK-generated VEs were run on a dual 733 MHz Pentium III personal computer (PC) operated under Windows NT (WinNT) 4.0 for the benefit of WTK. The hand-scale haptic device was interfaced to the PC via a standard PCI bus multifunction I/O card (Sensoray Co., Inc., model 626).

Because of the 10 msec scheduler resolution in WinNT, switching between WTK and haptic control applications was too slow. This limited haptic control rates to no better than 100 Hz—insufficient for maintaining stable interaction forces. Resorting to the 1 msec WinNT multimedia timer was also ineffective, because WinNT background tasks can still sporadically interfere with high priority tasks, creating unacceptable variability in haptic controller execution. Although commercial real-time WinNT kernel extensions could afford more deterministic regulation of CPU task scheduling, an understanding of computational loads expected for more complex future VE simulations suggested that haptic interface control should be offloaded onto a separate processor.

To ensure tightly regulated, temporally deterministic response, we selected a DSP-based architecture in order to isolate time-critical haptic interface control tasks from computationally intensive and more slowly updated VE simulation processes. The standalone DSP we developed is embedded inside the haptic interface itself, maintaining portability by allowing the device to be connected with different VE simulation computers. The inclusion of FPGA technology, which provides dedicated I/O for reading haptic interface sensors and commanding its actuators, specifically enables the fundamental enhancements to displacement measurement resolution and actuator torque control that are the focus of this chapter.

BACKGROUND

Our 3 DOF haptic interface is a joystick-like device that provides three-dimensional point force interaction over a three-dimensional translational work volume (Adelstein et al., 1996). The joystick linkage is a 10 rigid-link 12 revolute joint, "parallel" spatial mechanism, arranged in three closed kinematic loops. While it possesses structural stiffness properties typically associated with parallel mechanisms, the reachable proportion of our joystick's nonsingular workspace approaches that of similarly scaled serial or partially serial 3 DOF arm-like devices such as SensAble Technologies' PHANToM (Massie & Salisbury, 1994). However, unlike serial and partially serial devices, the movable portion of our joystick does not carry its motors' weight and stator inertia because all three actuator housings are fixed with respect to the common ground link.

Because our 3 DOF mechanism is composed solely of rigid links and rotary joints, it neither requires nor uses gear, cable-pulley, or other transmission elements. By eliminating such elements, the "lossiness" or attenuation associated with friction, backlash, and compliance in these components can be avoided, thereby enhancing force and motion transfer fidelity both from the device's actuators to the user's hand and vice versa.

Nonetheless, avoidance of such transmission elements does have potential drawbacks. First, "gearing down" by these elements permits smaller motors to turn more quickly (operating nearer their peak efficiency), while at the transmission output stage, delivering greater torques at slower, more appropriately scaled velocities. This design strategy of using smaller motors with geared down cable-pulley transmissions was adopted in both the PHANToM and Immersion's Impulse Engine. Second, this gearing down improves (by the transmission ratio) the resolution of output motion measurement and control while still using low-cost, small-sized, relatively low resolution sensors that are mounted directly on the now rapidly rotating motor shafts. Third, the aforementioned transmission lossiness contributes mechanical "filtering" that can be beneficial in masking motor torque imperfections such as cogging and ripple.

Alternatively, to increase available actuator torque in our haptic interfaces, we employ brushless DC (BLDC) motors rather than brushed motors such as those used in the PHANToM and Impulse Engine. BLDC motors are capable of delivering greater sustained torque per unit mass and volume because their construction enables efficient dissipation of winding induced heat. Furthermore, the motors in our device have slotless windings which eliminates cogging torque—the tendency for motors (even when unpowered) to seek out preferred angular positions because of the attraction between permanent magnets and exposed iron in conventional slotted windings.

Two significant deficiencies in our original hand-scale interface implementation hindered its use. The first was intrusively palpable levels of torque ripple stemming from trapezoidal commutation of the device's BLDC motors. Second, because of a direct-drive (i.e., transmission-free) system, measurements from a conventional motor-mounted rotary encoder yielded relatively coarse (nominally 160 µm, or 0.006 in) joystick endpoint displacement resolution, thus restricting achievable haptic control accuracy and dynamic range. These two shortcomings have been dealt with and eliminated as discussed in the remainder of this chapter.

ENHANCED DISPLACEMENT MEASUREMENT RESOLUTION

Optical Encoders

Incremental optical encoders measure shaft rotation angle by detecting the motion of a uniform radial grating pattern of alternating transparent and opaque lines arranged around the circumference of the disk fixed to the shaft (e.g., Slocum, 1992, p. 163). The varying transmission of light from a single source on one side of the disk through the rotating grating is monitored by a pair of photodetectors (typically labeled Channels *A* and *B*). The passage from transparent to opaque lines of the grating in front of a detector gradually obscures more light and produces a continuously varying output from the photodetector. Thus, as a succession of grating lines pass at a uniform rate, the raw voltage output pattern from an individual photodetector resembles a sinusoid. The channel *A* and *B* photodetectors are offset circumferentially from each other by one-quarter of the grating period such that there is a 90° spatial (termed quadrature) phase shift between the two sinusoidal output traces.

In conventional incremental optical encoders (such as those in the PHANToM, Impulse Engine, and our initial hand-scale interface), comparators threshold the sinusoidal output of the photodetectors to produce two-state (HIGH or LOW) digital logic signals. As shown in Figure 4-2, the 90° phase shift between channels *A* and *B* produces four possible states for each encoder line, with the order of state transitions indicating rotational direction. Counting the number of up-down state transitions therefore yields a fourfold improvement in rotation angle measurement resolution over the original encoder disk's grating line density. This resolution enhancement and subsequent angle accumulation (i.e., counting of state transitions) is typically carried out by integrated electronic quadrature decoder/counter circuits.

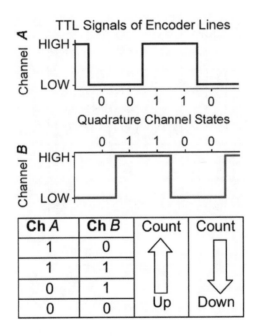

Figure 4-2: Digital encoder quadrature signals (top) and possible state transitions.

Sinusoidal Encoder Interpolation

We use sinusoidal encoders to implement the interpolation scheme to improve angular resolution to levels well beyond those achievable through quadrature decoding. These encoders' mechano-optical components operate like those described above but provide the individual 90° phase-shifted quadrature channels as differentially amplified, continuously varying analog sinusoid signals, without conversion into two-state digital logic levels.

To compute the interpolation, the continuous channel A and B signals first undergo analog-to-digital (A/D) conversion. A/D conversion of the sinusoids results in digitized signals that are discretized into uniform amplitude increments, as depicted schematically in Figure 4-3, for operation about a single encoder grating line. Interpolation of the phase angle for each sinusoid (i.e., $\alpha = \arcsin(A)$ and $\beta = \arcsin(B)$) requires calculation of the inverse sine of each signal. However, because the inverse sine function is a nonlinear mapping, the uniform A/D conversion (ADC) increments yield variable size angle increments. Consequently, interpolated phase angle increments plotted in Figure 4-3 show highest density sampling as the sinusoids' amplitudes approach zero from either above or below.

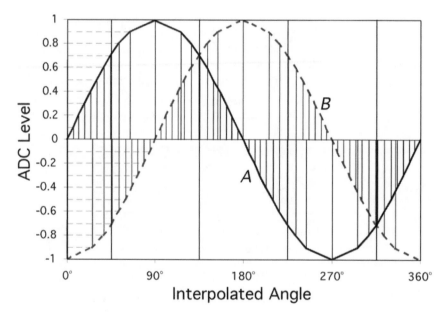

Figure 4-3: Nonlinear arcsine mapping of sinusoidal A and B channel quadrature output levels to rotation angle for one encoder line cycle. Equal ADC sample intervals (vertical axis) correspond to nonuniform interpolated angle increments indicated by drop-lines.

From the overlapping sinusoidal curves in Figure 4-3, it is seen that the higher phase angle sample densities span 90° segments that alternate between the two encoder channels A and B. (These 90° segments correspond to quarter rotations through individual grating lines equivalent to the conventional encoder quadrature resolution.). Thus, by switching every 90° between the two curves whenever they pass through ±0.707 of the peak amplitude, it is possible to maximize the effective angle interpolation resolution across each encoder grating cycle by using only the most densely sampled regions of each inverse sine function.

In practice, because there are a limited fixed number of discrete sinusoid ADC levels, it is more efficient to retrieve arcsine values from a precomputed lookup table (LUT) than it is to repeatedly carry out online floating-point calculations. Additionally, encoding LUT angle entries as fixed-point binary numbers enables the subsequently described interpolation steps to be carried out with simple Boolean operations, further avoiding costly floating-point math. Finally, limiting the size of the LUT helps reduce the memory space required for implementing the interpolation scheme. From Figure 4-3, it is noted that the alternating 90° high resolution regions for each channel (A or B) are composed of successive mirrored 45° segments, the first from the sinusoid's negative amplitude portion prior to the zero-crossing, and the second from the positive portion immediately following the zero crossing. Hence, by taking advantage of the signal's sign, the inverse sine LUT need in principle only have storage corresponding to 45° (1/8) of the sine wave. Thus, the arcsine LUT, when combined with the signs of the respective A and B segments, enables fine-resolution interpolation for each encoder grating line. Alone, the 90° phasing pattern between successive A and B sign changes is only sufficient for conventional coarse-resolution quadrature-based angle measurement, but can span multiple encoder revolutions.

Practical Resolution Considerations

The interpolation scheme was examined for the "efficiency" of various combinations of LUT size and ADC resolution. The amplitude resolution of the digitized sinusoidal encoder signals is dependent both on the A/D converter's analog input range and the number of bits produced by the ADC output. The interpolated angle resolution is limited principally by the amount of available space for LUT storage, as well as the address and data bus widths to access the table's memory locations. Ideally, the ADC and LUT resolutions selected should allow a 1:1 mapping back and forth between digitized sinusoid levels and the inverse transformed angle entries in the table. To be fully efficient 1) each ADC level should address its own unique entry in the LUT, and 2) points in the interpolation table should be uniformly distributed (i.e., identical differences between any pair of stored binary output values, or counts, in the LUT should represent identically sized physical angle increments anywhere in the rotation space) and reachable from their own specific ADC level. That is, there should be no unused LUT locations or ADC levels.

Consider the use of 8-bit A/D converters (i.e., typical, inexpensive integrated circuits) to digitize encoder channel outputs. For convenience, ADC circuit gain is most easily set so that the converters' 256 levels match the encoder channels' peak-to-peak (in our design, ±1 volt) output range. Successive positive and negative sine function peaks occur 180° apart at

±90°. Thus an interpolation table covering the full 360° cycle across an individual encoder grating line, if it were linear (i.e., a triangle profile relating phase angle to sensor amplitude), would need twice as many points, 512 entries or 9 bits, to be fully efficient. If such a hypothetically linear interpolation table spanning the 360° cycle had an 8-bit size (256 entries), only every second ADC level could address the table, leaving half of the A/D converter's levels unused (i.e., 50% ADC efficiency). Similarly, for a hypothetical linear 10-bit (1024 entry) LUT of uniformly spaced interpolation angles, only 50% of table entries would be addressable by the 256 ADC levels.

Nonetheless, because of the inverse sine function's nonlinearity, a 9-bit (360°) table, which was perfectly efficient for a hypothetical linear interpolation, is now inefficient in its use (depending on region) either of uniform increment ADC levels or LUT space. However, while 26 of 90 possible ADC levels within the critical 0° to 45° range (Figure 4-4(a)) are not unique (i.e., they point to the same lookup entries as their neighbors), all 64 LUT values in this region remain accessible, enabling uniform angular interpolation increments. Doubling the 360° table size to 10 bits (Figure 4-4(b)), eliminates ADC inefficiency with all 90 levels mapping into a unique interpolated angle, but still leaves inaccessible 38 of the 128 LUT entries over the 45° region. Because of the dispersion of the 38 points, output resolution is not uniform and varies locally. Thus, 10-bit interpolation of an individual encoder grating line's 360° single cycle, which on average produces finer resolution, has in the worst case resolution no better than the 9-bit version. Figure 4-4(a)(b) shows LUT segments for 9-bit interpolation. Stepped curves (full-scale plot and magnified insert) relate normalized sinusoid amplitude with corresponding ADC levels to interpolated angle with corresponding count or discretized table location. Bars emanating from vertical zero angle axis (full-scale and insert) to the left indicate ADC inefficiency. Bars to the right show inefficiency in LUT output. Absence of a bar indicates no inefficiency for particular ADC level and corresponding LUT entry.

Implementation

In our implementation, 8-bit differential A/D converters sample encoder channel A and B voltages, with the ADC output values spanning the integers from −128 to 127 for the resultant ±1 volt sinusoidal signal inputs. The quadrant of the current encoder position is simply determined from the sign of the ADC value of channel A and B (i.e., by checking the ADC most significant bit), as shown in Figure 4-5. As noted above, the signs, and therefore these quadrants, correspond to the standard encoder quadrature signals.

Within each quadrant, the interpolation input alternates every 45° between the higher resolution segments of channel A and B. For this reason, the LUT only contains values corresponding to positive ADC values between 0 and 90. As seen in Figure 4-5, the selection between channels A and B is based on which has the lesser absolute ADC magnitude.

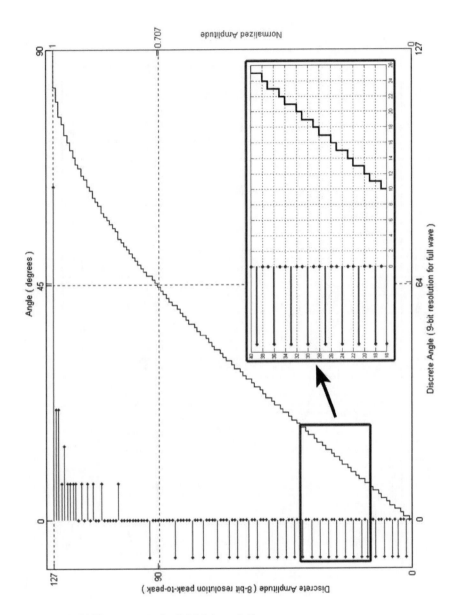

Figure 4-4(a): LUT segments for 9-bit interpolations.

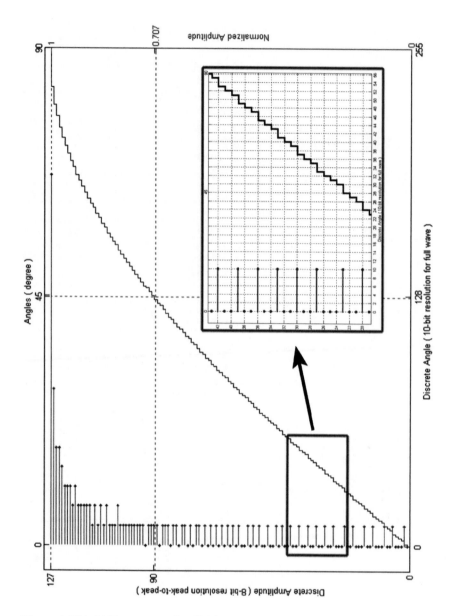

Figure 4-4(b): LUT segments for 10-bit interpolations.

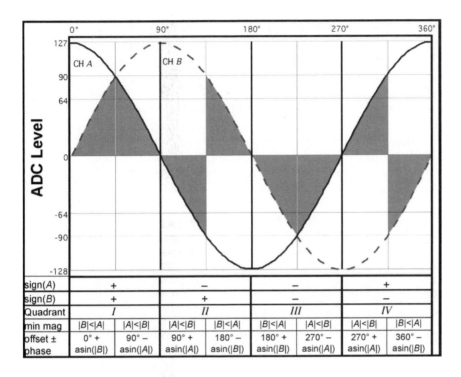

Figure 4-5: Angle interpolation procedure for channel *A* and *B* sinusoids. Shaded regions between 0 to 90 and 0 to −90 levels for 8-bit ADC indicate 45° segments for lookup table. Combination of quadrant (line 3) and minimum magnitude in each 45° segment (line 4) allow composition of 10-bit interpolation per encoder grating line (line 5).

Combining the *A/B* selection with the quadrant information allows computation of the interpolated phase angle between 0° and 360° for the individual encoder line. Thus the interpolation is composed from 2 bits for the four quadrature quadrants of the 360° cycle, 1 bit for which half of the quadrant is being interpolated, plus the 7-bit LUT density for the 45° segment, for a total of 1024 counts per single encoder grating line. For a 1024-line encoder, this amounts to 1,048,576 counts per revolution.

As discussed above, however, not all arcsine LUT locations are addressable by possible ADC levels, causing the interpolation resolution to fluctuate locally, thereby degrading the effective resolution to 524,288 counts per revolution, or 0.00069°. At a nominal 10 cm (4 inch) radius for the endpoint of our hand-scale haptic interface, the worst-case sensor resolution corresponds to a theoretical displacement (i.e., ignoring any possible linkage mechanism compliance, backlash, etc.) of 1.2μm (4.7×10^{-5} inch).

Sinusoidal Encoder Interpolation Bandwidth

The analog to digital converters used in our design, while rated to 20 MSPS (20 million samples per second), are run at one MSPS, synchronously with FPGA-based quadrature and interpolation circuitry. At 1 MSPS, the ADC and quadrature counters are theoretically capable of capturing all up-down transitions (four samples/line from Figure 4-2 $\times$ 1024 lines) for encoder speeds up to 244.2 rev/s (14.6 KRPM). However, since encoder quadrature in our case is derived from the sign of the sinusoidal signals, the coarse resolution (4×1024 counts per revolution) depends solely on each ADC levels' MSB (most significant bit).

Because the interpolation also operates at the 1 MSPS FPGA rate and because the interpolator output is written out to the data bus as a parallel word, full 19-bit high-resolution can be achieved up to the same 14.6 KRPM rotation speeds as the low resolution quadrature count. This performance is significantly different from that expected of the typical 10 to 20X commercially available interpolated encoders. Following the interpolation stage in these commercial sensors, the n-bit wide parallel output is converted back into a dual-track square-wave output so that the resulting quadrature signals can then be decoded and counted by the same interface boards and circuits employed for conventional low resolution (e.g., 1024-line) encoders. Consequently, these commercial devices are limited to operation at slow velocities in order to prevent intervening interpolation level transitions from occurring too quickly to contribute to the pulse pattern. If transitions between adjacent levels are not detected, the pulse train would fail to keep up with shaft rotation and, because of this slippage, the external quadrature counter circuits would therefore be inaccurate. For example, if our high-resolution output were to be converted back to a quadrature pattern at the full 1 MSPS FPGA rate, counts would be lost if the shaft speed were to exceed 114 RPM (i.e., 1.9 rev/s = 1 MSPS / 524,288 counts/rev).

Preliminary Interpolation Performance

We confirmed that quadrature-level resolution could be obtained from the encoder FPGA circuitry at rates far exceeding the minimum 1 kHz target for haptic interface control. Interpolated angle from the FPGA output was displayed via a digital-to-analog (D/A) converter on an oscilloscope. Approximately uniform input velocity produced by connecting a small DC motor to the encoder resulted in the expected sawtooth angle trace (ramp-up until digital value rollover) that could then be compared with the once-per-revolution encoder index pulse. No slippage between the index pulse and the ramp waveform was noted after several minutes at motor speeds of 150 rev/s (9000 RPM), indicating that the ADC quadrature update, and therefore the high-resolution interpolation output, could be maintained up to rates of at least 614.4 kHz (150 rev/s $\times$ 1024 lines/rev $\times$ 4 counts/line).

Experimental validation of the interpolator's spatial fidelity is currently underway. In particular, within each grating line's sinusoidal cycle, the interpolation is subject to inaccuracies (systematic errors) caused by the sensor's internal electro-optical properties, sensor misalignment at the time of assembly, and imprecise electronic adjustment. These factors can produce nonzero offsets and unmatched or improperly scaled gains for channel *A* and *B* encoder output signals, as well as imperfect (non-90°) phasing between the channels. Additionally, the encoder's signals can deviate significantly from the ideal sinusoidal profile (Venema & Hannaford, 1995). Moreover, the signals' waveform, gain, and offset may also vary from line to line around the circumference of the encoder disk.

Initial observations for our haptic interface's three encoders indicate that signal profiles are very closely sinusoidal, especially within the 45° segments employed by our interpolation. A preliminary analysis of interpolator fidelity was conducted by examining deviation of local angle from the expected best fit to constant velocity displacement. Systematic departures from the best-fit angle were 0.0027°, 0.0041°, and 0.0027° RMS (0.008°, 0.010°, and 0.0045° at worst case peaks) across individual grating lines for the haptic interface's three encoders—prior to any adjustment of LUT output, or external trimming of raw encoder offsets, gains, and phase. Stochastic variability in interpolation output due to sensor or other system noise typically amounted to ±0.0007° (1/500,000 rev) or less when the interface's servo amplifiers and actuators were not powered.

TORQUE RIPPLE ELIMINATION

Permanent Magnet Motor Basics

Permanent magnet DC (PMDC) motors are used in nearly all joystick-type haptic devices. Depending on the motor type, the permanent magnets can be located on either the rotor (the rotating element typically attached to the output shaft) or the stator (the stationary element fixed to the motor housing). Electrically conductive windings are contained in the opposing element, respectively the motor's stator or rotor. The force generated between the permanent magnets and the magnetic field generated by current flowing through different winding coils causes the rotor to align in different orientations with respect to the motor's stator. By modulating the current in the different winding groups (or phases) in the proper sequence (i.e., by the process of commutation), the motor can be made to rotate continuously.

In brushed PMDC motors, the windings are on the rotor and the permanent magnets on the stator. Commutation is accomplished by the wiping of brushes, which are fixed with respect to the motor housing, across pairs of conductive "bars" on the rotor that are separated by insulator strips in a circumferentially arranged commutator ring. The brushes are connected to an external power source (e.g., a servoamplifier), while the individual commutator bars are connected to opposite ends of their respective winding coils. As the rotor moves, the conductor bars advance under the brushes and alternately connect and disconnect different coils, thereby energizing different winding phases.

In BLDC motors, the permanent magnets are on the rotor. Because the windings do not move, mechanical commutation is impossible, and instead, specialized electronic controllers are used. In addition to eliminating electrical arcing and the consequent maintenance and hazardous environment concerns, the absence of brush-rotor contact in BLDC drives eliminates a source of shaft friction and is therefore beneficial to the "feel" of haptic interface hardware. Most importantly, we employ BLDC motors in our haptic devices because of their higher continuous and peak torque output per unit of actuator size or mass. The higher torque density is attributable to better heat dissipation by stator windings in direct thermal contact with the actuator housing. In contrast, the rotor windings of brushed PMDC motors are separated by the thermal insulation of the actuator's air gap from the stator and exterior housing.

Brushless Motor Commutation

Proper commutation of motor windings (i.e., the energizing of winding phases in the correct sequence) depends on knowledge of the instantaneous angular displacement between rotor and stator. Brushed drives, by design, ensure that the simple mechanical "switching" of the brushes between the rotating commutator bars will always activate the correct phases with respect to the permanent magnet field, without need for additional sensor feedback. In BLDC drives, there is no such direct mechanical connection to account inherently for the angular rotation between rotor magnets and stator windings. Thus trapezoidal and sinusoidal commutation, the most widely used commutation schemes for BLDC machines, depend on motor shaft angle sensors for this information.

Trapezoidal Commutation

In trapezoidal commutation, Hall Effect sensors are used to detect the orientation of the rotor magnetic field. Typically, three Hall Effect sensors are distributed around the stator circumference to match the 120° electrical offset between the three winding phases. The two-state signal transitions from the three Hall Effect sensors serve to divide the rotation into unique 60° wide segments for each motor magnetic pole pair. Switching logic under direct control of the Hall Effect sensor states directs currents among the trapezoidal amplifier's three output channels to produce the six-step four-level delta-connected winding current profiles depicted in Figure 4-6. This straightforward current switching strategy makes trapezoidal (sometime called "six-step", or "brushless DC") servo amplifiers and sensors simpler, less expensive, and, therefore, the most popular of the brushless commutation techniques.

A motor's back EMF (i.e., generator voltage) pattern in relation to uniform velocity, and equivalently the relation of its torque profile to constant drive current, depend on the design and construction of its winding coils and permanent magnets. Specifically, as discussed in the Appendix, sinusoidal windings generate sinusoidal torque patterns in response to constant current. Consequently, the application of trapezoidal commutation currents that are not matched to sinusoidal winding torque profiles induces spatially periodic deviations from commanded actuator torque termed "ripple." As illustrated in Figure 4-6 for the six-step commutation of sinusoidally wound, delta-connected BLDC machines, the theoretical peak-to-peak ripple (calculated per equation 4.15) is 13.4% of the highest torque—a level that is unacceptably palpable to the haptic interface user. (Note that related current patterns produce the same 13.4% torque ripple for the alternative wye-connected BLDC motor windings.) With six transitions per electrical period occurring as commutated current levels abruptly switch, the torque ripple cycle would repeat twelve times per shaft rotation, or every 30°, for our hand-scale device's four-pole motors.

Sinusoidal Commutation

The torque ripple arising from trapezoidal commutation can be seen from Figure 4-6 to coincide with significant departures in winding currents from the underlying sinusoidal current-to-torque (or back EMF) profile. Essentially, the BLDC motor ripple is caused by the four-level switched waveform's overly coarse sinusoid approximation and can therefore be remedied by refining the commutation profile. Ideally, by matching individual phase currents to the particular motor winding's spatial and temporal torque characteristics, sinusoidal commutation can completely eliminate torque ripple, as discussed in the Appendix and shown in Figure 4-7. However, a perfectly matched sinusoidal (also called "AC brushless") amplifier will reduce mean torque to ~91% (i.e., 1.5 / 1.65) of that obtainable with trapezoidal commutation for a given sinusoidally wound BLDC motor (Figures 4-6, 4-7).

Sinusoidal Commutation Implementation

Depending on the particular servo amplifier design, either encoders (with direct angular output) or resolvers (in which angle is intrinsically converted to commutation-ready sinusoidal waveforms) are typically required to provide the necessary rotation feedback for sinusoidal commutation. In our haptic interface, we employ the incremental encoders described above in conjunction with the appropriate three-phase servo amplifiers.

Unlike resolvers, which measure absolute rotation permanently referenced to stator orientation, incremental rotary encoders report angle relative to the quadrature counter's last initialization. Encoder angle may be referenced to the BLDC motor winding phases by several methods. Without resorting to secondary absolute rotation sensors, the encoder can be aligned at installation on the motor such that its index channel (an optional third disk track but with only a single grating line) produces a pulse when crossing through a single predetermined winding location. This location would, for example, coincide with the shaft angle of a Hall Effect transition, shown in Figure 4-6, if such a secondary rotation sensor were present. The encoder counter would be initialized upon the first index pulse crossing and would therefore from then on indicate the rotor relative commutation phasing.

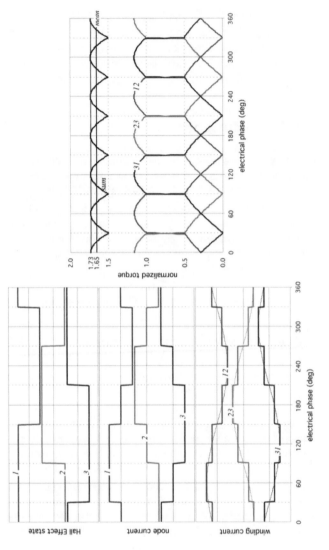

Figure 4-6: Torque output for six-step Hall Effect sensor-based trapezoidal commutation of sinusoidally wound delta-connected brushless DC motor. (Upper
left) Hall Effect sensor output; (middle left) three level brushless DC
servo amplifier channel input currents to delta-wound motor nodes;
(lower left) resultant four level delta winding currents superimposed over
underlying sinusoidal winding current-to-torque (back EMF-to-speed)
profile; (right) normalized individual phase torques and their sum.

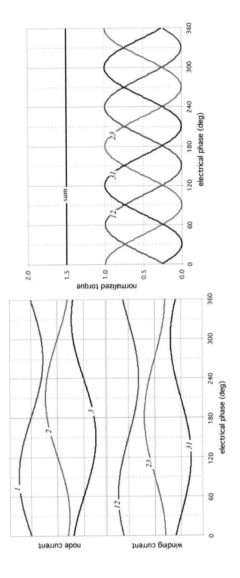

Figure 4-7: Torque output for sinusoidal commutation of sinusoidally wound delta-connected BLDC motor. (Upper left) sinusoidal brushless AC servo amplifier channel input currents to delta-wound motor nodes; (lower left) resultant sinusoidal winding currents coincident with underlying sinusoidal winding current-to-torque (back EMF-to-speed) profile; (right) normalized sum and individual phase torques.

Alternatively, once the index pulse is placed, absolute shaft angles for a unique pre-specified joystick linkage pose (imposed by a precision mechanical startup jig) can be measured and recorded. Provided that the jig is used for subsequent restarts, the encoders' initial angular offsets will be the exactly known prerecorded starting pose angles. Thus commutation could be initiated without first seeking out each encoder's index pulse or specified Hall Effect transitions.

The commercial pulse width modulated (PWM) servo amplifiers selected for the haptic interface—chosen because of their higher power efficiency and consequent lower heat losses than linear amplifiers—only provide a current-controlled output power stage. The amplifiers themselves do not produce the sinusoidal commutation pattern; it is instead generated onboard the FPGA circuitry described below. Each servo amplifier simply takes in a pair of control signals (presumed to be phased 120° apart) that already incorporate the modulation of the desired torque command by the commutation profile and produces three-channel PWM current output. Two of the amplifier output channels directly follow the input control phases. The amplifier derives the third phase internally under the assumption of balanced output—the three channels' instantaneous currents sum to zero. (In fact, because of access to the control signal on the FPGA, six-step or other balanced nonsinusoidal commutation patterns may also be implemented on the amplifiers.)

The modulation of the commanded input torque by the commutation profiles of the respective windings entails real-time multiplication on the FPGA of the torque command by the appropriate angle dependent sinusoidal levels. The commutation profile, pre-computed for equally spaced angle intervals, is stored on the FPGA as a single 256-point sine curve LUT. Though the LUT only covers the first quarter commutation cycle (0° to 90°), the same sine values can also be used for the remainder of the cycle—either directly (from 90° to 180°) or with a sign inversion (180° to 360°). Moreover, to span the entire 10-bit commutation cycle ($2^{10} = 4 \times 256$ points per segment), only the 11 most significant bits (two electrical cycles per mechanical revolution) bits of the interpolated encoder reading are required to address LUT angle entries.

The modulation process proceeds in the following order. First, prior to addressing the sine LUT, the encoder angles are adjusted for offsets between the initializing index pulse and the individual 120°-shifted winding phase orientations. Second, sine LUT output values for the offset-adjusted angles are then multiplied by the torque command. Finally, the two 120° shifted control signal channels resulting from the multiplication (i.e., the commutation-modulated torque commands) are issued via a pair of bipolar 14-bit digital-to-analog converters (DACs) to each servo amplifier. Since there is only one LUT for this process that is shared by the haptic interface's three motors, the sinusoidal profile cannot be applied simultaneously to each of the amplifier input channels. Instead, there is a 2 μs time skewing between the loading of successive DAC channels, contributing to a cumulative six-channel latency of 12 μs (6 × 2 μs). The individual DAC's 16 μs settling time, which limits the maximum commutation update rate, however, is long enough such that the commutation cycle is not further slowed by the accumulated interchannel delay. The resulting 31.25 kHz FPGA commutation update rate approximately equals the nominal PWM switchng frequnecy of our commercial servo amplifiers.

Subjectively, we observed that the implementation of sinusoid commutation in our hand-scale haptic device has eliminated any perceptible evidence of ripple, which had been so significant at 30° intervals under the prior trapezoidal commutation. We have not yet attempted formal calibration of the new motors and consequent overall haptic interface dynamics under the improvements afforded by the sinusoidal drives.

CONCLUSION

We have described in detail issues associated with the FPGA implementation of enhanced position resolution and improved BLDC motor commutation for a 3 DOF joystick-like haptic interface. The FPGA, along with its I/O, forms the lower level of a three-level haptic VE control architecture. The middle level, embodied on a DSP system, is at present responsible for calculation of the kinematic transformations specific to our haptic interface's mechanical configuration, servo (i.e., PD or impedance) control in Cartesian endpoint (hand-grip) coordinates, active compensation for unbalanced linkage mass, as well as linkage workspace boundary constraints. The third and highest level of control, which resides on an external desktop PC (or potentially on more powerful or networked computers), is where the governing VE model dynamics (i.e., virtual object interactions) as well as graphics for visual presentation are computed. The interconnection and signal communication between the low- and mid-level subcomponents are shown in Figure 4-8.

Together the mid- and low-level FPGA and DSP elements form a standalone embedded controller housed along with the motors and servo amplifiers inside the joystick's base enclosure. The embedded controller, because it contains all the required motor and sensor I/O components, eliminates the need for laboratory interface (data acquisition) cards in the PC. Portability of our haptic interface is therefore enabled by virtue of the embedded controller's small size and ready connection to any PC's standard serial (or USB) port.

The embedded controller serves to offload time-critical, high-update-rate tasks from the PC. Because of dedicated parallel processing on the FPGA, the low-level control components run the fastest, with the encoder interpolation updating at 1 MHz and the sinusoidal motor commutation at 31.25 kHz. On the DSP, the PD impedance control, workspace boundaries, and active mass balance operate concurrently at an overall rate of 5 kHz.

The specific improvements offered by the low-level FPGA components make feasible the use of BLDC motors in direct-drive haptic interface configurations. The sinusoidal commutation, which theoretically eliminates all torque ripple, when combined with cogging-free slotless stator windings, produces remarkably smooth BLDC motor actuation, without any noticeable spatially periodic variation in haptic interface force. Because the sinusoidal commutation signals are generated on the FPGA, the same embedded controller may be used with larger or smaller scale systems by simply swapping out the present servo amplifiers for PWM amplifiers with different power or current ratings.

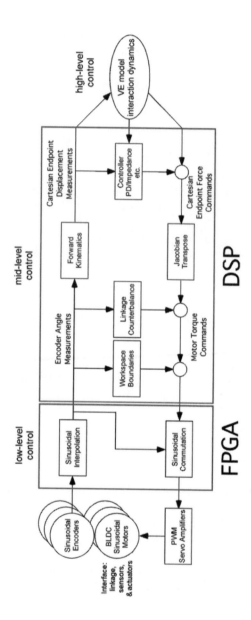

Figure 4-8: Standalone haptic interface controller comprising FPGA for low-level tasks and DSP for mid-level tasks. High level tasks on right may be assigned to single or multiple networked personal computers.

The sinusoidal encoder interpolation produces a theoretical angular resolution of 0.00069° at the motor shaft. This corresponds to a nominal worst case resolution of 1.2 μm for Cartesian endpoint motion of our hand-scale haptic interface—more than two orders of magnitude better than our prior standard quadrature decoding implementation, and also surpassing the resolution of similar scale haptic devices with geared-down cable transmissions.

BLDC motors with their superior torque enable higher sustained interface forces without incurring winding damage from overheating. At the lower end of the force dynamic range, smoother, ripple-free output torque should improve control accuracy. In principle, with better spatial and temporal displacement resolution, more robust velocity estimation and higher impedance gains will also be achievable.

APPENDIX

Three-Phase Motor Torque

The net torque produced by a three-phase BLDC motor is the sum of the torques of its individual phases

$$\tau_{sum} = \tau_{12} + \tau_{23} + \tau_{31} \tag{4.1}$$

The individual phase torques are functions of the respective stator phase currents

$$\tau_{12} = K_T i_{12} \qquad \tau_{23} = K_T i_{23} \qquad \tau_{31} = K_T i_{31} \tag{4.2}$$

where K_T is a torque constant assumed equal in all three windings.

Three-Phase Winding Currents

First, the winding currents, (i_{12}, i_{23}, i_{31}), must be related to the three phase servo-amplifier outputs, (i_1, i_2, i_3). For a delta-connected motor such as we use in our hand-scale haptic interface, the phase currents shown in Figure 4-9 can be expressed from the voltage drop across the individual winding coils

$$i_{12} = (v_1 - v_2)/Z \qquad i_{23} = (v_2 - v_3)/Z \qquad i_{31} = (v_3 - v_1)/Z \tag{4.3}$$

where impedance Z is presumed to be identical for all three phases. Summing the three equations in equation 4.3 yields

$$i_{12} + i_{23} + i_{31} = 0 \tag{4.4}$$

Beginning with the currents at each node

$$i_1 = i_{12} - i_{31} \quad i_2 = i_{23} - i_{12} \quad i_3 = i_{31} - i_{23}$$
(4.5)

three current differences can be written

$$i_1 - i_2 = 2i_{12} - (i_{23} + i_{31}) = 3i_{12}$$
$$i_2 - i_3 = 2i_{23} - (i_{12} + i_{31}) = 3i_{23}$$
$$i_3 - i_1 = 2i_{31} - (i_{12} + i_{23}) = 3i_{31}$$
(4.6)

Upon rearranging, equations 4.6 give

$$i_{12} = (i_1 - i_2)/3 \quad i_{23} = (i_2 - i_3)/3 \quad i_{31} = (i_3 - i_1)/3$$
(4.7)

enabling the motor torque in equation 4.1 and equations 4.2 to be stated in terms of servoamplifier output currents.

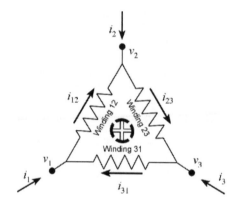

Figure 4-9: Four-pole, delta-wound brushless motor model.

Sinusoidal Three-Phase Currents and Torque

The balanced three-phase current (i.e., $i_1 + i_2 + i_3 = 0$) outputs of a sinusoidally commutated amplifier are

$$i_1 = i_0 \sin(\omega t) \quad i_2 = i_0 \sin(\omega t - 120°) \quad i_3 = i_0 \sin(\omega t - 240°)$$
(4.8)

where i_0 is commanded current, ω is the rotational speed of the motor in rad/sec, and t is time.

From equations 4.7, the individual winding currents become

$$i_{12} = (i_0/3)s_{12} \quad i_{23} = (i_0/3)s_{23} \quad i_{31} = (i_0/3)s_{31}$$
(4.9)

in which

$$s_{12} = \sin(\omega t - 120°) - \sin(\omega t) = \sqrt{3}\sin(\omega t + 30°)$$
$$s_{23} = \sin(\omega t - 240°) - \sin(\omega t - 120°) = \sqrt{3}\sin(\omega t - 90°) \tag{4.10}$$
$$s_{31} = \sin(\omega t) - \sin(\omega t - 240°) = \sqrt{3}\sin(\omega t + 150°)$$

Substituting equations 4.9 and 4.2 into equation 4.1 gives the total motor torque for three-phase sinusoidal drive current:

$$\tau_{sum} = (i_0/3)(K_T s_{12} + K_T s_{23} + K_T s_{31}) \tag{4.11}$$

If K_T were uniform for each winding phase, the total torque, τ_{sum}, in response to a constant current input, i_0, would vary cyclically as a function of the sinusoids described by equation 4.10.

In a sinusoidal winding, however, torque varies sinusoidally for constant applied current. This temporal-spatial sinusoidal variation is expressed in a new coupling factor for each phase, similar in form to equation 4.2:

$$\tau_{12} = \tilde{K}_T^{12} i_{12} \qquad \tau_{23} = \tilde{K}_T^{23} i_{23} \qquad \tau_{31} = \tilde{K}_T^{31} i_{31} \tag{4.12}$$

where $\tilde{K}_T^{12} = K_T s_{12}$, etc.

For a three phase sinusoidal winding, substituting equations 4.12 and 4.9 into equation 4.1 produces

$$\tau_{sum} = (K_T s_{12} i_{12} + K_T s_{23} i_{23} + K_T s_{31} i_{31}) = K_T (i_0/3)[s_{12}^{\ 2} + s_{23}^{\ 2} + s_{31}^{\ 2}] \tag{4.13}$$

By applying trigonometry, equation 4.13 reduces to the uniform, spatially invariant overall torque

$$\tau_{sum} = (3/2)K_T i_0 \tag{4.14}$$

illustrating the benefit of using sinusoidal current servo amplifiers to drive BLDC motors with sinusoidal windings (such as the motors used in our hand-scale haptic interface). If, however, sinusoidal windings are instead driven at constant current magnitudes (i.e., $i_{12} = i_{23} = i_{31} = i_o/3$)

$$\tau_{sum} = K_T (i_0/3)[s_{12} + s_{23} + s_{31}] \tag{4.15}$$

and the cyclic variation (i.e., torque ripple) described by equation 4.11 arises once again.

ACKNOWLEDGMENT

This work was supported by NASA-Ames Research Center Cooperative Agreement NCC2-1171 with the University of California, Berkeley under NASA RTOP 704-10-82 (IT Base).

REFERENCES

Adelstein, B. D., Ho, P., & Kazerooni, H. (1996). Kinematic design of a three degree of freedom parallel hand controller mechanism. *Proceedings, Dynamic Systems and Control*, DSC-Vol. 58 (pp. 539–546). New York: American Society of Mechanical Engineers.

Adelstein, B. D., Gayme, D. F., Kazerooni, H., & Ho, P. (1998). Three degree of freedom haptic interface for precision manipulation. *Proceedings, Dynamic Systems and Control*, DSC-Vol. 64 (p. 185). New York: American Society of Mechanical Engineers.

Colgate, J. E., & Brown, J. M. (1994). Factors affecting the Z-width of a haptic display. *Proceedings, IEEE International Conference on Robotics and Automation* (pp. 3205–3210).

Gupta, R., Sheridan, T., & Whitney, D. (1997). Experiments using multimodal virtual environments in design for assembly analysis. *Presence, 6*(3), 318–338.

Hayward, V., & Astley, O. (1996). Performance measures for haptic interfaces. In G. Giralt & G. Hirzinger (Eds.), *Robotics Research 7th International Symposium* (pp. 195–207). Springer Verlag.

Ho, C-H., Basdogan, C., & Srinivasan, M. (1998). Efficient point-based rendering techniques for haptic display of virtual objects. *Presence, 8*(5), 477–491.

Massie, T. H., & Salisbury, J. K. (1994). The PHANToM haptic interface: A device for probing virtual objects. *Proceedings, Dynamic Systems and Control*, DSC, Vol. 55-1 (pp. 295–301). New York: American Society of Mechanical Engineers.

Morrell, J. B., & Salisbury, J. K. (1995). Performance measurements for robotic actuators. *Proceedings, Dynamic Systems and Control*, DSC, Vol. 58 (pp. 531–537). New York: American Society of Mechanical Engineers.

Slocum, A. H. (1992). *Precision machine design*. Englewood Cliffs, NJ: Prentice Hall.

Venema, S., & Hannford, H. (1995). Kalman filter based calibration of precision motion control. *Proceedings of the IEEE/RSJ Conference on Intelligent Robots and Systems 95*, Pittsburgh, PA, Vol. 2 (pp. 224–229).

Six Degrees-of-Freedom Haptic Visualization

Ajith Mascarenhas, Stephen Ehmann, Arthur Gregory,
Ming C. Lin, and Dinesh Manocha[1]

Extending the frontier of visual computing, haptic interfaces, or force-feedback devices, have the potential to increase the quality of human-computer interaction by accommodating the sense of touch. They also provide an attractive augmentation to visual display and enhance the level of immersion in a virtual world. They have been effectively used for a number of applications including molecular docking, manipulation of nanomaterials, surgical training, virtual prototyping and digital sculpting. Given their potential, a number of research prototypes and commercial devices that can accommodate up to seven degrees of freedom (DOF) (Burdea, 1996) have been designed.

Compared with visual and auditory display, haptic rendering has extremely demanding computational requirements. In order to maintain a stable system while displaying smooth and realistic forces and torques, haptic update rates must be as high as 1000 Hz. This involves accurately computing all the contacts between the object attached to the probe and the simulated environment, as well as the restoring forces and torques, all in less than one millisecond.

Some of the commonly used haptic devices include the 3 DOF PHANToM arm (Massie & Salisbury, 1994) and the SARCOS Dexterous Arm (Nahvi, Nelson, Hollerbach, & Johnson, 1998), which compute point-object contacts and provide only force feedback. However, many applications like scientific exploration, virtual prototyping (e.g., assembly planning and maintainability studies), medical simulation, and teleoperation need to simulate arbitrary object-object interactions. A 6 DOF haptic device that provides torque feedback in addition to force display within a large translation and rotational range of motion is very useful for such applications. It gives a user the much-needed dexterity to feel, explore, and maneuver around other objects in the virtual environment.

Although a number of commercial and research 6 DOF haptic devices are becoming available, their applications have been limited. This is mainly due to the complexity of accurate calculation of all the contacts and restoring forces that must be computed in less than one millisecond, as outlined by McNeeley, Puterbaugh, and Troy (1999). The existing fast haptic rendering algorithms developed for 3 DOF haptic devices primarily deal with single point contact with the virtual models (Gregory, Lin, Gottschalk, & Taylor, 1999; Johnson & Cohen, 1998; Ruspini, Kolarov, & Khatib, 1997; SensAble Technologies, 1997) and are not directly applicable to accurate computation of object-object contacts. To date, only *approximate* haptic rendering techniques for mostly static environments, such as the one based on point-voxel sampling, have been proposed for haptic display using a 6 DOF haptic device (McNeely et al., 1999). Current algorithms for exact contact determination and response computation for general polygonal models are unable to meet the real-time requirements of 6 DOF haptic rendering.

In this paper, we present our system for six degrees-of-freedom haptic rendering of moderately complex polygonal environments and volumetric scientific data-sets. We assume that each polygonal object can be decomposed into convex primitives. Since the probe's position changes little between successive frames, our algorithm keeps track of the pairs of closest features between convex primitives (Lin & Canny, 1991). By exploiting the temporal coherence and spatial locality of closest features, we can take advantage of incremental computation by caching the last closest feature pair and performing a "greedy walk" to the current pair of closest features. We exploit motion coherence from extremely high haptic update rates to predict contact locations and minimize penetration between the probe and the virtual environment. The restoring forces are computed based on a concept similar to "virtual proxy" (Ruspini et al., 1997) extended to 6 DOF force feedback devices. The algorithm has been applied to haptic display of mechanical interaction between moderately complex structures composed of tens of convex primitives.

As compared to earlier approaches, our algorithm offers the following advantages:

- **Applicability to Dynamic Environments:** We do not assume the environment is static. Objects in the scene are free to move simultaneously. Our current implementation can only handle a few moving objects at the same time.

- **Accurate Contact Determination:** We do not need to trade off accuracy for performance, while maintaining required force update rates.

Haptic rendering of volumetric data-sets, like force-fields, is achieved by attaching a point-sampled rigid body to the haptic probe and calculating the force and torque acting on the rigid body as it moves through the data. We can handle uniformly sampled force-fields, tetrahedralized data-sets and arbitrary functions defined in three-dimensional space.

PREVIOUS WORK

In this section, we survey previous work related to haptic rendering, contact determination, and collision response.

Haptic Display

Several techniques have been proposed for integrating force feedback with a complete real-time virtual environment to enhance the user's ability to perform interaction tasks (Massie & Salisbury, 1994; Salisbury, Brock, Massie, Swarup, & Zilles, 1995). Iwata describes a 6 DOF haptic master and the concept of time-critical rendering at a lower update rate (Iwata, 1990). Ruspini et al. (1997) presented a haptic interface library (HL) that uses a virtual proxy and a multilevel control system to display forces effectively using 3 DOF haptic devices. Thompson, Johnson, and Cohen (1997) have presented a system for direct haptic rendering of sculptured models

Techniques for haptic visualization of the topology of vector fields were investigated by Helman and Hesselink (1990, 1991). Durbeck, Macias, Weinstein, Johnson, and Hollerbach (1998) have described a system for enhancing scientific visualization with the use of haptic feedback. The combined haptics/graphics display is used for displaying flow fields and vector fields. These systems were based on 3 DOF haptic devices that provided force feedback only. Iwata and Noma (1993) also proposed methods for presenting volume data by force sensation using a 6 DOF force reflecting master manipulator with update rates of one hundred Hz. Recently, Lawrence, Lee, Pao, and Novoselov (2000) presented a technique for shock and vortex visualization using a combined visual and haptic interface with a 5 DOF force feedback device.

Contact Determination

The problem of fast collision detection and contact determination has been well studied in computational geometry, robotics and graphics literature.

Convex Polytopes: A number of specialized algorithms have been developed for contact determination and distance computation between convex polytopes (Baraff, 1990; Dobkin, Hershberger, Kirkpatrick, & Suri, 1993; Ehmann & Lin, 2000; Gilbert, Johnson, & Keerthi, 1988; Lin & Canny, 1991).

Hierarchical Approaches: Some of the commonly used algorithms for general polygonal models are based on hierarchical data structures. These include bounding volume hierarchies where the bounding volume may correspond to a sphere (Hubbard, 1995), axis-aligned bounding box, oriented bounding box (Gottschalk, 1996), a k-DOP (Klosowski, Held, Mitchell, Sowizral, & Zikan, 1998) or a swept sphere volume (Larsen, Gottschalk, Lin, & Manocha, 1999). These algorithms can only compute all pairs of overlapping triangles and not the intersection region. Algorithms for separation distance computation based on bounding volume hierarchies have been proposed by Quinlan (1994), Johnson and Cohen (1998), and Larsen et al. (1999).

Intersection Region and Penetration Depth: Given two polyhedral models, algorithms for intersection computation and boundary evaluation have been extensively studied in solid modeling. Bouma and Vanecek (1993) used spatial partitioning approaches to compute the contact region. Ponamgi, Manocha, and Lin (1997) combined hierarchical representations with incremental computation to detect contacts between polygonal models. Snyder (1995) used temporal coherence to track penetration depth on spline models.

All these algorithms rely on a surface-based representation of the model. Their performance varies as a function of the size and relative configuration of two models.

Volumetric Approaches: Gibson (1995) and Avila and Sobierajski (1996) have proposed algorithms for object manipulation, including haptic interaction with volumetric objects and physically realistic modeling of object interactions. More recently, McNeely et al. (1999) have proposed a voxel sampling technique for 6 DOF haptic rendering, where point samples from one surface are tested against the voxel representations of the static environment. This approximation approach achieves constant query time at the expense of accuracy and correctness of haptic force display.

Collision Response

There is considerable work on dynamic simulation and response computation (Baraff, 1990, 1994; Mirtich & Canny, 1995). However, these algorithms do not guarantee real-time performance. Other algorithms propose an artificial coupling between the haptic display and the virtual environment (Colgate et al., 1994) or the notion of a "god-object" (Ruspini et al., 1997; Zilles & Salisbury, 1995).

OVERVIEW

Preliminaries

In general, the computation for haptic rendering at each time frame involves the following steps:

1. **Collision Detection:** The algorithm first detects if an intersection has occurred between an object (or a probe) held by the user and the virtual environment.

2. **Computing the Contact Manifold:** If an intersection has occurred, then the algorithm needs to compute the intersection points that form the *intersection region* and the *contact normal direction*.

3. **Estimating the Penetration Depth:** A measure or an estimation of penetration depth along the contact normal direction is computed from the intersection region.

4. **Computing Restoring Forces and Torques:** A restoring or contact force is often calculated based on penalty methods that require the penetration depth. Given the force and the contact manifold, restoring torques can be easily computed.

The *contact manifold* refers to the set of all points where the two objects come into contact with each other or may come into contact for predictive methods. For haptic simulation, the stability of force computation is extremely important. An accurate computation of the contact manifold at each frame also helps in smoothing the transition of force display from one frame to the next. This is crucial for the stability of the force feedback system with a human-in-the-loop, especially in a situation when there are multiple contacts between the object attached to the probe and the simulated environment.

None of the current algorithms and systems can perform force display of interaction between general polygonal models in an efficient and accurate manner. Given the time constraint of performing all these computations in less than a millisecond, our approach uses predictive techniques and incremental computation along with spatial and temporal coherence. As part of the pre-computation we initially decompose each object into *convex primitives* (Bajaj & Dey, 1992), if such a decomposition is not given. For the rest of the paper, we will refer to them as *primitives*. By exploiting the convexity of the objects, we can compute the contacts between a pair of convex primitives in expected *constant time*, with some simple preprocessing. As long as the number of contacts is bounded, our algorithm can guarantee the performance of force update rates.

6 DOF Haptic Rendering with a Virtual Proxy

The computation of our 6 DOF haptic rendering involves three components: (1) the use of virtual proxy (Ruspini et al., 1997); (2) contact manifold computation and penetration depth estimation; and (3) haptic response computation.

Extension of the Virtual Proxy: A virtual proxy is a representative object that substitutes for the physical object that the probe is attached to in the virtual environment. The motion of the virtual proxy is greedy in nature. It will move as long as it is not obstructed. Once it runs into a surface of some object in the environment, its motion is constrained to the surface location, in such a way that the actual object position will locally minimize the penetration depth. This is accomplished by predicting where the collision may occur between the two objects, based on the proxy position and velocity (also the actual probe position and velocity) from the previous frame and a simple linear interpolation along the travel path. At the beginning of the current frame, the object attached to the probe is constrained to travel no more than a safe threshold distance based on the predicted scheme, so as to minimize the amount of penetration.

Contact Determination and Penetration Depth Estimation: The contact determination algorithm initially narrows down pairs of primitives on different objects that are in close proximity, using a combination of an N-body "sweep-and-prune" test and "real-time scheduling." Then, it checks those pairs in close proximity for contacts. For a pair of convex primitives, we use an expected constant time algorithm to track the pair of closest features, thereby computing the contact manifold, the contact normal, and the estimated penetration depth. Moreover, a predictive approach is used to minimize penetration computations between the probe and the virtual environment.

Collision Response: The algorithm uses penalty methods to compute a force that is proportional to the penetration depth. It is then applied to the contact manifold in the direction of the contact normal.

HAPTIC RENDERING OF POLYGONAL OBJECTS

Contact Manifold and Depth Estimation

In this section, we present our algorithm for computing the contact manifold and estimating the penetration depth. Our algorithm uses convex decomposition to subdivide each object into convex primitives. The algorithm for contact determination uses a two-phase approach. In the first phase, it narrows down pairs of primitives in close proximity. The algorithm computes a tight fitting axis-aligned bounding box for each primitive, using incremental methods. It checks these bounding boxes for overlap by projecting them onto the coordinate axes and sorting them, using insertion sort (Cohen, Lin, Manocha, & Ponamgi,

1995). In the second phase, the algorithm performs exact contact determination tests on all pairs whose bounding boxes overlap.

Contact Determination between Convex Parts

We use a closest-feature tracking algorithm based on Voronoi regions for convex primitives, first proposed by Lin and Canny (1991). It is an incremental algorithm that keeps track of closest features between convex primitives from the previous frame. A *feature* corresponds to a vertex, edge, or face of the primitive. Using the external Voronoi regions of the convex primitives, the algorithm marches towards the new set of closest features in a greedy manner. The proof of correctness and the analysis of this algorithm is given in Lin, 1993.

Expected Constant Time Performance: The running time of this algorithm is $O_{(c)}$, where c is the number of features the algorithm traverses and is typically much smaller than the total number of features on a given polytope. The number of features that is traversed is expected to be constant due to coherence. When the bounding boxes of a pair of convex primitives overlap for the first time, coherence does not exist. In that case we use a directional lookup table (Ehmann & Lin, 2000) that has been precomputed for each convex primitive. It consists of nearest vertices to certain samples on a bounding sphere. The directional lookup table provides the means to find out quickly which vertex of a primitive is near a given direction by a simple lookup. The size of this table is determined by the resolution of directions on a unit sphere and is generally set to a constant. Given a constant size table, the table lookup time is also constant. Given the centers of two convex primitives and the vector connecting them, each primitive's table is used to look up a vertex in order to initialize the closest feature-tracking algorithm. This method can be used to help restore coherence and the closest features can be determined in expected constant time (a few microseconds) (Ehmann & Lin, 2000). The directional lookup table we used takes up less than a kilobyte for each convex primitive.

Contact Manifold Computation: The tracking algorithm always returns a pair of closest features for initializing contact manifold computation. There are six different feature combinations possible. If one of the features is a vertex, then the vertex and the closest point to it on the other feature are used. If both the features are edges, the closest points on the edges are used, assuming they are not parallel. If the two edges are parallel, the algorithm computes the projection of one edge to the other. For the edge-face and face-face cases, the algorithm uses a combination of edge-clipping and face-clipping routines.

Estimating Penetration Depth: The penetration depth is computed by extending the closest-feature algorithm. It is defined as the smallest distance that one of the primitives has to move so that the two primitives are just touching and not penetrating along the contact normal direction. This can be computed using the pseudointernal Voronoi region of each primitive (Ponamgi et al., 1997). For a convex polytope, the boundaries of the pseudointernal Voronoi region correspond to lines and planes, as opposed to quadric surfaces for general polyhedra. The pseudointernal Voronoi regions can be used to track and find all features that form the intersection volume. Given the intersection volume, we compute the penetration depth along the direction of the motion.

Real-Time Scheduling for Testing Convex Pairs

At each frame, the algorithm initially uses the sweep-and-prune technique (Cohen et al., 1995) to compute pairs of primitives in close proximity. The complexity of the sweep-and-prune algorithm is expected linear time (with a small constant, t_s) in terms of the number of primitives that the objects have been decomposed into. Let the total number of primitives be N and the total number of potential contacts be K. The total computation time for each update, T_h, for 6 DOF haptic rendering is bounded by:

$$T_h = N \times t_s + K \times t_c + M \times t_f \tag{5.1}$$

where t_f is the time required for computing the restoring force and torque for each of M resulting contact pairs, and t_c is an upper bound on the runtime performance of the closest features tracking between convex primitives. For large environments, it is possible that the algorithm cannot check all possible pairs for exact contacts in less than a millisecond.

As a result, we use a scheduling scheme to prioritize the pairs that will be checked for contact based on their importance. The pairs are assigned a priority based on the following:

- Pairs of objects that were in contact in the last frame are given the highest priority.

- The algorithm prioritizes the remaining pairs based on the amount of time since they were last checked for a contact (the greater the time, the higher the priority).

Given these criteria, the algorithm uses a simple greedy strategy. It sorts all the pairs based on increasing priority values into an array of fixed length. The length of the array is some constant derived from the maximum number of contacts the system can handle and still maintain the force update rate. The time of the pairs in this array is then updated to be that of the current frame, and they are checked for contacts.

Contact Forces and Torques

Given the contact manifold and estimated penetration depth between the probe and the virtual environment, we can compute the contact forces and torques for 6 DOF haptic rendering. In this section, we describe the basic formulation of 6 DOF force display and the use of predictive techniques to avoid penetration as much as possible.

Restoring Forces and Torques

We compute the restoring, or contact forces, based on the penalty methods. Using Hooke's law, we generate a spring force F_r that is proportional to the penetration depth:

$$F_r = k_s D_p \tag{5.2}$$

where k_s is the spring stiffness constant and D_p is the depth of penetration. We use 0.6 N/mm as the value of k_s in our implementation. The computed restoring force vector $\mathbf{F}_r$ is applied to the contact manifolds along the contact normal direction to resolve the penetration, thereby generating a sense of touch.

Restoring torques are generated by

$$\mathbf{T}_r = \sum_i \mathbf{R}_i \times \mathbf{F}_{ri} \tag{5.3}$$

where $\mathbf{F}_{ri}$ is the contact force vector applied at the point p_i and $\mathbf{R}_i$ is the radius vector from the center of the mass to p_i.

Predictive Collision Response

The computation of penetration depth is expensive in general. Furthermore, our depth estimation algorithm only computes a local approximation to the penetration depth. In conjunction with the use of virtual proxy, we minimize the frequency of computing the penetration depth by conceptually "growing" the actual surface along its surface normal direction by some small amount δ. Whenever the distance between two objects is less than δ, say $d < \delta$, we declare a collision. Then, we apply a restoring force

$$F_r = k_s (\delta - d). \tag{5.4}$$

If an actual penetration of D_p occurs, then we modify the contact force using the same principle by setting

$$F_r = k_s (\delta + D_p). \tag{5.5}$$

This fomulation reduces the need for computing penetration depth, which is relatively more expensive than computing the separation distance.

The value δ is a function of the upper bound on the magnitude of the current velocity v_c, which takes into consideration both the linear and angular velocity of the moving objects. δ is set to be:

$$\delta = v_c \times \Delta t \tag{5.6}$$

where Δt is 1 ms for typical haptic force update.

Force and Torque Interpolation

The displayed force is computed as a function of penetration depth, contact manifold, and contact normal direction. It is possible that the magnitude of contact forces can vary, thereby creating sudden jumps, and introduce sharp discontinuities between successive frames. We use a notion of *force and torque interpolation* that adopts the interpolated normals for "force shading," similar to that presented in Ruspini et al. (1997). We interpolate between two different force normals to achieve smooth force shading effects. In addition, we use a simple linear smoothing scheme to minimize discontinuity in force and torque display between successive frames.

Let F_0 be the force displayed at the previous frame and F_1 be the force generated during the current frame. Without loss of generality, let us assume that $F_1 > F_0$. Let F_{max} be the maximum amount of force difference allowed between successive updates. We use the following formulation to display the restoring force F_1:

$$\text{if } (F_1 - F_0) > 2F_{max}$$
$$\text{then } F_1 = F_0 + F_{max}$$
$$\text{else if } F_1 - F_0 > F_{max}$$
$$\text{then } F_1 = (F_0 + F_1)/2$$

DISPLAY F_1

We have considered other higher-order smoothing functions. However, this formulation seems to work reasonably well and is simple to compute. Due to the very fast force update rate, a more complex smoothing function may take unnecessarily long to compute and is likely to result only in very minute and subtle differences in the force and torque feedback to the user.

6 DOF HAPTIC VISUALIZATION OF VOLUMETRIC DATA-SETS

The ability to feel forces as well as torques enhances the user's ability to discover special regions in volumetric force-field data-sets like vortices, sinks, critical points, or higher order singularities. We now explain our algorithm for 6 DOF haptic visualization of arbitrary force-fields.

Uniformly Sampled Force-Fields

We assume the input data consists of a $N \times N \times N$ grid of force values, each force value being a 3-vector. To experience torque we need to have some object attached to the haptic probe. Currently, we feel the force-field using a simple rigid body like a cube or a sphere. The surface of the rigid body is point-sampled and moved virtually in the force-field using the haptic probe. The force exerted by the field on each of the sample points is calculated by indexing into the data. To ensure that the displayed forces are smooth, we use tri-linear interpolation within the grid cell indexed by the sample point. The calculated net force and torque on the rigid body are used to update the 6 DOF haptic rendering. Since computing force and torque due to a single sample point takes constant time, the total update time depends on the number of sample points on the rigid body.

Non-Uniformly Sampled Force-Fields

Our system can also haptically visualize volumes that are tetrahedralized with a force vector defined at each vertex. As described in the previous section, a point-sampled simple rigid body is moved through the tetrahedralization, and force and torque calculated at each point sample. For each sample point we use point location in the tetrahedralization to locate the tetrahedron containing the point. We then use the barycentric coordinates of the point to interpolate the force vectors at the vertices of the tetrahedron to get the force acting on the point. Torque is calculated using $T_i = R_i \times F_i$ where R_i is the radius vector from the center of mass to sample-point p_i and F_i is the force acting on the sample-point p_i.

Point location can be done by evaluating the point in the equation of each plane of a tetrahedron. We order the plane equation such that every point inside the tetrahedron evaluates to negative. If any plane evaluates to positive we walk across the plane to the adjacent tetrahedron and proceed till we locate the tetrahedron containing the point. The mesh data-structure maintains pointers from each tetrahedron to the neighboring tetrahedra that share a face with it. Traversing the mesh in this manner could, however, lead to long walks and does not guarantee a constant update time. To overcome this problem, we impose a uniform grid on the tetrahedralization and store a pointer to a tetrahedron contained in each grid cell. During point location we first index into the uniform grid cell containing the point. This can be done in constant time. We then start walking the mesh from the tetrahedron associated with the grid cell. By choosing an appropriate granularity we can restrict the walk to a few tetrahedra and can sustain the high update rate.

Force-Fields Defined by Functions

We can display forces described by an analytical function defined in three- or higher-dimensional space. As we move the rigid body through space, we evaluate the function, which returns a force vector, at each of the sample-points on the body. Arbitrary functions can be defined and the force can be visualized to enable the user to create test cases and interesting scenarios. The only restriction on the function is that it must be evaluated in real time without violating the haptic update requirements.

SYSTEM IMPLEMENTATION AND PERFORMANCE

In this section we describe our system and its application to haptic display of mechanical interaction between moderately complex structures and volumetric scientific data-sets. We used the 6 DOF PHANToM Premium 1.5 device (Chen, 1999) designed by SensAble Technologies.

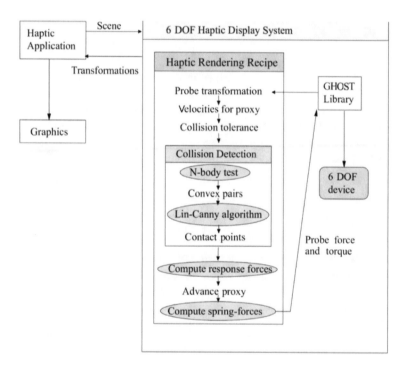

Figure 5-1: Overall architecture of the 6 DOF haptic display system.

Implementation

Haptic Rendering of Polygonal Models

The system consists of routines for hierarchical transformations, predictive methods, collision detection and contact manifold computation, and computing contact force/torque. It is interfaced with the provided GHOST® library as well as graphical display routines. The overall architecture of the system is shown in Figure 5-1.

The main loop of the system consists of three basic parts:

- **Contact Determination:** The probe proxy is typically attached to some object in the scene. The linear and angular velocities for this object are computed from the difference in the transformation between the proxy and the probe. Given the time slice for the current frame and the velocities of the moving objects, a conservative estimate is computed as a tolerance for collisions. Contact determination initially consists of applying an N-body algorithm based on sweep-and-prune. If the environment has too many potential pairs, it makes use of the scheduling scheme to prioritize the pairs as described earlier. For each pair in close proximity, it checks them for contact and computes the contact manifold between them. For convex objects the contact manifold can be used to compute a contact normal and a pair of contact points to apply the response forces.

- **Collision Response:** For each pair in contact, the algorithm uses the relative velocity at the contact points, the contact normal, and the distance between them to estimate the time of impact. If there are multiple contacts during the given time frame, the algorithm uses the one with the smallest time of impact. Each object is then advanced using its current velocities to the time of impact, and the contact forces are applied. Finally, it is advanced with its new velocities for the remainder of the time in the frame.

- **Computing Proxy Forces:** The actual force and torque being applied to the probe are computed using a simple spring model based on the transformation from the actual probe to its proxy at the end of the frame. After that a simple smoothing is applied to the force and torque vectors to make sure that the first derivatives of both the magnitude and the direction of these vectors have not changed drastically between frames.

- **Real-Time Constraints:** An important component of a high-fidelity haptic rendering system is that all the computations including contact determination and response computation have to be performed in less than a millisecond. In practice, this is a rather hard constraint and many portions of our system need to be optimized to achieve such performance. Currently, our system only works well on geometric models that can be decomposed into a few convex primitives (10–

30 convex primitives). The algorithm for collision detection between a pair of convex primitives takes just a few microseconds.

Haptic Visualization System for Volumetric Data-Sets

The haptic visualization code runs on a PC with Windows NT and we use an SGI R10000 to display the force-field and the rigid body proxy attached to the probe. The position and orientation of the rigid body are sent by the PC, over the network, to the display server. The pseudocode for the overall haptic visualization process is given in Figure 5-2.

In order to understand more fully the variations in forces and torques in data-sets that have a high dynamic range, our system allows for applying transfer functions to the data. We can window in on a small force range and apply an amplification filter to this range to emphasize the forces and thus feel the variations with greater fidelity.

The graphical rendering of a 3D volumetric data-set is important in the overall visualization. We have used the OpenGL Volumizer API available on the SGI platform for displaying our volumetric data-sets. A pseudocoloring scheme, similar to the traditional thermal spectrum, is used to color the data based on the magnitude of the force at each data point. The user can apply a filter to cutoff portions of the displayed data. In Figure 5-8(a)(b)(c) we see the data-set displayed with outer layers of the volume removed to view the inside layers. We achieve this by using a ramp cutoff filter. The user simply uses the mouse to position the ramp and also change its slope.

```
haptic_vis() {
    Points = rigidBody.samplePoints();
    For each update cycle do
    {
        netForce = [0, 0, 0];
        netTorque = [0, 0, 0];
        For each point p in Points do
        {
            (i, j, k) = Grid.findcell(p);
            f = interpolateForce(i, j, k, p);
            netForce = netForce + f;
            distV = p - rigidBody.centerOfMass();
            netTorque = netTorque + distV x f;
        }
        update6DOF(netForce, netTorque);
    }
}
```

Figure 5-2: Pseudocode for haptic display of the force field.

System Demonstration

Mechanical Interaction Between Gears

The gears are modeled and positioned in such a manner that the user can turn one gear with the other in either direction. The teeth are not so tightly interlocking that a collision always occurs. In the demonstration shown, the gears contain a few hundred polygons and about 20 convex primitives, as shown in Figure 5-3(a).

In order to aid the user in turning one gear with the other, constraints are applied to the gears so their position cannot be altered, and their rotation is constrained to be about an axis. In order to generate a correct response, these constraints are applied to the velocities at the beginning of the haptic frame and to the new transformations computed for the objects towards the end. As a result the user can feel the gears rotating against each other just as he or she would in a real mechanical part, as shown in Figure 5-3(b).

The user can attach the haptic probe to either gear in two different modes. Clicking the button towards the rim of the gear is like inserting a rod into a bicycle wheel. The probe's position remains at a fixed radius from the center of the gear, and its orientation is fixed so as to rotate with the gear at that radius. If the user clicks around the center of a gear, the probe effectively becomes the gear. Its position is fixed, and it is only allowed to rotate about one axis. In this mode, the user turns the gears and feels their interactions entirely through the torque of the probe handle. We encourage the reader to view the system demonstration on our website: *www.cs.unc.edu/~geom/6DHaptics*.

Figure 5-3(a)(b): The image on the left shows the contact scenario for the gear demo. We test the highlighted primitives against each other. The image on the right shows the user manipulating the gears using the 6 DOF PHANToM device.

Inserting a Peg in a Hole

In this scenario, the user attaches the probe to a rectangular peg and attempts to insert it into a rectangular hole. Often one or two pairs of the parallel faces are the pair(s) of the closest features and may be in contact. If any type of sampling technique is used, the number of contact points would be very high, since nearly all faces of the peg are in close proximity with the walls of the hole. Collision detection and contact determination for such a seemingly simple scene are actually rather difficult, due to the contact configuration and geometric robustness problem. A sequence of snapshots is given in Figure 5-4 (a)(b)(c) to demonstrate a successful attempt by a user to insert the peg into the hole with a 6 DOF haptic display.

Figure 5-4(a)(b)(c): Images from the peg-in-the-hole sequence. The user manipulates the rectangular peg into the rectangular hole. The jamming of the peg against the walls of the hole causes force and torque that constrain the peg to lie within the hole.

A Dynamic Scene of Multiple Moving Objects

In this scenario, all objects are moving simultaneously under the influence of gravity and impact due to collision with other objects. The user can pick up any of the objects with the probe and move it to hit other objects or feel other objects hitting it.

Sample snapshots are shown in Figure 5-5(a)(b)(c). In this particular setup, there are four cubes, four spheres (320 faces each), four ellipsoids (320 faces each) and a stick-like block. There are two types of simulated force. There is continuous force/torque such as gravity. There is also impulsive force/torque due to impact between the user-controlled object and other moving objects. The motion of all moving objects is simulated using impulse-based rigid-body dynamics. The continuous force can be felt quite well, but the impulsive ones currently feel like small blips. This is exactly what we expect, since the impulsive contact duration is very short. We are considering the possibility of force expansion over time or force amplification to exaggerate the feel of impulsive force/torque.

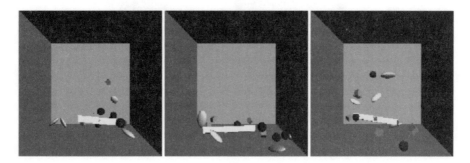

Figure 5-5(a)(b)(c): Scenes from a dynamic environment. The user can grab any of the several objects that move under the influence of gravity. Gravity results in a continuous force and collisions with the moving objects result in impulse forces and torque. The scene shows a stick-like object being manipulated by the user.

Uniformly Sampled Force-Fields

Our volumetric haptic rendering system has been applied to simple force vector fields generated using the 'streamlines' package, described by Turk and Banks (1996). We used a 2D vector field of 512×512 values and then extended the same force field along the third dimension. The system can directly handle any 3D vector field. In Figure 5-6(a)(b), we display the force fields using the streamlines superimposed to show the direction of the force. Each force vector is normalized and interpreted as a RGB triple to highlight the intensity value for that pixel in the image.

Non-Uniformly Sampled Data-Sets

We have run our system on the volumetric data-set, which we received from the University of Utah, of a human head. The data-set is composed of a tetrahedralization of the human head with three electric charges placed inside the volume. The electric field has been calculated at each tetrahedral vertex. There are $72 \, K$ nodes and $406 \, K$ tetrahedral elements in the data-set. Figure 5-7 and Figure 5-8(a)(b)(c) show the graphical display of the data-set. The region around the charges is seen in Figure 5-8(c).

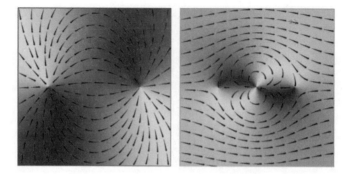

Figure 5-6(a)(b): The image on the left (a) shows the force-field generated by two charges of opposite polarity. The streamlines indicate the direction of the forces. The user feels forces directed away from the charge on the right and towards the charge on the left. The force-field for ideal flow around and inside a cylinder is shown in the image on the right (b). The region within the cylinder shows two flow regions separated by the horizontal axis. The flows meet at the right and proceed towards the left before diverging again. Small movements away from the horizontal will push the user in a semicircular path following the field.

Figure 5-7: View of the head data-set with the electric charges.

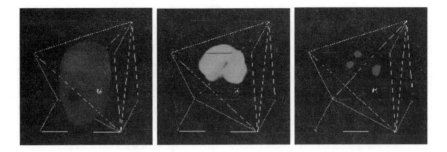

Figure 5-8(a)(b)(c): Volume visualization of the electric field in the human head data-
set. The image on the left (a) shows the entire data-set. The center image (b) shows the force-field around the brain. Filtering is used to display different ranges of the force-field. The image on the right (c) shows
the field around the three charges that are placed in the interior of the
head. Lighter shades stand for stronger field strength and darker shades
indicates weaker field strength. The small wire-frame cube in the center
of each image shows the position of the haptic probe.

DISCUSSION

Force display of mechanical interaction is useful in virtual assembly, maintenance
studies, and other electronic prototyping applications. In cases where the user has to interact
with the virtual environment through a sense of touch (e.g., a mechanic trying to remove a
virtual part from a virtual engine), haptic display appears to be the only means of human-
computer interaction. In many other cases (e.g., molecular graphics (Brooks, Ouh-Young,
Batter, & Kilpatrick, 1990) force display can provide additional means to visualize complex
systems or environments.

As overall scenes become more complex, the type of contact scenarios do *not* necessarily become more complex, since the contact configuration in most cases is only local to
the region of impact. In fact, in our gear-turning demonstration, the polygon count is much
higher than the *visually simple* peg-in-the-hole scenario. However, the collision detection
and contact determination problem becomes substantially harder for peg-in-the-hole insertion, since nearly the entire peg is in contact with the hole. Although there are already many
contact pairs between the interlocking gears, there are significantly many more contacts (in
theory infinitely many point contacts) in the peg-in-the-hole case. Haptic display becomes
much more difficult to control due to multiple contact forces generated in opposing directions. This is an extremely challenging scenario. Our approach can provide a more accurate
and smoother response than an approximate method. However, if the user exerts too much

force, causing a large amount of penetration, the control loop can become unstable or the device can shut down due to exceeding the force limit. Furthermore, if we incorporate a more complex and accurate dynamics model for simulating sliding/rolling friction, it would become even more difficult to maintain the required force update rate on hard surfaces. This is a research area deserving serious investigation.

CONCLUSIONS AND FUTURE WORK

In this paper, we have presented methods for 6 DOF haptic visualization of polygonal models and volumetric scientific data-sets using force feedback devices. We make use of a combination of incremental techniques, spatial and temporal coherence, and predictive methods to compute all the contacts accurately and force response in less than a millisecond. The system has been used for force display of mechanical interaction and volume data-sets. In terms of complexity, our current haptic rendering system for polygonal data-sets works well on geometric models that can be decomposed into few tens of convex pieces.

There are many directions for future work. We plan to use 6 DOF haptic rendering for display of more complex geometric models, as well as massively large vector field datasets. In terms of haptic display of complex polygonal models, a major issue is the accurate computation of all the contacts and the penetration depth between general polygonal models in less than 1 millisecond. Algorithms based on hierarchical approaches, for example OBBTree (Gottschalk, Lin, & Manocha, 1996), cannot guarantee to compute all the contacts in less than a millisecond for complex models. Extensions based on the approach presented in this paper hold some promise. In addition, we would also like to interface our system with scientific visualization systems for better understanding and analysis of complex data-sets. We have developed a generic system framework for haptic visualization of force fields (represented as volumetric data) using a 6 DOF force feedback device and have successfully applied it to some complex volumetric data-sets. Finally, we would like to perform some user studies on the benefits of multimodal display systems using 6 DOF force display over traditional visualization techniques.

ACKNOWLEDGMENTS

This research is supported in part by ARO DAAG55-98-1-0322, DOE ASCI Grant, NSF NSG-9876914, NSF DMI-9900157, NSF IIS-9821067, ONR Young Investigator Award, and Intel. The head data-set was provided by Chris Johnson and the Scientific Computing Group at the University of Utah.

REFERENCES

Avila R. S., & Sobierajski, L. M. (1996). A haptic interaction method for volume visualization. In R. Yagel & G. Nelson (Eds.), *Proceedings of IEEE Visualization'96* (pp. 197–204). ACM Press.

Baraff, D. (1990). Curved surfaces and coherence for non-penetrating rigid body simulation. *ACM Computer Graphics, 24*(4), 19–28.

Baraff, D. (1994). Fast contact force computation for nonpenetrating rigid bodies. In A. Glassner (Ed.), *Computer Graphics (Proceedings of SIGGRAPH '94)*(pp. 23–34). Boston: Addison Wesley.

Bajaj, C., & Dey, T. (1992). Convex decomposition of polyhedra and robustness. *SIAM Journal of Computing, 2*, 339–364.

Brooks, Jr., F. P., Ouh-Young, M., Batter, J. J., & Kilpatrick, P. J. (1990). Project GROPE—Haptic displays for scientific visualization. In F. Baskett (Ed.), *Computer Graphics (Proceedings of SIGGRAPH '90)*(pp. 177–185). Boston: Addison Wesley.

Bouma, W., & Vanecek, G. (1993). Modeling contacts in a physically based simulation. In *Second Symposium on Solid Modeling and Applications* (pp. 409–419). ACM Press

Burdea, G. (1996). *Force and touch feedback for virtual reality.* John Wiley and Sons.

Chen, E. (1999). Six degree-of-freedom haptic system for desktop virtual prototyping applications. In G. Subsol (Ed.), *Proceedings of the First International Workshop on Virtual Reality and Prototyping* (pp. 97–106).

Cohen, J., Lin, M., Manocha, D., & Ponamgi, M. (1995). I-collide: An interactive and exact collision detection system for large-scale environments. In P. Hanrahan & J. Winget (Eds.), *Proceedings of the ACM Interactive 3D Graphics Conference* (pp. 189–196). ACM Press.

Colgate, J. E., & Brown, J. M. (1994). Factors affecting the z-width of a haptic display. In H. Stephanou (Ed.), *Proceedings of the IEEE Conference on Robotics and Automation* (pp. 3205–3210). IEEE Computer Society Press.

Colgate, J. E., Stanley, M. C., & Brown J. M. (1995). Issues in the haptic display of tool use. In *IEEE/RSJ International Conference on Intelligent Robots and Systems* (pp. 140–145). IEEE Computer Society Press.

Dobkin, D., Hershberger, J., Kirkpatrick, D., & Suri, S. (1993). Computing the intersection-depth of polyhedra. *Algorithmica, 9*, 518–533.

Durbeck, L., Macias, N., Weinstein, D., Johnson, C., & Hollerbach, J. (1998). *Scirun haptic display for scientific visualization.* Paper presented at the PHANToM Users Group Meeting.

Ehmann, S. A., & Lin, M. (2000). Accelerated proximity queries between convex polyhedra by multi-level Voronoi marching. In H. Hashimoto (Ed.), *Proceedings of IEEE/RSJ International Conference on Intelligent Robots and Systems 2000* (pp. 2101–2106). IEEE Computer Society Press.

Gibson, S. (1995). Beyond volume rendering: Visualization, haptic exploration, and physical modeling of element-based objects. In R. Scateni, J. van Wijk, & P. Zanarini (Eds.), *Proceedings of the Eurographics Workshop on Visualization in Scientific Computing* (pp. 10–24). Springer-Verlag.

Gilbert, E. G., Johnson, D. W., & Keerthi, S. S. (1988). A fast procedure for computing the distance between objects in three-dimensional space. *IEEE Journal of Robotics and Automation, RA-4*, 193–203.

Gottschalk, S., Lin, M., & Manocha, D. (1996). Obb-tree: A hierarchical structure for rapid interference detection. In H. Rushmeier (Ed.), *Computer Graphics* (*Proceedings of SIGGRAPH'96*) (pp. 171–180). Boston: Addison Wesley.

Gregory, A., Lin, M., Gottschalk, S., & Taylor, R. (1999). H-collide: A framework for fast and accurate collision detection for haptic interaction. In L. Rosenblum, P. Astheiner, & D. Teichmann (Eds.), *Proceedings of Virtual Reality Conference 1999*. IEEE Computer Society Press.

Guibas, L., Hsu, D., & Zhang, L. (1999). *H-Walk*: Hierarchical distance computation for moving convex bodies. *Proceedings of ACM Symposium on Computational Geometry* (pp. 265–273). ACM Press.

Helman, J., & Hesselink, L. (1990). Representation and display of vector field topology in fluid flow data sets. In *Proceedings of the Eurographics Workshop on Visualization in Scientific Computing* (pp. 61–73). Springer-Verlag.

Helman, J., & Hesselink, L. (1991). Surface representations of two- and three-dimensional fluid flow topology. In *Proceedings of IEEE Visualization '91* (pp. 6–13). IEEE Press.

Hubbard, P. M. (1995). Collision detection for interactive graphics applications. *IEEE Transactions on Visualization and Computer Graphics, 1*(3), 218–230.

Iwata, H. (1990). Artificial reality with force-feedback: Development of desktop virtual space with compact master manipulator. In F. Baskett (Ed.), *Proceedings of SIGGRAPH '90* (pp. 165–170). Boston: Addison Wesley.

Iwata, H., & Noma, N. (1993). Volume haptization. In *Proceedings of IEEE VRAIS* (pp. 16–23). IEEE Press.

Johnson, D., & Cohen, E. (1998). A framework for efficient minimum distance computation. *IEEE Conference on Robotics and Automation* (pp. 3678–3683). IEEE Computer Society Press.

Klosowski, J., Held, M., Mitchell, J. S. B., Sowizral, H., & Zikan, K. (1998). Efficient collision detection using bounding volume hierarchies of k-dops. *IEEE Transactions on Visualization and Computer Graphics, 4*(1), 21–37. IEEE Computer Society Press.

Lawrence, D. A., Lee, C. D., Pao, L. Y., & Novoselov, R. Y. (2000). Shock and vortex visualization using a combined visual/haptic interface. In T. Ertl, B. Hamann, & A. Varshney (Eds.), *Proceedings of IEEE Visualization* (pp. 131–137). IEEE Computer Society Press.

Lin, M., & Canny, J. F. (1991) Efficient algorithms for incremental distance computation. In *Proceedings of the IEEE Conference on Robotics and Automation* (pp. 1008–1014). IEEE Computer Society Press.

Lin, M. (1993). *Efficient collision detection for animation and robotics.* Unpublished doctoral dissertation, University of California, Berkeley.

Larsen, E., Gottschalk, S., Lin, M., & Manocha, D. (1999). *Fast proximity queries with swept sphere volumes.* Technical Report TR99-018, Department of Computer Science, University of North Carolina at Chapel Hill.

Mirtich, B., & Canny, J. (1995). Impulse-based simulation of rigid bodies. In P. Hanrahan & J. Winget (Eds.), *Proceedings of ACM Interactive 3D Graphics* (pp. 181–188). ACM Press.

McNeely, W., Puterbaugh, K., & Troy, J. (1999). Six degree-of-freedom haptic rendering using voxel sampling. In A. Rockwood (Ed.), *Computer Graphics* (*Proceedings of SIGGRAPH '99)* (pp. 401–408). Boston: Addison Wesley.

Massie, T. M., & Salisbury, J. K. (1994). The PHANToM haptic interface: A device for probing virtual objects. In C. J. Radcliffe (Ed.), *Proceedings of ASME Haptic Interfaces for Virtual Environment and Teleoperator Systems* (pp. 295–301). ASME Press.

Nahvi, A., Nelson, D., Hollerbach, J., & Johnson, D. (1998). Haptic manipulation of virtual mechanisms from mechanical CAD designs. *Proceedings of the IEEE Conference on Robotics and Automation* (pp. 375–380). IEEE Computer Society Press.

Ponamgi, M., Manocha, D., & Lin, M. (1997). Incremental algorithms for collision detection between polygonal models. *IEEE Transactions on Visualization and Computer Graphics*, 3(1), 51–67.

Quinlan, S. (1994). Efficient distance computation between non-convex objects. In H. Stephanou (Ed.), *Proceedings of the International Conference on Robotics and Automation* (pp. 3324–3329).

Ruspini, D. C., Kolarov, K., & Khatib O. (1997), The haptic display of complex graphical environments. In T. Whitted (Ed.), *Computer Graphics* (*Proceedings of SIGGRAPH '97)*(pp. 345–352). Boston: Addison Wesley.

Salisbury, K., Brock, D., Massie, T., Swarup, N., & Zilles, C. (1995). Haptic rendering: Programming touch interaction with virtual objects. In P. Hanrahan & J Winget (Eds.), *Proceedings of the ACM Symposium on Interactive 3D Graphics* (pp. 123–130). ACM Press.

Snyder, J. (1995). An interactive tool for placing curved surfaces without interpenetration. In P. Hanrahan & J. Winget (Eds.), *Computer Graphics* (*Proceedings of SIGGRAPH '95)*(pp. 209–218). Boston: Addison Wesley.

SensAble Technologies, Inc. (1997). GHOST® Sofware developer's toolkit. *Programmer's Guide.*

Turk, G., & Banks, D. (1996). Image-guided streamline placement. In H. Rushmeier (Ed.), *Computer Graphics (Proceedings of SIGGRAPH '96)* (pp. 453–460). Boston: Addison Wesley.

Thompson, T. V., Johnson, D., & Cohen, E. (1997). Direct haptic rendering of sculptured models. *Proceedings of ACM Interactive 3D Graphics* (pp. 167–176). ACM Press.

Zilles, C., & Salisbury, K. (1995). A constraint-based god object method for haptics display. *Proceedings of the IEEE/RSJ International Conference on Intelligent Robotics and Systems* (pp. 146–151). IEEE Computer Society Press.

Lossy Compression of Haptic Data

Antonio Ortega and Yifan Liu

Other chapters in this book provide a detailed overview of modalities of haptic data and their use in various applications (see also Mishra & Shrikanth, 2000; Ruspini & Khatib, 2000; Son, Kim, Amato, & Trinkle, 2000). Many of these current and future applications will involve the communication, storage, and retrieval of haptic data. As examples of this scenario consider the remote manipulation of an object. Here, the user interacts through a haptic device with a virtual object, then the resulting information is captured and transmitted to a remote site where this interaction may be replicated on the actual object or may be shown through computer graphics. Alternatively, a training session where the user learns to manipulate the object can be stored, so that it can be replayed and analyzed at a later time. In these examples one could consider the transmission/storage of uncompressed data to be an option. This, however, would be a very inefficient approach. As an example, complex commercial haptic devices such as the CyberGrasp from Immersion Corporation have more than 30 sensors that can produce floating point data with sampling rates that can be selected and are usually between 10–100Hz (Shahabi, Barish, Kolahdouzan, Yao, Zimmermann, Fu, & Zhang, 2001). With devices like these, transmission/storage rates of around 100 kbits/s would not be unusual. While applications involving haptic data capture and transmission/storage are in their infancy, and indeed practical haptic devices are constantly updated and improved, we believe that future systems will have to incorporate some sort of compression in order to be practical.

Compression techniques can be divided into two general classes, namely lossless and lossy. Lossless compression exploits statistical redundancies in the data to achieve compression. The basic principle is to map each one of the discrete input symbols to a codeword with a length that is shorter for the more popular input symbols (i.e., those that occur more frequently). The selection of codewords is such that the mapping is one-to-one and the bitstream containing the variable length codes can then be parsed to decode the codewords and recover the input symbols. The overall process is lossless, so this type of compression is routinely used for computer files. A major drawback of standard lossless techniques, which were initially created to compress text files, is that they may not prove efficient for media data. This is because these algorithms do not take advantage of inherent properties in the data or because they become inefficient as the size of the input alphabet (total number of possible different inputs) becomes large. As an example, lossless compression of images using standard utilities such as Zip often fails to provide any compression, whereas using lossless compression specifically designed for images can lead to compression by a factor of two or more.

As an alternative, lossy compression is often used to compress media data, such as audio, images, or video. When lossy compression is used, the decoded media data is not an exact copy of the original. Lossy compression schemes are popular, however, in that they achieve substantially higher compression rates, while the decoded media displayed or played back is practically indistinguishable from the original. Thus high quality lossy compression schemes are designed to achieve decoded data that is *perceptually* indistinguishable from the original. As an example, the best lossless compression algorithms for images can achieve compression ratios of about two (i.e., the compressed file is half the size of the original file), while state-of-the-art lossy compression can achieve perceptually identical images with compression factors around 10. Thus lossy compression of media is prevalent in all consumer applications (from mp3 files to DVDs or speech coding for cellular phones). There are only a few applications that require the use of lossless media compression. These are applications where the decoded media have to be processed or have to be preserved exactly as captured. Examples include storage of medical images (for which legal considerations have precluded lossy compression from being seriously considered) and transmission of deep space images (where the cost of capturing data in the first place leads to preference for lossless compression).

From the above discussion it is to be expected that lossless coding of haptic data will tend to provide limited compression gains. Indeed this was shown by our experiments; for example, we observed lossless compression factors of about a factor of two, whereas a factor of 10 compression can be achieved easily with lossy techniques. In this chapter, therefore, we concentrate on lossy coding techniques. Obviously, as soon as lossy compression is considered, one has to select a "distortion" metric for the application at hand. This distortion metric should be targeted to the specific application so that it is possible to establish what constitutes "acceptable" distortion for a given scenario. Since there is a trade-off between compression ratio and distortion (the more we compress the data, the higher the distortion will be), having an application-specific distortion metric will enable us to compress just enough so that the degradation of the decoded data is still usable.

This opens up some very interesting research issues. For example, experimental work could be devoted to studying the perceptual impact of haptic data compression (i.e., determining whether a subject can tell the difference between "experiencing" two different haptic "sessions," one played with the original data, the other produced with the data resulting from a decompressed file). This will depend largely on the applications and is an area where we believe a lot of work is needed before any conclusions can be derived. Alternatively, the ultimate goal of compressing and storing haptic data may be to provide a record and the ability to analyze the data at a later time. In this case, the amount of error that can be present in the decoded data will in turn depend on the type of analysis being performed. We expect that many applications will not require a very precise analysis of the traces to be performed; for these applications, lossy compression should be well-suited. Only relatively limited work has been done towards analyzing the perceptual quality of haptic interaction (see for example Lawrence, Pao, Dougherty, Salada, & Pavlou, 2000 or Shahabi et al., 2000). In particular, perceptual evaluations of the effect of compression are still very preliminary.

This chapter investigates novel techniques for haptic data compression and demonstrates that even relatively simple, low-delay techniques can provide substantial levels of compression performance without introducing too much error in the signal. We provide algorithms where the level of error introduced can be adjusted so as to accommodate different applications, with each having a predefined error level that can be tolerated. While the results are specific to the haptic data type considered here (data generated with the PHANToM device), we believe that similar results can be obtained with other, more complex, devices. Further improvements can also be expected once knowledge of application-specific perceptual and/or analysis error criteria is incorporated into our algorithm.

This chapter is organized as follows. First we provide examples of haptic data acquired with the PHANToM device and outline a series of requirements that should be met by a practical compression system. Next we introduce a simple and low-delay coding scheme based on differential pulse code modulation (DPCM). We then propose an alternative coding approach that takes advantage of knowledge of the underlying graphical model being used. Finally, we provide some coding results and discuss directions for future work.

HAPTIC DATA

Haptic Systems

A typical haptic system includes a force-feedback sensory device where the human hand can interact with the sensory device by moving it and in turn feeling some force feedback. Usually this device can detect movement or give feedback at a speed as high as 1 kHz in order to enable all kinds of possible realistic motions. This force feedback sensory device is linked to a computer system, where data processing is carried out and the haptic virtual environment is simulated. Usually a haptic environment involves one or more geometrical objects formed by either parametrical or meshed surfaces. With various techniques the software can capture the movement of the haptic display to create both forward and reverse interaction, and create a 3D graphics display for the interaction if needed. The virtual object models in the computer do not just contain geometrical information. In addition, a complete haptic environment may also contain information about the specific material that is being simulated (e.g., describe its deformation properties).

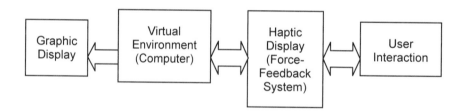

Figure 6-1: A typical haptic system.

Figure 6-1 provides an example of the various elements of a haptic system. We assume that the haptic display system is also capable of recording data. There are two alternatives in compressing the resulting data, both of which will be considered in this chapter. First, we can take the recorded data and compress it without any knowledge of the underlying virtual environment. In this case we assume that the data can take arbitrary values. For example, we consider the trajectory tracking the hand movements in 3D space as being essentially unconstrained. As an alternative, one can consider the interaction between the user and the virtual environment. For example, this would lead to compressing the hand trajectory relative to the position of the virtual objects in the scene.

A complete system to compress a haptic environment and associated interactions involves dealing with two types of information, namely the description of the geometrical models in the virtual haptic environment and compressing haptic movement trajectories. There has been substantial research in the area of multiresolution representation of geometrical models, which enable a model to be viewed at various levels of resolution (Bajaj, Pascucci, & Zhuang, 1999; Gueziec, Bossen, Taubin, & Silva, 1999; Gumhold & Straber, 1998; Popovic & Hoppe, 1997; Taubin & Rossignac, 1998). Most of this work is not specifically targeted at haptic environments but could be used within this context as well. The work by Kolarov (2000) is an example that explores the interaction between haptics and compression of geometric models. In this work a zero tree technique (Shapiro, 1993) is used to enable decoding only the area of the object that is being directly touched by the user. This enables a faster response in the application because, for example, as the object turns, only the portion that is exposed in the display needs to be decoded. To the best of our knowledge, however, coding of the haptic movement trajectory is still a relatively unexplored area of research. This may be due to the fact that the criteria that have to be applied in developing these systems are application-dependent, and applications requiring storage and retrieval of haptic data are only slowly emerging. Among the first attempts to compress haptic data, an approach based on adaptive sampling is worth mentioning (Shahabi et al., 2001). In this work, data is sampled at a relatively fast rate, but then it is subsampled based on the level of activity of the user. In this way, during periods of relatively low motion, it is possible to sample at a lower rate, while in high-motion periods the higher sampling rate is preserved. The main drawback of this approach is that it requires a delay, since the encoder will have to determine whether high or low motions are being observed based on a segment of input data.

The PHANToM Device and GHOST® Library

Before describing the details of our proposed techniques, we provide an overview of the device used in our experiments, namely the PHANToM device, produced by SensAble Technologies. Since our proposed algorithms are based on assumptions about the data being sensed over time, we expect that the results will not change substantially when other devices are considered and will depend more on the type of interaction.

The PHANToM device consists of a probing point (the so-called stylus, a wand-like instrument) that is attached to a servo system. The servo system is designed so that it can support whatever constraints are required by the application, such as inertia, force feedback, or vibrations. The system simulates a pen in 3D free space, with a light design that enables the user to maneuver without being disturbed by the equipment weight. The PHANToM 1.0 measurement system has 6 degrees of freedom (DOF), and its force feedback system has 3 DOF.

The software library used for creating the 3D haptic environment is called GHOST® (also produced by SensAble Technologies). It consists of device drivers and interface functions that interact with the PHANToM to exchange haptic information such as position, force, collision, and current control model (the default is a spring model). GHOST® also has library functions for building simple 3D scenes, like those incorporating basic geometrical shapes such as cubes or spheres. The PHANToM (hardware) and GHOST® (software) together provide a simple platform that enables haptic trajectory recording and replay. A more detailed description of this system can be found in Massie and Salisbury (1994).

There are other haptic devices on the market as well, but the PHANToM represents a simple general-purpose system with which it is easy to perform experiments. All experiments in this chapter were performed with data obtained using the PHANToM 1.0 device. Note that because the potential for compression depends primarily on how the user interacts with the device, rather than the device itself, we expect similar compression results to be achieved with more sophisticated haptic devices.

A haptic system usually has the ability to track the motion of the contact point, perform collision detection, and exert force reaction. In this chapter we are primarily concerned with encoding of the trajectory of the contact point. When the contact point moves into a geometrical object, a good system can detect the collision immediately and produce a prompt collision response. If the contact point slides over a smooth surface, the trajectory can be considered on the surface. Since most of the interaction will involve virtual objects, our second, model-based compression algorithm will seek to use the available knowledge about these objects to improve the compression performance.

Thus, while a haptic system has other properties of interest (e.g., friction or deformation properties), in this chapter we are only concerned with the geometric properties—the absolute position (and orientation) of the contact point as well as its position relative to the objects.

More specifically, the GHOST® library can provide various types of data from the PHANToM device, including

- Timing data
- Trajectory data
- Force feedback data
- Material property data

Typically, the force feedback and certain material properties can be interpreted from geometrical data. For example, the perpendicular feedback force from a wall is determined by how much the probing point moves into the wall. The deformation can be modeled by the change of the surface shape. Thus, studying geometrical data, such as the probing trajectory, provides enough information to replicate some of the other data (e.g., the force feedback), and our compression work focuses on compressing this trajectory.

To achieve acceptable resolution, and also satisfy the graphical display for visual feedback, the trajectory data is logged at the same rate as the screen refresh rate (about 30 samples per second). Because the Windows NT operating system is not a true real-time operating system, the sampling interval is not precisely fixed, so each sample has a time stamp.

In summary, the actual haptic data used for recording, replay, and analysis consisted essentially of temporal, positional, and collision-related information. Specifically, this included a series of logfile entries, which included for each sample

- Elapsed time from the start of the recording.

- Three-dimensional vector for spatial location (i.e. x, y, and z coordinates).

- Quadruple to represent *quaternions*, an efficient way to represent rotations. Quaternions are an alternative to rotational matrices.

- The ID of the facet involved in the collision if the probing point is on the surface of a virtual object. The virtual object could be stationary or moving. The interaction can be derived from the relative position of the probe and the facet.

In what follows we will refer to samples as any of the elements (coordinates or quaternions) captured by the haptic device. We compress each of these data streams independently of each other.

Figure 6-2 shows an example of a trajectory in 3D space. It is easy to see that the trajectory is smooth, which suggests a coding approach that uses previous points in the trajectory to encode the current one.

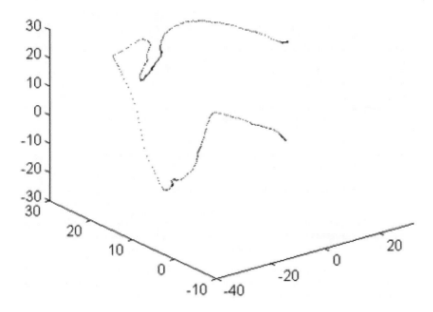

Figure 6-2: A typical haptic trajectory captured at 30 samples per second.

Haptic Data Encoder Requirements

Haptic data is captured in real time and may have to be transmitted with the minimum possible delay, especially if we are considering an interactive application. As an example, consider an interactive distributed game application where two or more users are sharing a virtual environment with which they interact through the haptic device. In this case data obtained from each user has to be quickly sent to the central server (or the other users) so that the environment gets modified accordingly (e.g., when an object has been displaced).

The volume of data collected is directly related to the complexity of the device that records or retrieves that data, but it is also related to the complexity of the geometrical objects that exist in the virtual environment. With the GHOST® library, the 3D scenes could potentially become very complicated. For our preliminary work we choose a simple scene in order to maintain a relatively simple computation. In addition to low delay an effective haptic coding system will likely be required to be simple enough that it can be run in real time.

Of the two systems presented below, the DPCM approach is of very low complexity and has extremely low delay (only one sample). By comparison techniques such as those used in Shahabi et al. (2000) adapt their sampling rate on a segment-by-segment basis. That means that the encoder has to wait until it has captured and stored a relatively long segment of data before it can decide what sampling rate to choose. Thus there will be an end-to-end latency in the system related to the length of the segment. This can be a drawback in interactive applications.

The model-based coding discussed below requires significantly higher complexity than that of the low-delay predictive coding approach but is also low-delay in nature, since only the current and previous sample values are needed to encode.

LOW-DELAY PREDICTIVE CODING

To motivate our proposed algorithm consider the trace of Figure 6-2 above and the data shown in Appendix 6-A. The figures in Appendix 6-A show the quantized differences between consecutive samples in each of the dimensions (i.e., x, y, z positions and quaternions). These figures clearly indicate that, as was to be expected given the example shown in Figure 6-2, a typical interaction is such that there exists very strong correlation between the values of consecutive samples. In other words, at consecutive sampling times the values of the data captured tend to be similar (e.g., the x-coordinate position is almost the same from one sampling time to the next). In terms of the figures in Appendix 6-A, which depict the differences between successive samples, this can be easily seen by observing that most of the time the difference between consecutive samples is very close to zero.

This observation leads to *predictive coding* as a natural choice to compress haptic data. Predictive coding (see, for example, Jayant & Noll, 1984) is a well known technique in coding of speech and audio. The basic principle is to use previously quantized and reconstructed samples to generate a predicted value for the current sample. For example, the simplest predictor would be one that uses the previous decoded sample to predict the current one (e.g., the previous x-axis position is used to predict the current x-axis position). It is important that prediction be based on the previously *decoded* samples, because the prediction algorithm will also be run at the decoder, and the decoder obviously does not have access to the original data.

In our experiments a first order predictor (prediction is based on only the most recent sample) is used. Once the difference between the predicted value and the actual sample is computed, the next step is to quantize this difference. As can be seen from the figures in Appendix 6-A, this difference tends to be small but can also be occasionally large. A simple explanation for this phenomenon is that the haptic interaction has periods of slow and fast motion. During a slow motion period most consecutive samples will be similar, whereas the differences will be larger (when the sampling rate is the same) when the motion increases.

This motivates us to use an adaptive DPCM scheme (ADPCM), where the quantization step-size is increased during periods of fast motion and decreased in periods of slow motion. Assume that the quantization step-size remained constant; it would then make sense to use a quantization step-size that can accommodate fast changes (i.e., large step-size), which would lead to inefficiency in slow motion situations. In our system we fix the number of outputs from the quantizer (1000 levels in our experiments). What each quantizer output represents depends on the current step-size. If the difference exceeds the maximum range of the quantizer (± 500*step-size) then we transmit the original sample, rather than the difference. This sample is then transmitted in integer format with an escape code to indicate that no prediction is used. In our experiments out-of-range data occurred less than 1% of the time.

The adaptation mechanism works as follows. A circular buffer (length chosen to be 10 in our experiments) stores the most recent quantized differences. When the maximum value in this buffer is larger than a threshold, a decision is made that high motion is being observed and the step-size is multiplied by a factor (1.6 in our experiments). Conversely, if the maximum is lower than a threshold, the step-size is multiplied by a different factor to make it smaller (0.6 in our case). The two thresholds used in this algorithm are obtained through training. As an example, one can consider the average value of the difference between consecutive samples in a training set and use that to compute the threshold (the high motion threshold could be, for example, double the average difference as in our experiments.)

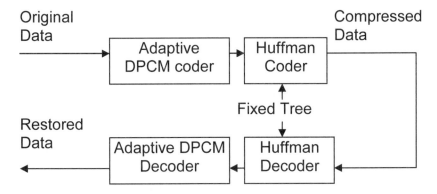

Figure 6-3: Codec structure.

It should be noted that obviously many of the parameters used in our system (e.g., the thresholds, the multiplicative factors to change the step-size, etc.) could be optimized to achieve even better performance. The results shown later in the chapter indicate that even this simple approach achieves good results. Further optimization will be considered in the future, especially once better experimental data is available and better statistical characterization of "typical" haptic trajectories is available.

Figure 6-3 shows a diagram of our adaptive DPCM coder. In addition to the already described adaptive quantizer the codec includes a Huffman coder designed with a fixed tree, where the code was constructed based on the statistical analyses of a few sets of haptic data. As discussed before, the principle of this Huffman coder is to assign shorter codewords to the most likely data. Thus, considering the graphs in Appendix 6-A, it is easy to see that quantization outputs close to zero will be mapped to short codes, while larger values will be mapped to longer codes.

MODEL-BASED CODING

Driven by research in areas like virtual reality, there has already been much work done in compression of geometrical models with the goal to reduce the bandwidth required in transferring these models through networks. For example, coding triangular mesh models has become part of the standard of VRML. Most of the coding algorithms are based on cutting (partition into tree structures), surface striping, then DPCM (Choi, Kim, Lee, Park, Lee, & Ahn, 2000; Deering, 1995).

In our work, we assume that geometric models will be available at both encoder and decoder and concentrate on techniques to code the haptic trajectory data using the geometric models to code trajectory. As an example, consider a user who is probing a known geometric model. In this process the probing point will tend to touch the surface of the model frequently, as the user explores the contours of the object. In this section we outline a coding technique, currently under development, that takes advantage of this fact.

Our basic assumption is that hand movements are almost constantly probing the surface of the object. At each sample time one can map the position in 3D space to the nearest point in the surface. It is then possible to locate the position in 3D space by transmitting the trajectory on the surface of the object (which could be further constrained to traverse only the center of each of the triangles, for example). Several factors affect how good this approach will be, including the resolution of the mesh and how closely the user is indeed following the surface of the object.

Let us assume that the trajectory remains always at a relatively close position to a facet. Then assume that we can locate the object facet that is nearest to the position of the probing point. Since the facets of the object have limited connectivity (i.e., one facet is connected only to a discrete number of neighboring facets), the coding strategy could consist of transmitting a sequence of facets (in some cases the probing point would remain closest to one of the facets so the same facet would be transmitted). This sequence would then be amenable to differential coding. Consider for example a triangular mesh where each facet has exactly three neighbors, where the sequence of facets could be coded with two bits to indicate whether the same facet is the nearest or whether one of the three neighboring facets became the closest. After this sequence of facets is generated we need to send a difference vector from the center of the facet to indicate the position of the probing point in 3D space.

There are several alternative ways of coding the remaining information given the facet. For example, one could pick the center of each facet as the standard reference point and then send a 3D vector. Or, alternatively, one could send the orthogonal projection of the point to the facet surface (a point within the facet) and then the magnitude of the vector that leads to the probing point (normal to the surface). Intuitively, this algorithm will work best whenever the trajectory is smooth and remains close to the object, because in this case the energy of the residue (i.e., the data needed once the facet is known) will be small and it will be possible to code it with few bits.

Our experiments so far have been inconclusive as regards the potential of this technique, primarily because of the complexity involved in mapping 3D points to the nearest point on the surface. An exact localization of the nearest facet may require operations on each of the facets of the object, which would be very complex. Alternatively, an approximate algorithm may lead to a fast localization of a facet, but one that is not as close, thus leading to coding inefficiency. Overall, this lack of accuracy and the complexity have led to our results being insufficiently good to merit our choosing this approach over the simple and efficient ADPCM approach. Further work is in progress to improve our results.

EXPERIMENTAL RESULTS, CONCLUSIONS, AND FUTURE WORK

Figure 6-4 shows the result of the adaptive DPCM coder on a typical set of haptic data (one trajectory). Error here is measured as the root mean squared error. For each sample we measure the distance between original and decoded position in 3D space and take the average. This average error per sample is measured in millimeters. Under the assumption that an average error of less than 0.1 mm is acceptable, the compression rate is a factor of 10 (i.e., the compressed file is one-tenth the original size). It should be noted too that even higher compression ratios are possible if one is willing to accept increased distortion. For example, if errors close to 1 mm on average are acceptable, then a compression rate of 25 is possible, as shown in Figure 6-4.

The throughput of our adaptive DPCM coder and decoder is about 13k samples per second on a Pentium III 500Hz PC. This coding speed is more than 10 times the rate needed to process samples at the maximum sampling rate of the PHANToM, 1 kHz.

Recording haptic movement was done at about 30 samples per second; replay, however, could not be this fast because the power for the PHANToM system is not strong enough to stabilize the probe at each sample step under the default spring model. Delays were inserted between each step. Experimental experience tells us that the replay speed is at least 10 times slower than recording in order to achieve a stable replay. This speed can be improved if other control techniques are adopted.

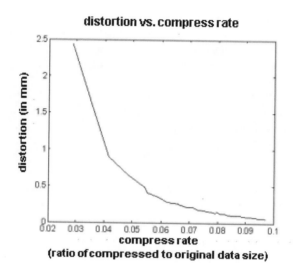

Figure 6-4: Rate distortion plot for DPCM coder.

With haptics hardware and software still under development, haptic coding appears to be an interesting research topic to explore. Our results indicate that even simple approaches can lead to fast and efficient compression of haptic data. Future work will be devoted to further study of model-based techniques for haptic data compression, as well as additional modeling of the differential data to improve further the performance of ADPCM based techniques. A key area of investigation that has not been considered in this chapter is the evaluation of the effects of compression error. Some applications may require small error (e.g., 0.1 mm or less) so compression rates can be correspondingly higher.

APPENDIX

Below we include histograms of the quantized differences between consecutive samples in each of the dimensions being compressed. This includes the differences between the time samples, between the x-y-z coordinates, and between the four quaternion coordinates (denoted x, y, z, w). The step size is normalized for each of these parameters so that the differences are in the range of -100 to 100 steps. Our main goal here is to show how there is indeed a very strong correlation between the values of successive samples taken by the system. This explains the compression performance provided by simple predictive systems. User interactions from which these results were obtained can also be regarded as typical.

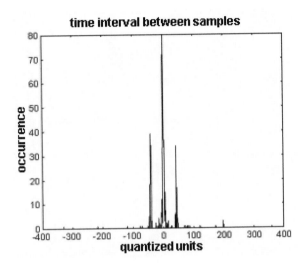

Figure 6-5: Histogram for quantized time intervals.

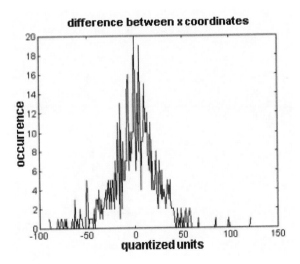

Figure 6-6: Histogram for differences between adjacent *x* coordinates.

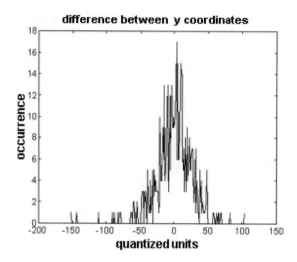

Figure 6-7(a): Histogram for differences between adjacent *y* coordinates.

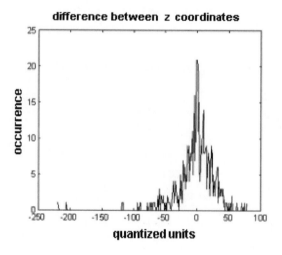

Figure 6-7(b): Histogram for differences between adjacent *z* coordinates.

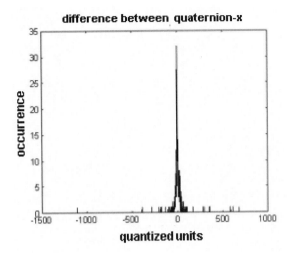

Figure 6-8: Histogram for differences between adjacent quaternion-*x*.

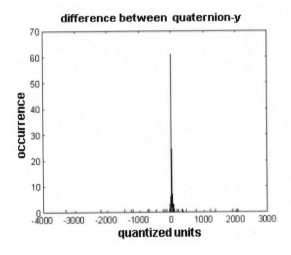

Figure 6-9: Histogram for differences between adjacent quaternion-*y*.

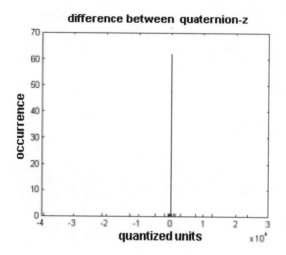

Figure 6-10: Histogram for differences between adjacent quaternion-z.

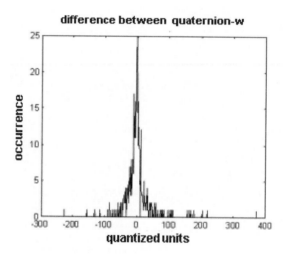

Figure 6-11: Histogram for differences between adjacent quaternion-w.

ACKNOWLEDGMENTS

This research has been funded in part by the Integrated Media Systems Center, a National Science Foundation Engineering Research Center, Cooperative Agreement No. EEC-9529152.

REFERENCES

Bajaj, V., Pascucci, V., & Zhuang, G. (1999). Single resolution compression of arbitrary triangular meshes with properties. *Proceedings of the Data Compression Conference*, Snowbird, UT.

Choi, J. S., Kim, Y. H., Lee, H-J., Park, I-S., Lee, M. H., & Ahn, C. (2000). Geometry compression of 3-D mesh models using predictive two-stage quantization. *IEEE Transactions on Circuits and Systems for Video Technology, 10*(2), 312–322.

Constantinescu, D., Chau, I., DiMaio, S. P., Filipozzi, L., Salcudean, S. E., & Ghassenmi, F. (2000). Haptics rendering of planar rigid-body motion using a redundant parallel mechanism. *Proceedings of the 2000 IEEE International Conference on Robotics & Automation*. San Francisco, CA.

Deering, M. (1995). Geometry compression. *Computer Graphics (Proceedings of SIGGRAPH '95)* (pp. 13-–20).

Guéziec, A., Bossen, F., Taubin, G., & Silva, C. (1999). Efficient compression of non-manifold polygonal meshes. *Proceedings of the Conference on Visualization '99: Celebrating Ten Years* (pp. 73–80).

Gumhold, S., & Straber, W. (1998). Real time compression of triangle mesh connectivity. *Computer Graphics (Proceedings of SIGGRAPH '98)*(pp. 133–140). Boston: Addison Wesley.

Jayant, N. S., & Noll, P. (1984). *Digital coding of waveforms: Principles and applications to speech and video*. Prentice Hall.

Kolarov, K. (2000). Graphical and haptic interaction with large 3D compressed objects. *Proceedings of the IEEE International Symposium on Robotics with Applications*.

Lawrence, D. A., Pao, L. Y., Dougherty, A. M., Salada, M., & Pavlou, Y. (2000). Rate-hardness: A new performance metric for haptic interfaces. *IEEE Transactions On Robotics and Automation, 16*(4), 357–371.

Massie, T. H., & Salisbury, J. K. (1994). The PHANToM haptic interface: A device for probing virtual objects. *Proceedings of the 1994 ASME International Mechanical Engineering Congress and Exhibition,* VOL DSC 55-1 (pp. 295–302).

Mishra, R. K., & Srikanth, S. (2000, November). *Genie – A haptics interface for simulation of laparoscopic surgery*. Paper presented at the 2000 IEEE/RSJ International Conference on Intelligent Robots and Systems.

Popovic, J., & Hoppe, H. (1997). Progressive simplicial complexes. *Proceedings of the 24th Annual Conference on Computer Graphics & Interactive Techniques* (pp. 217–224).

Ruspini, D., & Khatib, O. (2000). A framework for multi-contact multi-body dynamic simulation and haptic display. *Proceedings of the 2000 IEEE/RSJ International Conference on Intelligent Robots and Systems* (pp. 1322–1327).

Shahabi, C., Barish, G., Kolahdouzan, M. R., Yao, D., Zimmermann, R., Fu, K., & Zhang, L. (2001, June). *Alternative techniques for the efficient acquisition of haptic data*. Paper presented at the ACM SIGMETRICS/Performance Conference 2001, Cambridge.

Shapiro, J. M. (1993). Embedded image coding using zerotrees of wavelet coefficients. *IEEE Transactions on Signal Processing, 41*(12), 3445–3462.

Son, W., Kim, K., Amato, N. M., & Trinkle, J. C. (2000). Interactive dynamic simulation using haptic interaction. *Proceedings of the 2000 IEEE/RSJ International Conference on Intelligent Robots and Systems.*

Taubin, G., & Rossignac, J. (1998). Geometric compression through topological surgery. *ACM Transactions on Graphics, 17*(2), 84–115.

Vahora, F., Temkin, B., Krumml, T. M., & Gorman, P. J. (1999, June). *Development of real-time virtual reality haptic application: Real-time issues*. Paper presented at the 12th IEEE Symposium on Computer-Based Medical Systems, Stamford, CT.

Wu, J-L., & Kawamura, S. (2000). Quantitative analysis of human tactile illusory characteristic under visual environment and a haptic device of two-dimensional curved surface. *IEEE Transactions on Robotics and Automation, 16*(6).

A Robust System for Haptic Collaboration over the Network

Ichiro Fukuda, Soju Matsumoto, Mitsuharu Iijima, Kenji Hikichi,
Hironao Morino, Kaoru Sezaki, and Yasuhiko Yasuda

In recent years, computer networks have become ubiquitous, as data transmission speeds increased rapidly. In parallel, compression and streaming technology of audio and video information have exhibited significant development. As a consequence, network-aware applications have diversified, and media such as text, audio, video, and three-dimensional objects are transmitted simultaneously in full-duplex communication.

The haptic medium has also been displaying significant development. The haptic interface has unique characteristics: It requires simultaneous and interactive input and output by the haptic device, requiring high update rates (up to about 1 kHz). Moreover, the amount of information increases in proportion to the complexity of the Shared Virtual Environment

(SVE). This data can congest the network, causing delay, jitter, and loss of information, potentially resulting in system misbehavior.

According to Basdogan (1998), full-duplex haptic interaction can improve cooperation among remote users in SVEs. One of the main concerns in transmitting real-time data such as audio and video on the Internet is the synchronization between the distinct media streams. An additional concern is the synchronization among clients in SVEs. Audio and video media synchronization has been studied by a number of researchers (for example, Blakowski & Steinmetz, 1998) who have attempted to identify QoS (Quality of Service) synchronization requirements (Steinmetz, 1998). However, in the case of haptics, such studies are few, and QoS requirements are not yet clear. Our goal is to examine the characteristics of haptic media, clarify the required QoS, and then construct a system adapted to realistic network conditions.

In this work, we use a "Position Input-Force Output" type of PHANToM as the haptic interface and construct the new haptic communication system. Our proposed system is composed of the following modules: haptics; graphics; communications; codec; and prediction/interpolation. We clarify the characteristics of our system based on subjective and objective evaluation experiments.

HAPTICS OVER A NETWORK

For proper representation of stiffness in virtual environments, the haptic interface must be controlled at a high update rate (for example, the PHANToM needs to be updated at 1 kHz). When we share the virtual environment among clients through the Internet where delay and jitter occur, the haptic devices cannot be controlled at the required update rate.

In conventional haptic communication systems over the network, a server manages all the information for the shared virtual environment, and clients only display the updated information received from the server (Hirose, Hirota, et al., 2000). The system flow is as follows:

1. Clients send position data from the haptic interface to the server, synchronizing with the haptic device loop.

2. At the server side, the state of the virtual environment is updated and reaction forces for each client are calculated using the position information received from clients.

3. The server sends to the clients the updated state of the virtual environment and the reaction forces.

4. At the client side, the reaction force is applied to the user and the graphics are displayed with the updated state received from the server.

We confirmed that, in this system, users perceive a disorder in the sense of touch when the delay reaches about 30 ms. This is caused by the fact that the reaction force is calculated in proportion to the interpenetration between the haptic device and the virtual objects.

When the delay between client and server is approximately zero, the haptic device reacts immediately when users touch virtual objects, because the reaction force is sent to the haptic interface at the same time the force is calculated. However, when there is a delay between the calculation of the reaction force and its display, the depth of interpenetration between the haptic interface and the virtual objects may be excessive, causing a reaction force that is too large.

It is very difficult for the current Internet infrastructure to meet a 30 ms maximum delay requirement. Therefore, we must compensate for this delay if we want to achieve haptic communication over the Internet. Some methods have been proposed to solve the delay problem. The work on "Passive Transmission Line Modeling" (Wilson, Kline-Schoder, Kenton, & Hogan, 1999) determines the stiffness coefficient and mass of the virtual object based on linear circuit theory. This method guarantees the stability of the system but cannot allow arbitrary physical parameters for the virtual object.

PROPOSAL FOR A HAPTIC COMMUNICATION SYSTEM

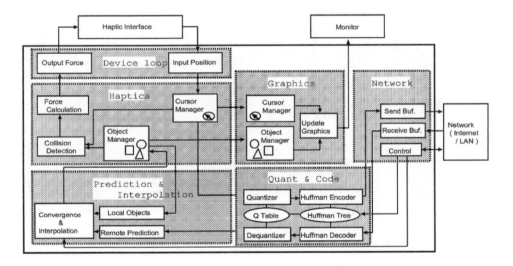

Figure 7-1: Haptic communication system.

Outline of System

In this section, we examine the processing flow in the haptic communication system between two or more clients sharing a virtual environment. All clients are equipped with PHANToM devices and graphic displays. We propose a new haptic network-tolerant force-feedback algorithm to solve the excess-force problem. We describe which processes should be placed at the server and the client sides and we also specify which information should be transmitted between server and clients. The haptic communication system proposed in this chapter (Figure7-1) is composed of the following five modules.

Haptic Processing Module (HPM)

The Haptic Processing Module updates the state of the virtual environment and calculates reaction forces to be applied to the users, synchronizing them with the haptic interface loop. It manages the properties of objects in the virtual environment (size, weight, shape, etc.) and their state (position and rotation).

Graphical Processing Module (GPM)

The Graphical Processing Module draws graphics of the virtual environment managed by the HPM, using OpenGL. The drawing rate is 30 Hz, and this loop is independent of the ones within the HPM.

Prediction and Interpolation Module (PIM)

Since the haptic medium is less tolerant toward loss of information than other media like audio and video, the Prediction and Interpolation Module is necessary to achieve stable operations. When the required information does not arrive on time the Prediction and Interpolation Module statistically predicts the movement and rotation of virtual objects based on the previous data. Later, when the correct data is received, this module gradually corrects the estimate to the true value so that the user does not feel the incompatibility. Using this technique, the transmission rate can also be reduced.

Codec Module (CM)

The position of the PHANToM—which is called the "cursor" and is obtained from the HPM—is compressed and encoded by the CM. The transmission bit rate is controlled by the quantization step (Q value), which is chosen taking into account the condition of the network and the control strategy, based on the results of the subjective evaluation. When the cursor comes in contact with a virtual object, the Q values for the cursor and object are decreased; otherwise they are increased.

Network Interface Module (NIM)

The state of the communication channel is monitored using time stamps and sequence numbers. The communication is controlled based on QoS parameters obtained from the subjective evaluation. The state of the channel is fed back to control the system by, for example, affecting the Q value of the CM or the parameters the PIM when the QoS has deteriorated due to a reduction of the transmission rate.

System Details

Haptic Processing Module (HPM)

In this research, a new technique was used to solve the excess-force problem of conventional force-feedback systems, preventing excessive penetration of the PHANToM cursor into the virtual object. This technique consists of calculating the reaction force applied to the user on the client side.

This method has no influence on the physical parameters of the objects in SVEs, keeps the correspondence of the collaboration, and prevents haptic disorders caused by the network delay. The processing flow for this technique is described below:

Processing Flow:

1. The encoded position of the PHANToM cursor is transmitted from the client to the server at 1 kHz.
2. The state of the SVEs maintained at the server side is updated using the data received from the client.
3. The compressed state of the SVEs is transmitted from server to client.
4. The reaction force to be applied to the user is calculated at the client side using the SVE information obtained from the server and the position data collected from the PHANToM at the time the data arrive. The graphics display is also updated using the position and rotation data of the virtual object received from the server.

This module has the following functions:

Cursor Manager:

It obtains position data from the PHANToM and sends it to the CM. This is synchronized with the device loop.

Object Manager:

It updates and manages the state of the SVE, using the data obtained from the PIM. The object properties (size, weight, etc.) are shared beforehand among all clients and the server. This function works in synchronization with the Collision Detection and Force Calculation functions.

Collision Detection and Force Calculation:

It detects collisions and calculates contact forces, using the PHANToM cursor and object position/rotation data obtained from the Object Manager. The module then sends the force value to the haptic device. The PHANToM requires force value at the rate of 1 kHz.

Prediction and Interpolation Module (PIM)

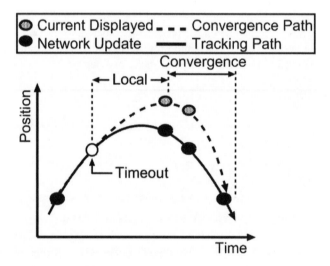

Figure 7-2: Convergence technique.

The prediction and interpolation module is set up to prevent the haptic rendering from becoming unstable due to data loss and network delay. This module consists of an internal prediction part and an error concealment part.

This module has two buffers: the internal prediction buffer and the remote buffer. The internal prediction buffer stores the state of objects (predicted using the past state in this buffer). The update information from the server is stored in the remote buffer after decoding in CM.

If update data arrive too late from the server, or are lost in the network, the module statistically predicts the state of objects when the HPM requires updated information, using past data stored in the internal prediction buffer. In the absence of update data, internal prediction is iterated to provide the HPM with the predicted state of objects. But as more packet losses occur, the prediction error accumulates and the receiver cannot be synchronized with the other hosts. Later, when update data from the server are received, the error concealment part of this module gradually corrects the state of objects in the HPM to the true value (received data) so that the user does not feel the incompatibility. Thus, when network congestion causes restriction of the transmission rate, the update rate is not the rate required by the haptic device. This module statistically predicts and interpolates the state of objects to compensate for this shortfall, thereby acting as an interface between the rate of transmission and the haptic device loop (Figure 7-2).

Past-state information is used to predict the state of objects and other cursors that exist in SVEs. Since the autocorrelation of each object's state is high, it is possible to predict the object state accurately, even if simple prediction techniques are used. Therefore, we use two simple techniques to predict and interpolate. The PIM dynamically switches between the prediction methods by detecting the rapid state change of object and cursor, for example when collision between cursor and object occurs. The behavior of the change is classified as follows: 1) Contact and the change are gradual; or 2) contact and the change are abrupt.

When not in contact, it is possible to predict (using environmental information such as gravity, air resistance, etc.) state information. When in contact, if the change is gradual, the state is predicted quadratically. When the change is abrupt, the state is predicted linearly. A prediction error threshold is set to distinguish whether the change is gradual or abrupt. This threshold is determined by the Q value below which humans cannot perceive error. However, when loss of data occurs, prediction uses only the velocity to avoid the error increment caused by the quadratic predictor.

At the receiver side, this module compensates for lost data by thinning out at the sender side or network congestion

Codec Module (CM)

The Codec Module (CM) consists of a quantizer and a Huffman coder. The position of the PHANToM cursor obtained from the HPM is quantized and encoded. In this module the Q value used by the quantizer is the maximum value that does not perceptibly damage the system operation. After that the bit rate is decreased using Huffman coding.

When we analyze position data, its distribution is almost uniform. Therefore it is not efficient to compose a Huffman tree in every case by reading the characteristics of application and users.

When we pay attention to the time-continuous nature of the position, the correlation between adjacent sample values of the PHANToM position information is high, and the height of the correlation is maintained even if the samples are some milliseconds away from each other. Therefore, differential pulse code modulation (DPCM) or DPCM using linear prediction analysis based on the former value of position information (predictive DPCM:

PDPCM) can be applied. It is known that the distribution of difference information between adjacent samples values is concentrated about zero, and a great decrease in the bit rate becomes possible. It is possible to decrease up to a range of about 4 to 8 bits on average with the quantizer and the encoder, depending on the movable range of the value of Q, while the local system requires 64 bits for each sample.

The CM module transmits bits that represent the quantized (not encoded) value in a certain interval. Sending differential data through the network makes the application very sensitive to packet loss; therefore, absolute values must be sent periodically. Moreover, one of the characteristics of haptic applications is that collisions are not always between objects and the device. The bit rate can be decreased further by controlling the state transition as follows. When the possibility of contact is low, the system is said to be in the no-contact section and the Q value is enlarged, and when the possibility is high, it is in the contact section and the Q value is set to be small. We also examined the degree of deterioration in application QoS by the quantization step in preparation for interpretation.

Network Interface Module (NIM)

Each sample of the SVE state, such as the position of the PHANToM, object positions, and rotations, is represented by 64-bit data. Due to the 1 kHz update rate, 192 kbps is required for the data that are uploaded to the server and more than 384 kbps for the download from the server. Actually the amount of data downloaded from server to client increases in proportion to the number of objects. A transmission rate of 384 kbps or more is needed if the haptic update rate is 1 kHz, and stable operation cannot be guaranteed on the Internet with a sudden change in delay. Therefore it is necessary to introduce real-time streaming technology.

In future work, we hope to implement the transmission protocol using Real-Time Transport Protocol (RTP) (Shulzrinne, 1996). Additional functions (such as time stamping and sequence numbering) are needed for control when the SVE state is being streamed using multicast. Extra information may be needed at the upper layer of RTP for adaptive QoS control in the haptic communication system.

EXPERIMENT ON QOS MEASUREMENT

The experiments on subjective and objective assessments for measuring QoS against the network delay and Q value were done using the system described above. The measurement technique of the subjective assessment and the objective assessment are as follows.

Subjective Assessment of Haptic Interface

There are several studies of subjective assessment of haptic collaboration. We propose a subjective assessment method to evaluate haptic communication systems, such as our prototype system and those developed by others. The basic method of the subjective assessment is ITU-R Rec. BT500-10 (ITU-R Recommendations, 2000).

Classes of Subjective Assessment

In general, there are two classes of subjective assessments:

1. **Quality assessments**: Assessments that establish the performance of the system under ideal conditions.
2. **Impairment assessments**: Assessments that establish the performance of the system under nonideal conditions (e.g. with network delay).

Table 7-1: Five-grade scale.

Score	Quality	Impairment
5	Excellent	Imperceptible
4	Good	Perceptible, but not annoying
3	Fair	Slightly annoying
2	Poor	Annoying
1	Bad	Very annoying

Evaluation Condition

There are two groups of assessors, expert and nonexpert users. The assessor in group one is accustomed to the operation of the haptic interface or was trained, while in group two, the user is unaccustomed to the operation of the haptic interface. The evaluation condition was divided in this manner to investigate the dependence of the results on user expertise.

Settings of haptic interface: The device is positioned at shoulder height on the side of the monitor corresponding to the user's dominant arm. The initial height of the haptic interface is set up at the center of the monitor.

Instruction of the assessment: Assessors should be carefully introduced to the method of assessment, the sequence and timing of impairment or quality factors (network delay and Q value) to change, and the grading scale. Training sequences demonstrating the range and the type of the impairments to be assessed should be used with presenting conditions other than those used in the test, but of comparable sensitivity.

In the case of quality assessments, quality may be defined as consisting of specific perceptual attributes. It is thought that manipulating/operating the virtual object with a haptic interface is difficult for the nonexpert user, so we must train them to operate the interface.

Evaluation of System

One purpose of the evaluation is to verify the effectiveness of each module in the system. The other is to investigate the characteristics of haptic media under delay. Moreover, collaboration characteristics are evaluated to confirm the necessity of distributed synchronization. Figure 7-3 shows the SVE in this experiment. This virtual environment uses physical simulation with gravity, air resistance, a collision of the object, and friction.

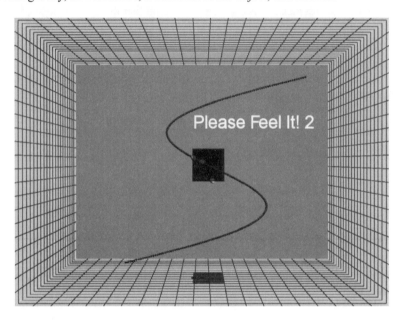

Figure 7-3: Shared virtual environment.

Task

A basic task was to manipulate the virtual object (rigid body cube with no transformation) along the track (Figure 7-4). The target sphere moves on the track for ten seconds, while the assessor operates the cube to keep it in contact with the target sphere. Additionally, there was a difference in the evaluation according to the skill of the operator with the PHANToM. The depth degree of freedom in virtual space was limited so the result would not depend on the evaluator's skill

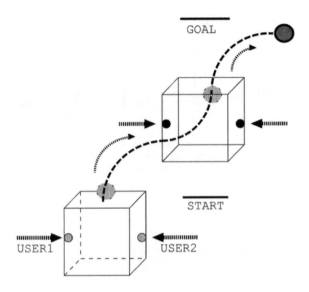

Figure 7-4: Task of evaluation.

System Specification

Server
OS: Windows NT4.0
CPU: Pentium 600MHz
RAM: 128MB SDRAM
Client
OS: Windows NT 4.0
CPU: Pentium 850MHz
RAM: 512MB SDRAM
Display-Adapter: ELSA Gloria-XXL
Force Device: PHANToM PREMIUM 3.0

Assessment

Subjective Assessment: In the experiment, the task through the network was evaluated by using impairment assessment referring to DSIS Variant I (ITU-R Recommendations, 2000), because the system can be characterized under non-ideal conditions. The system with ideal conditions (which is the reference) and the system with non-ideal conditions are continuously and alternately presented as a pair (Figure 7-5).

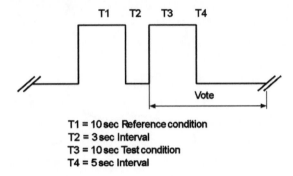

T1 = 10 sec Reference condition
T2 = 3 sec Interval
T3 = 10 sec Test condition
T4 = 5 sec Interval

Figure 7-5: Presentation of test conditions.

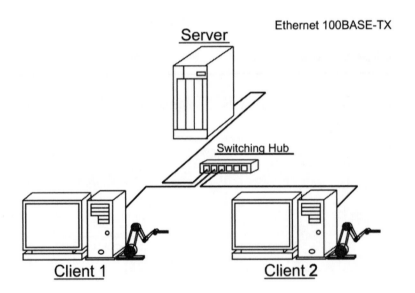

Figure 7-6: Evaluation system.

The scale for measuring deterioration ranged from 5 ("The delay was imperceptible") to 1 ("The delay was very annoying"), based on the five-step deterioration standard shown in Table 7-1. A numerical straight line of 100 mm in length was drawn, and each point of the score was plotted on the straight line.

Objective Assessment: In the task shown above, the target object, which moves on the track, is pursued, and the total time of contact is assumed to be an objective evaluation value.

Evaluation Item: The items that are used to evaluate the proposed haptic communication system (Figure 7-6) are listed below.

1. Verification of the reaction force calculation model of the client side against network delay.

2. Verification of the system against the Q value.

3. Verification of the necessity of distributed synchronization and characteristics of collaboration among multiple users.

Experimental Results

The performance of the modules that compose the proposed system is evaluated. An allowable limit is assumed that a relative value from the reference is −1.5 in DMOS (Degradation Mean Opinion Score). Characteristics of the client side's reaction force calculation model are shown in Figures 7-8(a)–7-8(c). This result shows that users can control the virtual object under the condition of the 100 ms delay in the proposed system, and it improved about 100 ms of time delay compared to conventional force feedback architecture (Figures 7-7(a)–7-7(c)). The results of objective evaluation also show the improvement of the task performance, operating the virtual cube along the track and keeping contact with the target sphere.

Characteristics of the system against the Q value are shown in Figures 7-9(a) and 7-9(b). From the data, the allowable limit of the Q value is 1.5 mm. Users felt impairment with an increase in Q value, but their objective score did not decrease until 1.0 mm (Figure 7-9(c)). Moreover, users were barely able to perceive impairment within the range from 0.01 to 0.4. If 10 bits or more are allocated to each sample, the transmission rate from each client to the server can be compressed up to 24 kbps or less using Huffman coding. Generally, the distributed synchronization technique of conventional media such as audio and video is the queued state control method. In the case of haptic media, Figure 7-10(a)-10(c) show that it is not necessary to synchronize the state of virtual environments. This result is quite different from conventional media. Annoyance about the task deterioration depends heavily on the sense of touch at the local interface.

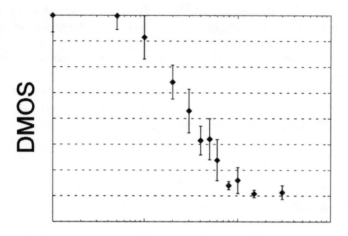

Figure 7-7(a): Conventional force feedback architecture with respect to operationality.

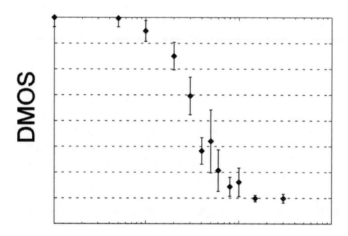

Figure 7-7(b): Conventional force feedback architecture with respect to accomplishment.

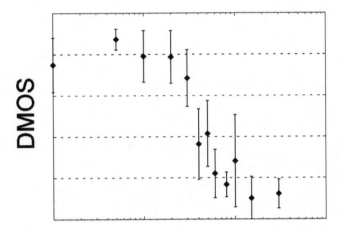

Figure 7-7(c): Conventional force feedback architecture with respect to objective
score.

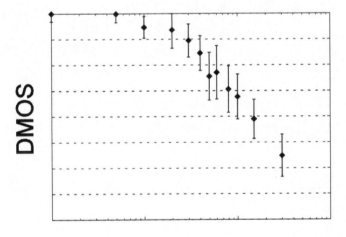

Figure 7-8 (a): Force calculation at client side's architecture with respect to operationality.

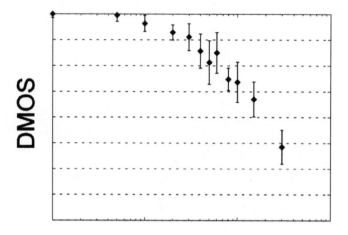

Figure 7-8 (b): Force calculation at client side's architecture with respect to accomplishment.

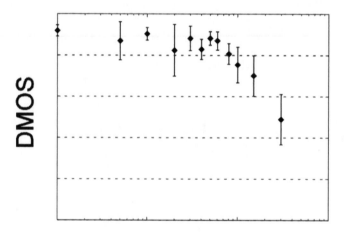

Figure 7-8 (c): Force calculation at client side's architecture with respect to objective
score.

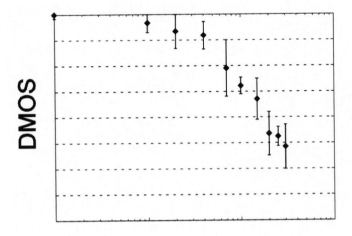

Figure 7-9(a): Quantization characteristics with respect to operationality.

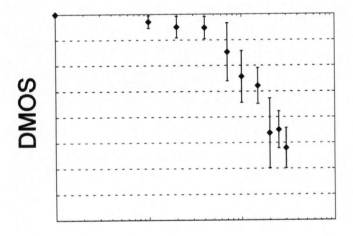

Figure 7-9(b):Quantization characteristics with respect to accomplishment.

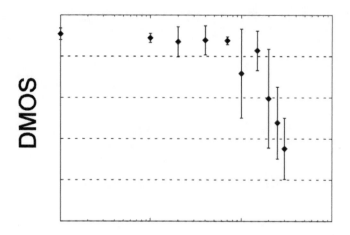

Figure 7-9(c): Quantization characteristics with respect to objective score.

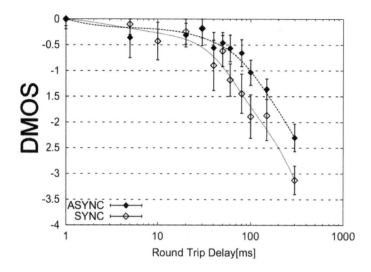

Figure 7-10(a): Collaboration characteristics with respect to operationality.

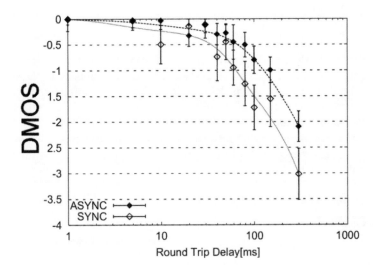

Figure 7-10(b): Collaboration characteristics with respect to accomplishment.

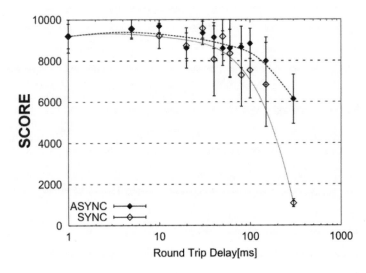

Figure 7-10(c): Collaboration characteristics with respect to objective score.

CONCLUSION

In this paper, we introduced an adaptive haptic communication system, showed performance of the system using force calculation at the client side to compensate for network delay, and introduced the Q value of virtual state (position, rotation). Moreover, we showed the necessity of distributed synchronization and examined the characteristics of collaborative tasks through the fixed delay network.

In future work we hope to implement adaptive state control architecture over the Internet and assess its performance. We will also examine not only rigid-body objects but also soft and deformable objects.

ACKNOWLEDGMENT

This work is partially funded by the Inamori Foundation.

REFERENCES

Basdogan, C., Ho, C-H., Slater, M., & Srinivasan, M. A. (1998). The role of haptic communication in shared virtual environments. In J. K. Salisbury & M. A. Srinivasan (Eds.),*Proceedings of the Third PHANToM Users Group Workshop, PUG98*. AI Technical Report no. 1643 and RLE Technical Report no. 624. Cambridge, MA: MIT.

Blakowski, D., & Steinmetz, R. (1996). A media synchronization survey: Reference model, specification, and case studies. *IEEE Journal on Selected Areas in Communications, 14*(1), 5–35.

Fukuda, I., Matsumoto, S., Hikichi, K., Morino, H., Sezaki, K., & Yasuda, Y. (2000). *Media synchronization of haptic collaboration system*. IEICE Tech. Report IN2000-126, 1–6. (In Japanese)

Hirose, M., Hirota, K., et al. (2000). Construction of haptic server for remote cooperative work. *Prceedings of the VRSJ Fifth Annual Conference* (pp. 269–272). (In Japanese)

ITU-R Recommendations. (2000). *Recommendation 500-10; Methodology for the subjective assessment of television pictures*. Rec.ITU-R BT.500-10, 1–16.

Kuwako, Y., & Sezaki, K. (1998). *Media synchronization on distributed environment*. IEICE Tech.Report SSE98-100, 67–72. (In Japanese)

Massie, T. H., & Salisbury, J. K. (1994). The PHANToM haptic interface: A device for probing virtual objects. In *Proceedings of the ASME Winter Annual Meeting, Symposium on Haptic Interfaces for Virtual Environment and Teleoperator Systems*, Chicago, IL.

Matsumoto, S., Fukuda, I., Hikichi, K., Morino, H., Sezaki, K., & Yasuda, Y. (2000). The influences of network issues on haptic collaboration in shared virtual environments. *Preprints of the Fifth Annual PHANToM Users Group Workshop*, Aspen, CO.

Shulzrinne, H., Casner, S., Frederick, R., & Jacobson, V. (1996). *RTP: A transport protocol for real-time applications*. RFC1889, 1–75.

Steinmetz, R. (1996). Human perception of jitter and media synchronization for use of the Internet: analysis and implementation. *Proceedings of IEEE GLOBECOM* (pp. 893–398).

Wilson, J. P, Kline-Schoder, R., Kenton, M. A., & Hogan, N. (1999). Algorithms for network-based force feedback. In J. K. Salisbury & M. A. Srinivasan (Eds.), *Proceedings of the Fourth PHANToM User's Group Workshop*, AI Lab Technical Report No. 1675 and RLE Technical Report No. 633. Cambridge, MA: MIT.

Zilles, C. B., & Salisbury, J. K. (1995). A constraint-based God-object method for haptic display. *Proceedings of the IEEE/RSJ International Conference on Intelligent Robots and Systems (*pp. 146–151). Pittsburgh, PA.

Haptic Collaboration over the Internet

João P. Hespanha, Margaret L. McLaughlin, and Gaurav S. Sukhatme

In many applications of haptics it will be necessary for users to *interact with each other* as well as with other objects. In this article, we propose an architecture for haptic collaboration among distributed users. We focus on collaboration over a nondedicated channel (such as an Internet connection) where users experience stochastic, unbounded communication delays (Hespanha, Sukhatme, McLaughlin, Akbarian, Garg, & Zhu, 2000; McLaughlin, Sukhatme, Hespanha, Shahabi, Ortega, & Medioni, 2000; Sukhatme, Hespanha, McLaughlin, Shahabi, & Ortega, 2000).

The area of haptic collaboration is relatively new. There have been a few prior studies that we briefly review here. In a study by Basdogan, Ho, Slater, and Srinivasan (1998), partners at remote locations were assigned three cooperative tasks. Experiments were conducted with visual feedback only and with both visual and haptic feedback. Both performance and feelings of togetherness were enhanced in the dual-modality condition. Durlach and Slater (1998) note that factors that contribute to a sense of copresence include being able to observe the effect on the environment of actions by others with whom one interacts and being able to work collaboratively with copresent others to alter the environment. Buttolo, Oboe, and Hannaford (1997) note that when people at distributed sites share the same virtual environment, there may be registration problems. Representations of the virtual object must coincide, but the distributed nature of the communication, especially over the Internet, may introduce considerable latency whose effects may be hard to predict.

VIRTUAL HAPTIC WORLD

Imagine you decide to go to a handicraft museum. There is a map of the museum at the door showing different galleries in the museum, each containing a group of handicrafts. Upon entry into a gallery, you can see the handicrafts and the other people in that room. You can touch all of the objects in the room and interact with them. In a real museum, all of the above are familiar experiences, except for the last one. As a matter of practice, touching art objects is usually strictly prohibited.

The scenario described above motivates the research presented here. Our goal is to design an architecture that will support collaborative touch in virtual environments. We term such environment a *virtual haptic world*. As shown in Figure 8-1, users may have different kinds of haptic devices, such as the PHANToM, CyberGrasp, or a FEELit mouse, or they can just be viewers. Some of the participants in the haptic world may only provide virtual objects as a service to the remaining users. This would be the role, for example, of a museum's server.

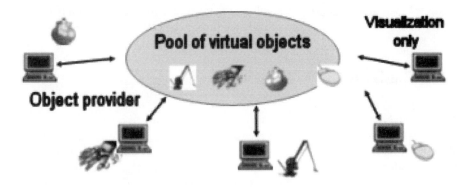

Figure 8-1: A virtual haptic world.

From a computational perspective, a haptic world consists of a network of nodes. Each node corresponds to a computer whose operator is part of the shared virtual environment. The operator will typically interact with virtual objects through a haptic device, but some users may interact with the haptic world using other modalities, like simple visualization.

Some nodes may operate autonomously (i.e., without a human operator) and simply provide virtual objects for the haptic world.

Each node in the haptic world contributes to the shared environment with virtual objects. These can be static (e.g., a sculpture "bolted" to the ground) or dynamic (e.g., a teapot that can be virtually manipulated). We view the haptic devices that the human operators use to interact with the haptic world as dynamic objects. Each object in the haptic world is *owned* by one of the nodes, which is responsible for defining how its dynamic properties evolve. Typically, a node that is physically connected to a haptic device owns the object that represents the device.

Two databases are used to represent a haptic world. The *node database* contains information about the node network. It stores the logical identifiers and the IP addresses of all nodes, as well as the latency and available bandwidth between all nodes. The need for this information will become clear later. This database is dynamic because new nodes may join or leave the haptic world at run time. The *object database* contains the information about all objects that are part of the haptic world. Each record in this database refers to a particular object and it contains the object identifier, the identifier of the node that owns it, its static properties (shape, size, color, etc.), and its dynamic properties (position, orientation, velocity, etc.).

The force control algorithms used for haptic rendering generally require high sampling rates (typically, on the order of 1 kHz) and low latency (typically, on the order of a few milliseconds) (Wilson, Kline-Schoder, Kenton, & Hogan, 1999). This means that the databases need to be queried very frequently and with very low delay. Because of this it is necessary to distribute these databases by keeping local copies at each node. This allows for very fast access to the data about the objects that are needed for the force-feedback loops at the expense of the added complexity introduced by issues related to the consistency between the databases. Much of what follows is precisely related to the problem of keeping the databases synchronized so that all nodes have roughly the same perspective on the shared environment.

DATABASE SYNCHRONIZATION

Since the objects database contains data that is dynamic, the local copies of this database that exist at each node must be kept synchronized by a periodic exchange of data. This is done by a very simple mechanism that uses the concept of object ownership introduced earlier: Periodically, the owner of each object broadcasts the dynamic properties of its objects to all other nodes. Each node must then continuously listen to the other nodes for updates on the dynamic properties of the objects that it does not own. This is represented schematically in Figure 8-2.

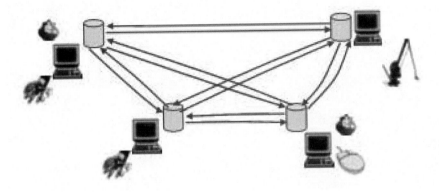

Figure 8-2: Object database synchronization in the haptic world.

Table 8-1: Pseudocode for Object Database Synchronization

While (1)

{

       Listen for dynamic properties of objects owned by other nodes and update local object database

       Query haptic rendering system for dynamic properties of objects owned

       Broadcast dynamic properties of objects owned

       Wait for one synchronization period

}

Typically, the haptic rendering system uses the following fairly standard algorithm as given in Table 8-2.

Table 8-2: Pseudocode for the Update of Dynamic Properties of Objects

Compute amount of overlapping between objects owned and all other objects

Compute forces on objects owned (assuming spring–damper system)

Transmit forces to haptic device

Integrate forward in time to predict dynamic properties of objects owned at next sampling time

When the number of nodes is large, the broadcast of object properties required by the algorithm in Table 8-1 may be costly unless the synchronization period is large. We will address this issue later.

Another main challenge arising from the distributed nature of the databases that store the information about the haptic world is related to the addition and removal of nodes from the haptic world. When a new node joins the haptic world, it must first receive the current node and object databases from some other node in the haptic world. It must then add itself to the node database and add its objects to the object database. Finally, it must inform all other nodes of these changes to the databases. This is implemented by the pseudocode shown in Table 8-3 that must run in every node.

Table 8-3: Pseudocode for the Creation of a New Node in the Haptic World

Request copy of node database

Request copy of object database

Add self to node database

Add objects owned to object database

Broadcast request to add new record to node database

Broadcast request to add new records to object database

While (node active)

{

Listen for requests to:
    send node/object database
    add/remove record to/from node database
    add/remove record for/from object database

}

Broadcast request to remove self from node database

Broadcast request to remove owned objects from object database

LOCAL GROUPS

The broadcast required by the synchronization algorithm in Table 8-1 can be very costly when the number of nodes is large. Because of this, the synchronization period may need to be fairly long. For static objects this poses no problems, but the same is not true for dynamic objects (i.e., objects that can move). When two or more dynamic objects touch each other, the resulting motion must be computed by simulating Newton's laws using an algorithm similar to the one in Table 8-2. However, when the same node does not own all the objects involved in a close interaction, each object only observes the effect of its motion in the motion of other objects at a relatively low sampling rate, determined by the synchronization period. This leads to very unrealistic motions (and possibly instability), because the algorithm in Table 8-2 no longer provides a good approximation to Newton's law.

We reduce the potential for unrealistic motion and instability by creating small groups of nodes that engage in very fast and very frequent exchanges of synchronization data for objects in close interaction. The creation of these groups is, of course, only possible when the bandwidth between the nodes is sufficiently large and the latency is sufficiently small. Because of the high cost of local groups, these should only be maintained while the objects are interacting. As explained above, to resolve the motion of objects involved in close interaction, a high bandwidth/low latency synchronization mechanism is needed. In our architecture this is achieved by introducing the concept of a *local group*. A local group consists of a group LG of objects, whose owners enhance the basic synchronization algorithm for those objects in LG, by decreasing the synchronization-sampling period. The local group synchronization algorithm, given in Table 8-4, is very like the basic one provided in Table 8-1.

Since each local group determines the positions of all the objects in that local group, each object should belong to, at most, one local group. This does not prevent a node that owns several objects from being involved in several local groups. Moreover, the fast synchronization within the local group requires high bandwidth and low latency between the nodes involved. Special care must therefore be paid to the creation of local groups.

Table 8-4: Pseudocode for Local Group Synchronization

Input: G = {list of objects in local group}

While (1)

{

    Listen for the dynamic properties of objects in G owned by other nodes and update local object database

    Query haptic rendering system for dynamic properties of objects owned

    Broadcast to the owners of the objects in G the dynamic properties of objects in G owned by self

    Wait for one local group synchronization period.

}

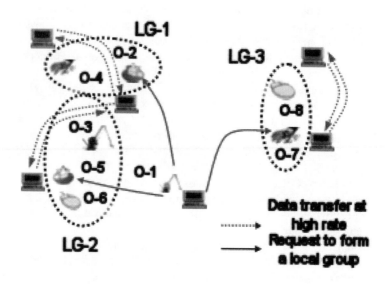

Figure 8-3: Haptic world with three local groups and a node asking to create a local group.

We use an example to illustrate the issues involved in the management of local groups. Consider the haptic world shown in Figure 8-3. In this figure we see three local groups: LG-1 is formed by the set of objects {O-2, O-4}, LG-2 is formed by {O-3, O-5, O-6}, and LG-3 is formed by {O-7, O-8}. Note that the same node owns the objects O-2 and O-6 but they are part of distinct local groups. This means that, although belonging to the same node, these objects are not in close proximity and therefore their motions are independent.

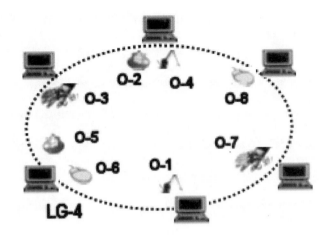

Figure 8-4: New local group, after the request in Figure 8-3.

Table 8-5: Pseudocode to Create a New Local Group

Input: T = {desired list of objects in new local group}

L = Expand (T)% determine list of all objects that need to be included in new local group

If Feasible (L)

{   % Only create local group if all nodes involved

       % satisfy the bandwidth and latency requirements

   For each l ∈ L

       Request owner of object to destroy the local group to which it belongs

   For each l ∈ L

       Request owner of object to create a local group for objects in L

   Return Success

}

Else

Return Failure

Suppose now that the user at the node that owns O-1 wants to use O-1 to manipulate the objects O-2, O-5, and O-7 (Figure 8-3). This requires the creation of a local group that contains $T = \{$O-1, O-2, O-5, O-7$\}$. However, since some of these objects are already part of other local groups, the old local groups LG-1, LG-2, and LG-3 must be destroyed and a new local group LG-4 must be created, containing the objects in T as well as those in the old local groups LG-1, LG-2, and LG-3 (Figure 8-4). This only occurs if the network connections between all the nodes that own the objects in question have sufficiently large bandwidth and sufficiently low latencies for the local group synchronization.

The pseudocode in Table 8-5 implements the algorithm used to create a new local group. The pseudocode in Table 8-3 also needs to be modified as shown in Table 8-6 to process the requests generated by the algorithm in Table 8-5.

Table 8-6: Modification in the Pseudocode in Table 8-3 to Process the Requests Generated by Table 8-5

```
{...}
While (node active)
{
Listen for requests to:
      send node database
      send object database

    add/remove record to node database

     create/destroy a local group
}
{...}
```

Conclusions and Future Work

We have proposed an architecture for the real-time collection and simultaneous broadcast of haptic information to multiple haptic session participants, so that collaborative exploration of objects is possible, even when users are distributed across a network. The architecture relies on two distributed databases: the node and the object databases. These two databases are dynamic and need to be kept coherent among all nodes in the virtual haptic world. We presented pseudocode for the algorithms that keep these databases synchronized. These algorithms are independent of the actual haptic devices employed by each user.

In future work, we hope to make significant progress on the registration of the haptic display systems in collaborative networked environments. We will also examine the necessary entities to achieve networked collaboration with disparate haptic devices (pen-based versus glove-based, small versus large workspace). We plan to address not only integration issues but also questions related to the interaction process itself, including feelings of co-presence and performance satisfaction, and how these variables are affected by the exploration modality (vision, vision plus haptic, or haptic only). Another line of research is the development of force control algorithms tailored to a distributed haptic environment. These algorithms must be robust with respect to the stochastic delays caused by the communication network.

ACKNOWLEDGMENT

This research has been funded by the Integrated Media Systems Center, a National Science Foundation Engineering Research Center, Cooperative Agreement No. EEC-9529152.

REFERENCES

Basdogan, C., Ho, C-H., Slater, M., & Srinavasan, M. A. (1998). The role of haptic communication in shared virtual environments. In J. K. Salisbury & M. A. Srinivasan (Eds.), *Proceedings of the Third PHANToM Users Group Workshop, PUG98.* AI Technical Report no. 1643 and RLE Technical Report no. 624. Cambridge, MA: MIT.

Buttolo, P., Oboe, R., & Hannaford, B. (1997). Architectures for shared haptic virtual environments. *Computers and Graphics, 21*(4), 421–429.

Durlach, N., & Slater, M. (n.d.). *Presence in shared virtual environments and virtual togetherness.* Retrieved from www.cs.ucl.ac.uk/staff/m.slater/BTWorkshop/durlach.html.

Fukuda, I., & Matsumoto, S. (2001). A robust system for haptic collaboration over the network. In M. L. McLaughlin, J. P. Hespanha, & G. S. Sukhatme, *Touch in Virtual Environments.* IMSC Series in Multimedia. New York: Prentice Hall.

Ho, C., Basdogan, C., Slater, M., Durlach, N., & Srinivasan, M. A. (1998). *An experiment on the influence of haptic communication on the sense of being together.* Paper presented at the British Telecom Workshop on Presence in Shared Virtual Environments, Ipswitch.

McLaughlin, M. L., Sukhatme, G., Hespanha, J., Shahabi, C., Ortega, A., & Medioni, G. (2000). The haptic museum. *Proceedings of the EVA 2000 Conference on Electronic Imaging and the Visual Arts,* Florence, Italy.

Sukhatme, G., Hespanha, J., McLaughlin, M., Shahabi, C., & Ortega, A. (2000). Touch in immersive environments. *Proceedings of the EVA 2000 Conference on Electronic Imaging and the Visual Arts*, Edinburgh, Scotland.

Wilson, J. P, Kline-Schoder, R., Kenton, M. A., & Hogan, N. (1999). Algorithms for network-based force feedback. In J. K. Salisbury & M. A. Srinivasan (Eds.), *Proceedings of the Fourth PHAN-ToM User's Group Workshop*, AI Lab Technical Report No. 1675 and RLE Technical Report No. 633. Cambridge, MA: MIT.

Perceiving Complex Virtual Scenes without Visual Guidance

Gunnar Jansson

Three-dimensional (3D) properties of two-dimensional (2D) pictures can easily be perceived visually, which is not the case when pictures are read tactually. In fact, a classic problem with tactile pictures is how to present 3D aspects in a readable way. The problem is not that it is impossible to perceive the third dimension via touch in general, but that it is not possible to perceive a 2D picture tactually to be a 2D surface and a representation of a 3D scene at the same time, as it is visually (J. J. Gibson, 1979, Chapter 15). It is a common opinion among producers of tactile pictures that it is an unachievable, or at least a very difficult, task to read such pictures representing 3D scenes. A corollary is that 3D objects therefore should be avoided or should at least be simplified by presenting them in front view or profile (cf. Edman, 1992, pp. 128–130). This means a serious restriction on the availability of pictorial material for the visually impaired.

On the other hand, there are experimental reports that some kinds of perspective information in pictures can be picked up by touch, such as information in outlines making up line drawings (Heller, Calcaterra, Tyler, & Burson, 1996; Kennedy, 1993) and in texture gradients of surfaces (Holmes, Hughes, & Jansson, 1998; Jansson & Holmes, in press). It should be noted, however, that so far only relatively simple pictures have been investigated in these studies. It remains to be seen to what extent these results can be generalized to more complex pictures.

A solution to this long-term problem may be haptic[1] displays, such as the PHANToM (SensAble, Inc), as they can present virtual objects with 3D properties to be explored haptically. However, there are several issues to take into account when considering the usefulness of haptics displays.

It may be questioned to what extent haptics can render 3D aspects in general, but that is not the main issue. When functioning naturally in real environments, haptics has a very high potential (cf. J. J. Gibson, 1966; Katz, 1925/1989). A main issue is that the information provided via the haptic displays built so far differs in critical aspects from the information obtained via natural haptics. It cannot be assumed that haptics can handle these situations as well as it can natural situations.

Another main issue is that haptics used as a replacement for vision by visually impaired people has to function without the close cooperation with vision that plays such an important role when both senses are available. Therefore, haptics alone may not function optimally when it cannot cooperate with vision.

A main restriction for haptics on its own is that the instantaneous haptic "field of view" is small. It is often reduced to the direct contacts between skin and object, but can be perceptually enlarged by encompassing the space between two or more contacts. However, there is no correspondence in haptics to peripheral vision. Enlargement of the haptic field has to be achieved through exploration over time. This is one of the restrictions imposed on haptics when it is used alone without visual guidance. This means loss of help with identification of objects and loss of suggestions about interesting features in the environment to explore further. Haptics and vision cooperate normally by providing complementary as well as redundant information.

That people with severely impaired vision have to use haptic displays without any aid from vision means that the usefulness of these displays in this context has to be studied separately. To demonstrate their usefulness when vision is available is not sufficient to demonstrate utility when vision is missing.

---

[1]The term "touch" (and the related adjectives "tactile" and "tactual") is traditionally used for the sense in the skin that informs about contacts with objects. This includes the hand, considered as a perceptual system. However, if you want to emphasize that exploratory activity is an important aspect of the hand as a sense, the terms "active touch" or "haptics" (with the adjective "haptic") are preferably used. It is proper to use this term in connection with displays rendering virtual objects to be explored by the hands.

NUMBER AND SIZE OF AREAS OF HAPTIC CONTACT

A very significant difference between the information a PHANToM provides to the haptic observer and the information provided in natural contexts is the number and size of areas of contact between the user and the objects presented. A standard three degrees-of-freedom PHANToM provides only one point of contact at a time between the virtual object and the user. A real object explored naturally usually has several larger simultaneous contact areas with the user. The use of more than one PHANToM or the six degrees-of-freedom PHANToM may improve things, but the situation is still far from natural. The entire over-view has to be based on successive contacts with a PHANToM. Reduction of the skin area involved to one small point of contact has significant effects on several kinds of perform-ance, as demonstrated by Lederman & Klatzky (1999) in experiments where the skin area available for natural haptics was artificially reduced.

Perception of Texture

A reduction in the contact area available for exploration may not be an equally vexing problem for the perception of surface texture. The 1000 Hz updating is sufficient for detailed perception of an extended surface, and experiments have demonstrated that judgments of surface properties may not be much affected by the reduction to one point. In the Lederman and Klatzky study roughness was judged similarly when the skin area was reduced and when it was not. Jansson et al. (1999) found that the roughness of real and virtual sandpapers, in both cases explored with a stylus, was not judged to be significantly different. A reason for these results may be that when a surface is explored in order to judge texture properties common to the whole surface, the exact path is not important; the critical stimulus properties are not dependent on the relative position of the fingers but on features that are not bound to specific locations and can be picked up along any movement path.

Perception of 3D Form

Perception of 3D form is quite different and probably more complicated. The sensors in the skin are involved, as are the sensors in the muscles and the joints. When a virtual ob-ject is explored with a standard PHANToM, there is no simultaneous information from two or more locations; rather all the information about form has to be obtained successively. This has similarities to what a visual exploration would be if an object were explored via a small hole in a cover moved over a surface. In spite of this restriction at least some 3D forms of objects can be perceived this way. Jansson et al. (1999) found that simple geometric 3D forms (cylinder, cone, cube, and sphere) in dimensions of 10 to 100 mm could be identified via a PHANToM stylus with relative accuracy (above 75%) within a mean exploration time of about 10 to 35 seconds. However, this is far from the quality of performance for real ob-jects explored naturally by a hand. In another experiment real objects of the same forms as the virtual ones, down to dimensions of 5 mm, were correctly identified to 100% after a mean exploration time of 2 seconds (Jansson & Billberger, 1999, summarized in Jansson, 2000).

Effects of Size of Object

Object size has an important effect on performance with the PHANToM. A threshold of 75% correct identification around 7 mm is suggested by the results of an experiment by Jansson & Billberger (1999). In contrast to the results with 100% correct identification for real objects, such a performance was not reached within a size range of up to 100 mm; the highest percentage reached as a mean for all forms was 96% (Jansson et al., 1999). Exploration time was negatively correlated with correct identification in both experiments, and the mean time in these experiments varied between 15 and 37 seconds (Jansson, 2000). Larger objects were not studied, but it is reasonable to assume a U-form for exploration times, as it is logical to assume that exploring very large objects takes time.

COMPLEXITY OF THE RENDERED SCENE

An important problem that is just beginning to be investigated is to what extent it is possible to perceive complex objects with a PHANToM when vision is not available. The experiments mentioned above were concerned with texture or simple 3D geometric forms. In order to be generally useful, a haptic display must allow perception of more complex scenes correctly and without excessively long exploration times. What the limits may be is an open question.

Exploratory movements are basic for the functioning of haptics, and there is a great repertoire of such movements (Lederman & Klatzky, 1987). Many of them include coordinated movements of several fingers. That haptic exploration methods differ in efficiency has been demonstrated for tactile pictures (Berlà, 1982; James, 1982). Haptic displays often require specific exploration methods not used in natural contexts that are thus new to the observers.

Instantaneous overview obtained via vision is increasingly difficult to duplicate with tactile exploration as complexity grows. Exploration takes time and puts a heavy load on the perceptual integration of the movement path. The integration is made still more difficult because of frequent deviations from the object's surface when following it with a probe. The number of unintended deviations probably increases with the complexity of the object's form. The existence of deviations means that the observer cannot base the integration on the whole movement path but must build it on the instances when the stylus is in contact with the virtual object and on interpolation of the spaces in between the contacts. There seem to be no reports in the literature on how such integration is accomplished. In vision, missing parts of a figure are compensated for by gestalt building. That similar laws may be operating in haptics as well is indicated by the fact that perception of form can be achieved even though the hand does not cover the whole object. However, in the case of one-point-at-a-time contact the integration has to be over time (Jansson, 2001).

PERFORMANCE IMPROVEMENT THROUGH PRACTICE

Experiments on the usefulness of haptic displays are usually conducted over short sessions, and the participants often have very limited experience in using the haptic display. It is reasonable to assume that performance with such a display would improve with practice, as most activities do. However, it is not self-evident how much practice improves performance in specific tasks.

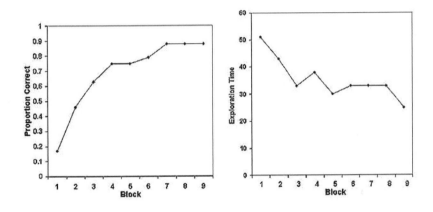

Figure 9-1(a)(b): Most improved participant's performance, Jansson & Ivås experiment. Proportion Correct to the left (a) and Exploration Time to the right (b).

Jansson & Ivås (2001) designed an experiment to investigate if brief practice in using a haptic display would be useful. In their experiment the participants identified nine blocks of 24 simple virtual 3D objects by exploring them with the stylus of a PHANToM 1.5A. The nine blocks were distributed over three days, and the three blocks each day took up to about an hour. The result was that the mean performance of the whole group improved both in terms of proportion of correct identifications and in terms of exploration time. However, there were large individual differences. In addition to a majority that improved, there was also a minority of participants who did not show any improvement. On the other hand, some participants improved dramatically. The results for the participant with the largest improvement are shown in Figure 9-1. These results demonstrate that there is a substantial probability of underestimating the usefulness of a haptic display if only untrained participants are used.

SIMPLIFICATION OF COMPLEX SCENES

When 2D tactile pictures are produced for visually handicapped people, complex representations are sometimes divided into simpler pictures that can be read separately. For instance, geographical information about an area may be presented on separate maps for borders, mountains, rivers, and towns. Reading these simpler pictures may provide some of the information wanted, but it may also be possible to read more complex pictures after having experienced the simpler ones. Something similar may also be useful in the case of virtual 3D objects.

Perception is very adaptive. It can handle not only the real world, but also many kinds of representations of it. This ability is utilized in many contexts. Ordinary 2D pictures are well-known examples. Despite the fact that pictures are 2D, 3D aspects of a real scene can usually be perceived easily by looking at them, as discussed above. We are so used to this visual ability that we may not think of how remarkable it is. Another example is the perception of a sketch of an object; it may be even more informative for specific purposes than a detailed representation of the real thing. Further, vision can identify representations deviating considerably from realism, such as caricatures (Rhodes, 1996). The potential of vision to perceive nonphotorealistic representations is beginning to be utilized in several ways. (For a review, see Lansdown & Schofield, 1995.)

To what extent similar laws apply to haptics has received very little attention. One case is the perception of tactile pictures as discussed above. Others include *nonrealistic haptic rendering* and *haptic rendering with successively increasing complexity*.

Nonrealistic Haptic Rendering

The aim for nonrealistic haptic rendering is twofold: to reduce the information to a few important aspects and to simplify orientation and navigation through the scene (König, Schneider, & Strothotte, 2000). The method is to render 2D planes of the 3D virtual object and to provide nonpictorial information about the relations between these planes, as well as the opportunity for exploratory movements on these planes. The 2D planes are equipped with information about 3D constructions related to them, such as surface textures and low representations of walls and other objects. In this way they are similar to tactile pictures and may more precisely be described as 2½D. To this may be added information that is not haptic—for instance speech and other sounds, activated at specific positions of the planes—and available to observers when they pass the area during navigating on the plane. So far, the observers' perception of the rendered scenes has not been investigated.

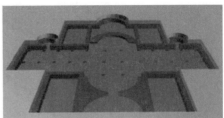

Figure 9-2(a)(b): A 3D virtual castle (a) and its 2½D ground plane (b). From König (1999).

The nonrealistic haptic rendering has been applied to an architectural model of a castle (Figure 9-2(a)); a 2D plane, shown in Figure 9-2(b), represents the foundation that is the starting point for exploration (König, 1999). This plane gives a general presentation of the layout of the building and its parts within the plane. An advantage of this representation is that a 2D plane is more easily explored than a 3D space. However, other aspects, such as the height of the rooms and details about other objects in them, are not presented here. If this information is considered to be important, it has to be provided in some other form.

An unsolved problem is the integration of the different 2D planes to a perception/understanding of the whole building. Even if the information for integration is available, it cannot be taken for granted that it is really useful for the observer. This is true for vision, and possibly to a larger degree for haptics.

Haptic Rendering and Successively Increasing Complexity

How complexity should be defined is a difficult question, but examples can easily be found. A 2D plane of a building is less complex than the whole building, as discussed above. Another example is that a human head is more complex than a sphere. The head surface has many protrusions and indentations that are important for identification, while a spherical object does not. For vision, complexity is not much of a problem; a well-known human face can be identified in practically no time. The significant features of the face are easily perceived visually, possibly even without any exploration. When a virtual object, such as a face, is haptically explored with a PHANToM, one point is following along its surface, and the exploration path is critical. Significant features may easily be missed.

The potentially useful method for haptic presentation of complex objects to be described is inspired by a general theory of perceptual learning (E. J. Gibson, 1969, 1991). This theory states that we learn to perceive more efficiently by detecting significant features of objects and improving our discrimination of them. This means that objects that are perceived as similar when first encountered may be perceived as different after repeated exposures. One example is perception of faces. At first babies probably do not discriminate between faces at all, but they learn to discriminate caregivers' faces from other faces to begin with, and then among other faces in increasing number. Another example is that adults may have problems in distinguishing between people belonging to a group other than their own, but this difficulty disappears with repeated exposure.

The theory describes a process where observers repeatedly come upon complex objects and discriminate between them with improved success. This may happen over long periods in real life, but it also occurs during relatively short experimental sessions. It is thought to be a process that to a large extent is spontaneous and does not necessarily require instruction. In real life multifaceted objects in all their complexity are constantly encountered. The hypothesis to be examined in this context is that the same mechanism also works for virtual objects explored haptically. A drawback may be that a spontaneous process takes considerable time.

Figure 9-3(a)(b): Examples of a simple (a) and a more complex (b) synthetic human head.

An alternative option is to see if the detection of critical features can be facilitated by presentation of a complex scene by a series of scenes successively increasing in complexity. For instance, the presentation of a human head could start with a sphere modified in the three dimensions roughly corresponding to those of a real head. Then the other components of the head—nose, ears, eyes, lips and so on—are successively added. At the end a complete head can be presented.

A series of experiments in planning will study if such a method, using presentation of successively more complex scenes, can be successful with virtual synthetic human heads explored with a haptic display (the PHANToM). The reason for using synthetic heads is that this method allows easy systematic variation of physical parameters of the head properties. It may thereby be possible to describe potential limits in object complexity that can be perceived with such a display.

Figure 9-3 presents some examples of visual representations of virtual heads to be used. They are constructed of combinations of simple geometric forms (spheres, cones, cylinders, and tori) modified in one or more dimensions. The software used when constructing them is the ENCHANTER program (Fänger & König, 1998). In the experiments the performance of observers during successive presentations of increasingly complex scenes will be studied.

DISCUSSION

Haptic displays may be a solution to provide people who have severe visual impairment with useful representations of 3D scenes, but it is wise to be cautious in judging their potential. A three degrees-of-freedom device (the PHANToM) has been shown to be useful in presenting textures and simple 3D forms in a way that is readable for observers with visual impairment. A major remaining problem is to determine how useful such a display is when the scenes are more complex.

A solution discussed here is to present a complex scene in parts with the expectation that the observer can integrate the parts to some kind of representation of the full scene. Two efforts were presented above. Neither of them is fully developed, and much research remains to be done before their usefulness can be judged. However, they indicate potential paths to a solution.

An important property of currently available haptic displays is that they require ways of exploration that are very different from those used in natural haptic exploration. New displays may permit methods closer to the natural ones. However, a completely natural exploration method can probably not be expected. Practice will probably be necessary for effective use of a haptic display. It is important to take this into account when conducting evaluations of haptic displays and when planning for their general use.

In the method of haptic rendering with successively increasing complexity discussed above, only the direction of change from simple to complex objects was mentioned. In practice, changes in both directions can be expected to be useful. The information with the complex scene will arrive at the observers' computers in complete form. With suitable software the observers choose what levels of complexity they want to try and go back and forth between different levels. How this software should be constructed in order to be generally useful for all possible scenes requires research in both perception and informatics.

REFERENCES

Berlà, E. P. (1982). Haptic perception of tangible graphic displays. In W. Schiff & E. Foulke (Eds.), *Tactual perception: A sourcebook* (pp. 364–386). Cambridge: Cambridge University Press.

Edman, P. K. (1992). *Tactile graphics*. New York: American Foundation for the Blind.

Fänger, J., & König, H. (1998). *Entwicklung einer Modellierungs- und Experimentierumgabe für eine Kraftrückskopplungsgerät* (Development of a form production and experiment environment for a force feedback device). Praktikumsdokumentation. Magdeburg, Geermany: Otto-von-Guericke Universität, Institut für Simulation und Graphik der Fakultät für Informatik.

Gibson, E. J. (1969). *Principles of perceptual learning and development*. New York: Appleton-Century-Crofts.

Gibson, E. J. (1991). *An odyssey in learning and perception*. Cambridge, MA: The MIT Press.

Gibson, J. J. (1966). *The senses considered as perceptual systems*. Boston: Houghton-Mifflin.

Gibson, J. J. (1979). *The ecological approach to visual perception*. Boston: Houghton-Mifflin.

Heller, M. A., Calcaterra, J. A., Tyler, L. A. & Burson, L. L. (1996). Production and interpretation of perspective drawings by blind and sighted people. *Perception, 25*, 321–334.

Holmes, E., Hughes, B., & Jansson, G. (1998). Haptic perception of texture gradients. *Perception, 27*, 993–1008.

James, G. A. (1982). Mobility maps. In W. Schiff & E. Foulke (Eds.), *Tactual perception: A sourcebook* (pp. 334–363). Cambridge: Cambridge University Press.

Jansson, G. (2001). The potential importance of perceptual filling-in for haptic perception of virtual object form. In C. Baber, M. Faint, S.Wall, & A. M. Wing (Eds.), *Eurohaptics 2001 Conference Proceedings (Educational Technology Research Papers, ETRP 1)* (pp. 72–75). Birmingham, England: The University of Birmingham.

Jansson, G. (2000). Basic issues concerning visually impaired people's use of haptic displays. In P. Sharkey, A. Cesarani, L. Pugnatti, & A. Rizzo (Eds.), *The 3rd International Conference on Disability, Virtual Reality and Associated Technologies—Proceedings*, 23–25 September, Alghero, Sardinia, Italy (pp. 33–38).

Jansson, G., & Billberger, K. (1999). The PHANToM used without visual guidance. *Proceedings of the First PHANToM Users Research Symposium (PURS99)*, May 21–22, 1999, Deutsches Krebsforschungszentrum, Heidelberg, Germany.

Jansson, G., Billberger, K., Petrie, H., Colwell, C., Kornbrot, D., Fänger, J., König, H., Hardwick, A., & Furner, S. (1999). Haptic virtual environments for blind people: Exploratory experiments with two devices. *International Journal of Virtual Reality, 4*, 10–20.

Jansson, G., & Holmes, E. (in press). Can we read depth in tactile pictures? Potentials suggested by research in tactile perception. In E. Axel & N. Levant (Eds.), *Art education for the blind teachers' resource guide.* New York: Art Education for the Blind.

Jansson, G., & Ivås, A. (2001). Can the efficiency of a haptic display be increased by short-time practice in exploration? In G. Goos, J. Hartmanis & J. van Leeuwen (Series Eds.) & S. Brewster & R. Murray-Smith (Vol. Eds.), *Lecture Notes in Computer Science: Vol. 2058. Haptic Human-Computer Interaction* (pp. 85-91). Heidelberg, Germany: Springer.

Katz, D. (1989). *The world of touch.* (L-E. Krueger, Trans.) Hillsdale, NJ: Erlbaum. (Original work published 1925).

Kennedy, J. M. (1993). *Drawing and the blind: Pictures to touch.* New Haven, CT: Yale University Press.

König, H. (1999). *Geführte nichtvisuelle Exploration eines virtuellen Gebäudes* (Guided non-visual exploration of a virtual building). Diplomarbeit. Magdeburg, Germany: Otto-von-Guericke Universität, Institut für Simulation und Graphik der Fakultät für Informatik.

König, H., Schneider, J., & Strothotte, T. (2000). Haptic exploration of virtual buildings using non-realistic rendering. In R. Vollmar & R. Wagner (Eds.), *Computers helping people with special needs. ICCHP 2000* (pp. 377–384). Vienna: Österreichische Computer Gesellschaft.

Lansdown, J. & Schofield, S. (1995). Expressive rendering: A review of nonphotorealistic techniques. *IEEE Computer Graphics and Applications, 15,* 29–37.

Lederman, S., & Klatzky, R. L. (1987). Hand movements: A window into haptic object recognition. *Cognitive Psychology, 19,* 342–368.

Lederman, S., & Klatzky, R. (1999). Sensing and displaying spatially distributed fingertip forces in haptic interfaces for teleoperator and virtual environment systems. *Presence, 8,* 86–103.

Rhodes, G. (1996). *Superportraits: Caricatures and recognition.* Hove, East Sussex, UK: Psychology Press.

Perceiving Texture through a Probe

Roberta Klatzky and Susan Lederman

People physically contact objects in the world by touching them, not only with their hands but through tools. David Katz (1925/1989) observed that when we feel a surface with a tool, we feel the surface, not the tool. When I stir a pot with a spoon, I can tell vividly and immediately that the food is sticking; I do not pause to analyze the pattern of pressure on my fingertips, which constitutes the stimulation to my sensory system.

Our work is concerned with feeling surface texture through one form of tool, a rigid probe. The specific aspect of texture that we are studying is roughness, one of the most salient attributes of objects that are being felt. The roughness of an object can be a compelling cue to its identity (Klatzky & Lederman, 1995) and strongly influences the forces that must be applied in manipulation (Johansson & Westling, 1990).

As will be explained in more detail below, when a textured surface is felt with the bare skin, the sensory system appears to make use of a spatial code, at least for textures formed by elements separated by a millimeter or more, and possibly for finer textures as well (e.g., Johnson & Hsiao, 1994; Taylor & Lederman, 1975). The spatial code is provided by mechanoreceptors within the skin that give a sustained response and provide a pressure map of 1 mm resolution. However, when the surface is felt through a probe, the pressure map on the skin is determined not by the surface elements, but by the portion of the probe that is in contact with the fingers. Because the pattern of pressure is no longer correlated with the surface being explored, there must be some other code that is used to determine the surface roughness. The obvious candidate for such a code is vibration.

Our work addresses several theoretical questions and has implications for various application domains. It asks, first, whether the vibratory input resulting from passing a probe across a surface is sufficient to provide a perceptual impression of its roughness. Second, when surface characteristics are varied and a psychophysical function is obtained, we ask whether the function resulting from exploration with a probe is similar to the function resulting from touching the physical surface directly with the skin. In other words, does the impression of roughness vary in the same way with surface parameters for direct and indirect contact? Third, we ask the same question with regard to exploratory parameters, in contrast to surface parameters. That is, does roughness vary similarly with variables such as the speed and force of contact, depending on whether the surface is touched with the skin or with a probe? Fourth, we ask why the effects of surface and exploratory parameters arise.

This last question is part of a more general goal: namely, to develop a model of vibration-based roughness perception that takes into account the mechanics of the interaction between exploratory effector and surface, the properties of the skin, and the psychological processing that ultimately gives rise to a roughness percept. Given such a model, it should be possible to produce virtual textures by simulating the appropriate vibratory input. This effort is well worthwhile, because of the many different contexts in which virtual textures could be of use.

One domain is electronic commerce. Roughness constitutes an important aspect of the quality and/or aesthetic value of goods, such as floor coverings, woven fabrics, or leather. We envision a low-cost haptic interface that would convey surface roughness by means of vibration, in conjunction with a visual display and vendor-supplied data about surfaces. An auditory display yoked to the haptically perceived vibrations could augment the impression of the touched surface. Haptic information about commercial products would prove useful for everyone; moreover, it could prove critical for enabling low-vision populations to judge electronically purveyed goods.

Synthetic textures would also be useful for remote medical diagnosis and intervention. Surface texture reveals important tissue properties. For example, dermatologists use skin texture to diagnose and evaluate many skin conditions. Using realistic vibratory displays, specialists could evaluate skin diseases or check on the progress of skin grafts in patients remote from the treatment site, using data transmitted by a local physician. In the longer term, for minimally invasive or robotic surgical procedures with instrumented tools, abrupt transient vibrations could be used to indicate initial contact with an underlying structure (e.g., tumor or bone) and transitions between types of tissue. The same type of feedback used in real surgeries could also be conveyed to trainees when practicing complex surgical operations on virtual patients.

More generally, force feedback, including vibration, is needed for teleoperation, the situation in which a human operator controls an end-effector at a remote site. Vibratory feedback may be particularly useful for remote surface inspection, allowing explorers to evaluate a surface in an inaccessible or dangerous environment, when vision provides insufficient information. Examples of such environments are undersea salvage operations, planetary exploration, and hazardous materials handling.

MODELS OF ROUGHNESS PERCEPTION FROM DIRECT SKIN CONTACT

Texture is a multidimensional construct, encompassing, for example, roughness, slipperiness, and tackiness. Behavioral and neurophysiological research on texture has concentrated on roughness as a highly salient aspect of texture. As indicated above, the model that has emerged (e.g., Johnson & Hsiao, 1994; Taylor & Lederman, 1975) implicates spatial coding as the basis for roughness perception with the bare skin. Psychophysical studies have shown that a principal determinant of roughness is the spacing between the raised elements that constitute a textured surface. The reported magnitude of roughness increased directly with the interelement spacing over a range of .5–3.5 mm, a point at which the texture is sufficiently sparse that observers are reluctant to evaluate it in terms of its perceived roughness.

In their mechanical model of roughness perception, Lederman and Taylor proposed that spatial coding is used (Lederman & Taylor, 1972; Taylor & Lederman, 1975; see also Lederman, 1974, 1983). This model related roughness magnitude to the total area of skin that was instantaneously indented from a resting position while in contact with a surface. It accounted for several important psychophysical effects observed when linear gratings were used as the textured surface, including a substantial increase in roughness with increasing groove width and a smaller, but still noteworthy, increase in perceived roughness with increasing net contact force applied. A smaller effect due to ridge width and comparatively little effect due to speed were also observed. All effects were assumed to be mediated by their influence on the amount of skin surface that was deformed. Total skin deformation, which the Taylor/Lederman model proposes to be the basis for roughness perception, represents the stimulus in terms of a unidimensional magnitude. Representation of a stimulus property in terms of such a single-valued metric is referred to as *intensive* coding.

Taking a neurophysiological approach, Johnson and associates have developed a model assuming that the nervous system computes a measure of instantaneous spatial variation in a pressure map on the skin (for a review, see e.g., Johnson & Hsiao, 1994). The initial pressure map is provided by slowly adapting mechanoreceptors. The map is transmitted to the primary somatosensory area in the brain, where activity over multiple units is used to compute spatial variability across the map. This information, which has been spatially preserved until this point, is ultimately integrated within the secondary somatosensory area.

Thus the roughness model begins with spatial coding, but culminates in a single intensive code that pertains to the magnitude of spatial variation. Klatzky and Lederman (1999) have therefore called this a spatial-intensive coding model.

With textures spaced at 1 mm and above, there has been considerable evidence for spatial-intensive coding but little evidence for vibratory coding. Speed effects, which would be expected if vibration were the basis for perceived roughness, are small relative to the effects of interelement spacing (Lederman, 1974, 1983). Further, roughness is unaffected by the spatial period of the elements (Lederman & Taylor, 1972). Moreover, initially adapting the finger to vibration does not affect the roughness judgment (Lederman, Loomis, & Williams, 1982). On the other hand, vibratory coding has been implicated for very fine textures felt with the bare skin (Hollins, Bensmaia, & Risner, 1998; Hollins & Risner, 2000; LaMotte & Srinivasan, 1991).

ROUGHNESS PERCEPTION THROUGH A PROBE

When a rigid probe passes over a surface with raised elements, vibrations ensue. The amplitude and frequency of those vibrations arise from the physical interaction between the probe tip and the surface. They are transmitted through the probe shaft and then filtered by the viscoelastic layers of the skin and deeper tissue. The resulting input excites four mechanoreceptor populations within the skin. These populations are known to be frequency-tuned, so that the extent to which they are excited depends on the parameters of vibration. For example, the Pacinian Corpuscles lie deep in fatty tissue and have peak responses in the neighborhood of 250 Hz.

The vibrations at the distal site, that is, where the probe and surface interact, depend on two classes of parameters: geometric parameters describing the structure of the probe and plate, and exploratory parameters such as the speed and force with which the probe is moved over the surface. Figure 10-1 indicates how one geometric variable—the spacing of the elements on the plate—will affect the vibratory input. When the spacing is dense, the probe tip rides along the tops of the elements; when the spacing is sparse, the tip drops between elements and rides along the underlying substrate, where it occasionally encounters individual elements; and at a moderate spacing, the tip drops between adjacent elements and then is lifted above them on a more regular basis. A goal of this research is to provide a model of the vibratory input to the mechanoreceptors, including the vibrations at the probe/plate interaction and the filtering of the skin. The filtered vibrations can be modified by the known response functions of the mechanoreceptors to determine how the various populations respond. We will then relate these model-derived responses to the psychophysical functions produced when people rate the roughness of a plate that is explored with a probe.

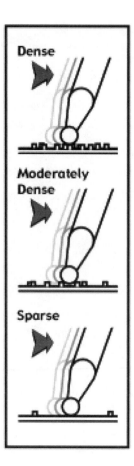

Figure 10-1: The interaction between probe and a plate at various levels of interele-
          ment spacing.

Although the vibratory input is critical, higher-order factors are also likely to influence the psychophysical outcome. For example, when people explore a plate actively, they have knowledge of the speed at which they are moving, based on the sensory responses in muscles, tendons, and joints. They may use this knowledge to account for speed-based changes in the vibratory pattern, thus achieving what is known as a "constancy," a perceptual response to a stimulus that does not change, despite changes in the input due to irrelevant factors. (An example of constancy is the continual perception of the form of a rotating square as a square, despite the changes in the shape of the retinal image as it rotates.)

PSYCHOPHYSICAL RESEARCH ON ROUGHNESS PERCEP-
TION THROUGH A PROBE

We have conducted a number of studies that investigate the effects of geometric and exploratory parameters on roughness perception through a probe. The results of these studies will be used to test the model. In addition to the standard variable of interelement spacing (surface geometry parameter), the variables of interest have been probe tip size (probe geometry parameter), speed (exploratory parameter), and force normal to the surface (exploratory parameter).

In our experiments, blindfolded subjects were required to scan a textured surface lightly with either the bare finger or with a probe held in the hand. Textured surfaces consisted of spatially jittered raised dot patterns, with some fixed mean interelement spacing for each plate. Masking sounds were played over earphones to eliminate touch-produced auditory cues. Subjects were taught to use a magnitude estimation procedure to estimate apparent roughness: For each surface, they generated the number that best represented the magnitude of perceived roughness—it could be a whole number, decimal, or fraction (but not zero). To control for different scales being used by different subjects, the magnitude estimates for a given subject are divided by the subject's mean and multiplied by the grand mean, then logarithmically transformed to produce more nearly normal distributions. The log magnitudes are then plotted against the log of the interelement spacing, and a best-fit function is determined. When the bare finger is used to explore the surfaces, this typically produces a monotonic function within the range of spacing values from .5—3.5 mm, which is well fit by a linear trend.

Effects of Probe Size

This variable was initially investigated by Klatzky and Lederman (1999) in our first study of perceiving roughness with a probe. Subjects explored a series of plates with the bare finger or with one of two probes, having contact diameters of 2 or 4 mm. (In this study, the tips were not spherical; subsequent studies use spherical tips and base the analysis of tip size on the diameter of the sphere rather than on the contacting surface.)

Results of this study were somewhat surprising, in the face of the literature on roughness perception with the bare finger, where a linear trend typically characterizes the psychophysical function relating log roughness magnitude to log interelement spacing. Although the typical trend was confirmed with the bare finger in these results, exploration with the probes—particularly the smaller probe—produced a function with a clear quadratic trend. We characterize this quadratic by three parameters: the location of the peak along the x-axis, the height of the peak on the y-axis, and the curvature of the function (how sharply it approaches the peak). The peak of the quadratic occurred at an interelement spacing of ~2 mm, the same value as the diameter of the probe. This result clearly pointed to the geometric relation between the probe and the plate as an important determinant of the roughness magnitude.

In all subsequent experiments involving surface exploration with a probe, we have confirmed the quadratic trend in the psychophysical roughness function. Moreover, we have consistently found that the peak of the function moves toward smaller interelement spacing values as the probe tip diameter decreases in size. Data from a study with 1, 2, and 3 mm probes are shown in Figure 10-2 (Lederman, Klatzky, Hamilton, & Grindley, 2000). These functions show a statistically reliable effect of probe diameter not only on the location of the peak of the quadratic, but also on its height.

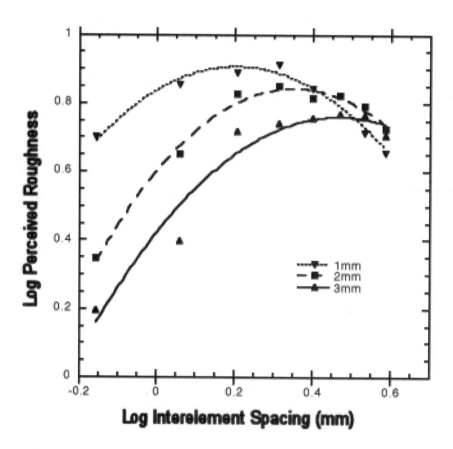

Figure 10-2: Effect of probe tip diameter on roughness magnitude as a function of interelement spacing (log scales). Quadratic functions have been fit to the data. Reprinted with permission from the ASME.

An analysis of the geometry of the probe/surface interaction was used to determine the minimum spacing between elements such that the probe tip could just drop between adjacent elements (the "drop point"). (Note that the elements on the surfaces used in this study were shaped like truncated cones, so that at the drop point, the tip must pass fully down the side of the cone until it rests on the substrate below the elements.) The drop point increases as the probe tip diameter increases—for probes of 1, 2, and 3 mm, the tip could fully drop to the bottom of the plate at 1.2, 1.7, and 2.2 mm. We did not expect that the drop point, as determined by a static geometric analysis, would precisely predict the spacing value at which subjects experienced maximum roughness, however. Certainly the dynamics of exploration must enter into the model. The effects of speed were investigated in subsequent experiments.

Effects of Exploration Speed

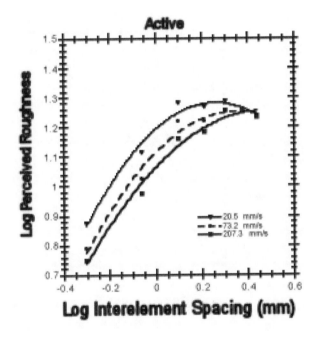

Figure 10-3(a): Effect of speed on roughness magnitude as a function of inter-element spacing (log scales), for active presentation. Quadratic functions have been fit to the data. Reprinted with permission from *Haptics-E*.

Lederman, Klatzky, Hamilton and Ramsay (1999) investigated the effects of speed using a specially designed apparatus. The stimulus plate was placed on a platform at the front end of a balance arm, which was balanced by a counterweight at the rear. The subject was instructed to apply a force just sufficient to keep the balance arm horizontal. This force was set at .29 N, the average force that was measured when a group of subjects freely explored the surfaces. To control speed, a motor and cam allowed the balance arm and platform to be moved side to side at a specified average speed. This constituted a passive exposure condition. A speed-matched active condition was implemented by training the subject to move his or her arm between the endpoints of a specified scan width to the sound of a metronome.

Figure 10-3(a)(b) shows the results of a speed variation of approximately 10:1 in the active (a) and passive (b) conditions. Speed affected two parameters of the quadratic functions. The magnitude (absolute value) of curvature decreased with increasing speed, indicating that the roughness percept is more finely tuned at a slower speed. In addition, the peak of the function moved rightward as the speed increased. This indicates that exploratory parameters, and not just probe geometry, influence the perception of roughness through a probe.

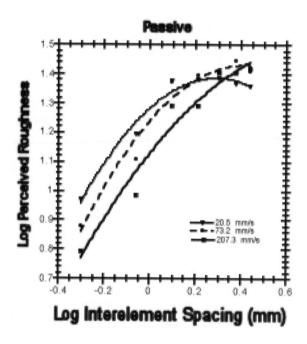

Figure 10-3(b): Effect of speed on roughness magnitude as a function of inter-element spacing (log scales), for passive presentation. Quadratic functions have been fit to the data. Reprinted with permission from *Haptics-E*.

The effect of speed can be characterized by calculating, for each stimulus surface, the ratio of the greatest roughness obtained at any speed to the least roughness obtained at any speed, then taking the maximum of this value across stimuli. From Figure 10-3(a)(b) it can be seen that this ratio is maximum at the densest plate (.5 mm spacing between elements), where it is the ratio of roughness for the slow speed to roughness for the fast speed. For the active condition, this ratio is 1.3; for the passive it is 1.5. Thus a 10:1 change in speed gave less than a 2:1 change in roughness. In comparison to this speed effect, the effect of spacing is much greater, as has been found for the perception of roughness with the bare finger. Considering the plates spaced from .5 mm to 2.0 mm, where the functions in Figure 10-3 tend to hit their maximum observed value (before turning downward), the 4:1 change in inte-relement spacing gives approximately a 3:1 change in roughness. This 3:1 effect is virtually unaffected by speed.

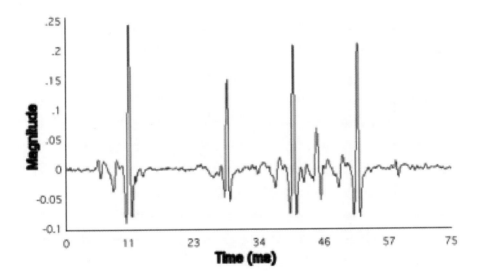

Figure 10-4: Accelerations from running a probe over a surface with raised elements.

A simple model of texture perception through a probe would propose that the vibratory profile is dominated by encounters with the raised elements of the surface, which produce high-amplitude forces at an interval that depends on interelement spacing and speed. Figure 10-4 shows the vibrations resulting from running a probe over a sparsely dotted plate, as measured by an accelerometer mounted on the probe (note that the elements were not equally spaced on the plate). There are clear peaks corresponding to contact with the raised elements, supporting the argument that these encounters are a key aspect of frequency. The finding that the effect of spacing does not depend on speed over a spacing range from .5 mm to 2.0 mm is inconsistent with this simple model, however, since the range of frequencies experienced across the spacing values is substantially different at slow and fast speeds.

Why should spacing be so much more powerful than speed in a domain where vibra-tion is thought to be the basis for the roughness percept? It appears that subjects achieved a substantial degree of speed constancy. Kinesthetic cues to speed could be used for this purpose when exploration is active, and even in the passive condition, our design could give rise to speed cues. For example, the highest frequencies must be produced by the fastest speed. Further research on this issue is clearly necessary, but one conclusion we can draw is that the level of perceived roughness is not simply a function of vibratory frequency.

Effects of Force

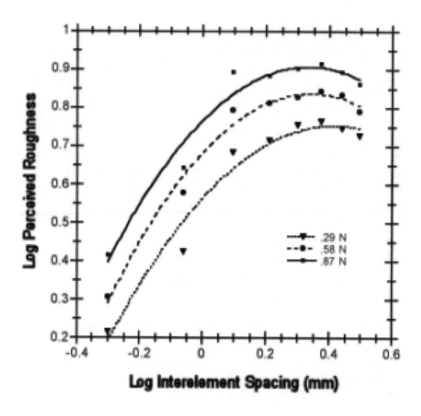

Figure 10-5: Effect of force on roughness magnitude as a function of inter-element spacing (log scales). Quadratic functions have been fit to the data. Reprinted with permission from the ASME.

Employing the same apparatus that was used to control speed but varying the counterweight on the balance arm enabled us to vary the force exerted by the subject normal to the surface of the stimulus plate, under active control (Lederman, Klatzky, Hamilton & Grindley, 2000). Three levels of force, .29 N, .58 N, and .87 N, were implemented, with a probe tip diameter of 3 mm. Figure 10-5 shows the effects of this manipulation. Statistical analysis showed a small but statistically reliable shift in the peak of the function toward slightly lower interelement spacings as force was changed from low to high values. More importantly, the height of the function shifted, indicating that the overall roughness magnitude increased with the force level applied normal to the surface. Force may affect the frequency or amplitude of vibration or both, but to the extent that exploratory speed—and hence rate of encountering elements on the plate—was passively controlled in this study, vibratory amplitude appears to be strongly implicated in the overall magnitude of perceived roughness.

Conclusions and Future Directions

The emerging picture from psychophysical and theoretical work is that exploration with a probe is sufficiently informative that people perceive a range of roughness values. However, the level of roughness they perceive is not governed by variations in the stimulus in the same way as when a texture is felt with the bare skin. In particular, increases in spacing of elements in the textured surface lead to a nonmonotonic variation in perceived roughness that depends further on exploratory parameters such as speed and force.

Our static geometric analysis placed the location of the peak roughness value near the "drop point," that is, the point at which the exploring tool just began to drop between elements in the surface. But the location of the peak was also affected by exploratory speed and, to some extent, by force.

We considered a simple assumption that the vibratory profile critically depends on the probe's contacting the raised elements in the surface. Under this assumption, our analysis of the frequencies that would be experienced by subjects over the range of spacing values and speeds indicated that, at least in conditions where subjects have cues to speed, the frequency of the vibratory profile cannot by itself account for variations in roughness. Nor would we expect this to be the case, given the possibility that subjects perceive speed directly and use it to compensate for speed-induced variations in vibration. The amplitude of vibration has been indicated by our work to be important in determining the overall magnitude of roughness, if not its relation to interelement spacing.

In future work, we intend to develop the theoretical model of the mechanics of probe/plate interaction and skin filtering. We also plan to verify the model by measuring vibrations at the probe/skin contact site. Psychophysical work with an improved apparatus for force and speed control is also planned. We can then relate the psychophysical roughness functions to the vibratory signal that has been modeled and measured.

An eventual goal of this research is to use the model to determine effective vibratory inputs for virtual texture perception. Synthetic textures have important domains of application, as we have indicated. Effective rendering of textures will also facilitate further psychophysical work, allowing us to vary the geometry of virtual surfaces without the need to manufacture real surfaces. In this way we can investigate the effects of element shape, height, spatial regularity, and the like.

We envision ubiquitous and inexpensive haptic interfaces that will enable vibratory textures to be perceived realistically and at high levels of sensitivity. These initial experimental and theoretical efforts contribute toward that vision.

REFERENCES

Connor, C. E., Hsiao, S. S., Phillips, J. R., & Johnson, K. O. (1990). Tactile roughness: Neural codes that account for psychophysical magnitude estimates. *Journal of Neuroscience, 10*(12), 3823–3836.

Hollins, M., Bensmaia, S., & Risner, R. (1998). The duplex theory of tactile texture perception. *Proceedings of the 14th Annual Meeting of the International Society for Psychophysics* (pp. 115–120).

Hollins, M., & Risner, S. R. (2000). Evidence for the duplex theory of tactile texture perception. *Perception & Psychophysics, 62*, 695–716.

Johansson, R. S., & Westling, G. (1990). Tactile afferent signals in control of precision grip. In M. Jeannerod (Ed.), *Attention and performance XIII* (pp. 677–713). Mahwah, NJ: Erlbaum.

Johnson, K. O., & Hsiao, S. S. (1994). Evaluation of the relative role of slowly and rapidly adapting afferent fibers in roughness perception. *Canadian Journal of Physiology and Pharmacology, 72*, 488–497.

Katz, D. (1925). *Der aufbau der tastwelt* (The world of touch). Translated by L. Krueger (1989). Mahwah, NJ: Erlbaum.

Klatzky, R. L., & Lederman, S. J. (1995). Identifying objects from a haptic glance. *Perception & Psychophysics, 57*(8), 1111–1123.

Klatzky, R. L., & Lederman, S. J. (1999). Tactile roughness perception with a rigid link interposed between skin and surface. *Perception & Psychophysics, 61*, 591–607.

LaMotte, R. H., & Srinivasan, M. A. (1991). Surface microgeometry: Tactile perception and neural encoding. In O. Franzen & J. Westman (Eds.), *Information processing in the somatosensory system* (pp. 49–58). Macmillan Press.

Lederman, S. J. (1974). Tactile roughness of grooved surfaces: The touching process and effects of macro- and microsurface structure. *Perception & Psychophysics, 16*(2), 385–395.

Lederman, S. J. (1983). Tactual roughness perception: Spatial and temporal determinants. *Canadian Journal of Psychology, 37*(4), 498–511.

Lederman, S. J., Klatzky, R. L., Hamilton, C., & Grindley, M. (2000). Perceiving surface roughness through a probe: Effects of applied force and probe diameter. *Proceedings of the ASME Dynamic Systems and Control Division, International Mechanical Engineering Congress & Exposition*, Orlando, FL.

Lederman, S. J., Klatzky, R. L., Hamilton, C.L., & Ramsay, G. I. (1999). Perceiving roughness via a rigid stylus: Psychophysical effects of exploration speed and mode of touch. *Haptics-e, The Electronic Journal of Haptics Research* [Online], *1*(1).

Lederman, S. J., Loomis, J. M., & Williams, D. A. (1982). The role of vibration in the tactual perception of roughness. *Perception & Psychophysics, 32*(2), 109–116.

Lederman, S. J., & Taylor, M. M. (1972). Fingertip force, surface geometry and the perception of roughness by active touch. *Perception & Psychophysics, 12*(5), 401–408.

Taylor, M. M., & Lederman, S. J. (1975). Tactile roughness of grooved surfaces: A model and the effect of friction. *Perception & Psychophysics 17*, 23–26.

Haptic and Auditory Display in Multimodal Information Systems

Wooseob Jeong and Dan Jacobson

Since the inception of virtual reality (VR) environments, interaction has been predominantly visual, especially in conveying spatial information. However, in many situations vision is not enough or is not available. For example, for the visually impaired over-reliance on visual display denies them access to the information. Even for the general population, if there is no light or weak light, a visual display is not optimal for conveying information. Recently a number of researchers have tried to add other modalities, such as sound or haptics, to overcome the imitations of visual display.

Nearly all the digital representations of spatial or georeferenced data, such as maps, diagrams or graphs, are designed to be read primarily by vision. This is not surprising, as vision is widely considered to be the spatial sense par excellence.

The reasons for presenting information in modalities other than vision are compelling. Three broad areas for applied research have been identified. The first is to provide nonvisual access when vision is not available due to a sensory loss (i.e., blindness). Here efficient access to spatial information is vital for independence, mobility, education, and employment.

Second, there are many situations where the visual modality may not be available or may not be the optimal sense for "reading" of spatial data. Such situations would include driving vehicles where visual attention is diverted, low light, and a visual disability that may preclude the sole use of vision. In virtual environments, and similar displays used in medicine, another object or feature may visually occlude information, and then another modality should be used for the additional information.

The third reason for investigating multimodality is for the augmentation (rather than replacement) of visually displayed spatial information. This has the potential to aid visualization and data representation. As the presentation of information becomes ever more complex—both in terms of detail and resolution of the data itself, and the nature of the representation—users need larger bandwidth to avoid "being lost." For example, in a geographic information system, if we open multiple windows on a screen it may be the case that to view one window we need to hide other windows, and we lose the information represented by vision. Multimodal representation can solve this problem by providing information through other channels.

As a basic research issue, what is the potential for haptic and auditory navigation within geographic information systems? Can visual information be augmented with the presentation of information via other modalities—namely, haptics and audition—and if so, to what extent?

In this study, we tested an auditory and haptic display with persons who were not visually impaired to explore the benefits of nonvisual multimodality for the general population. By augmenting visual information with an auditory and haptic interface, it is possible to convey information that is often obscured or hidden by the nature of display. Our purpose in this study is to find out how effective haptic and auditory displays are when they are individually represented and when combined together, and whether there is any interference between the two modes when they are combined.

RELATED LITERATURE

Theoretically speaking, cognitive load theory (Sweller, 1993, 1994) provides a framework for investigating multimodality. The theory assumes that people possess a limited working, or short-term, memory and for effective information processing, users need to reduce all unnecessary cognitive loads. Since each mode has its own working memory (Baddeley, 1992), cognitive load theory leads directly to Paivio's (1990) dual-coding theory, in which information can be encoded in different modal working memory for different purposes.

According to the dual-coding theory, visually presented information is processed in visual working memory, whereas auditory information is processed in auditory working memory (Mayer & Moreno, 1998). Effective working memory capacity can be enlarged by using multiple channels, so the cognitive load associated with split attention can be reduced by presenting information with dual rather than a unitary mode (Mousavii, Low, & Sweller, 1995).

Edwards (1992) explained the benefits of multimodality using the concept of redundancy. Redundancy is a natural part of communication in the real world. By using multiple modes in human-computer interfaces, it is possible to incorporate a degree of redundancy into the interaction. Such redundancy helps users by providing "back-up" information.

Numerous multimodal studies have been done in various fields such as education, scientific visualization, exploratory data analysis, and human-computer interaction. Geographic information systems (GIS) are not an exception. Adding the auditory mode to vision has been dominant in GIS (Gluck, Yu, Ju, Jeong, & Chang, 1999; Krygier, 1994; Weber, 1994), but recently haptic and other modes have begun to gain attention (Jacobson, 1998; Oviatt, 1997).

EXPERIMENT I

Experimental Design

The interface was built with Immersion Studio and Immersion Web Designer.[1] For haptic display, different forces were created in Immersion Studio's periodical effect, especially with the vibration option. Since the periodical effect provides only 0 to 10,000 units of magnitude,[2] and the vibration's psychophysical exponent is 0.95, which is approximately 1, according to Stevens's Law (Stevens, 1957), it is reasonable to set an equal interval scale. Since the experiment had 10 different forces, each force has a 1000-unit difference (i.e., 1000, 2000, 3000, 9000, 10,000).

To create the musical tones for the auditory display, 10 piano keys from middle C to the E one octave above (i.e., C, D, E, F, G, A, B, C, D, and E) were used. They were played by a Yamaha PSR-185 keyboard and recorded by Windows98 Sound Recorder in WAV format.

The final interfaces were designed using Immersion Web Designer. They had 10 different icons in a circle format with different strength or pitch. For the haptic display, Logitech's WingMan Force Feedback Mouse was used. Headphones were used to minimize the sound of the force-feedback mouse. A mouse-over event triggered auditory, haptic, or combined display. In other words, when a subject moved the mouse over an icon, the system

---

[1] These programs are available at *www.immersion.com* at no cost.
[2] According to the software company, the actual force will be variant depending the output devices. They arbitrarily defined the maximum force as 10,000 and the minimum force as 0, regardless of the device.

produced a tone, a force of vibration, or both, so that the subject could hear and feel the stimulus.

Experimental Procedure

Before the experiments, subjects were asked to fill out a pretest questionnaire that asked them to indicate their gender, age, musical competency, musical performances, and experience with haptic devices. Subjects were asked to have three learning sessions (auditory only, haptic only, and both) with three icons and three main experimental sessions under the same conditions, with 10 icons. During the learning session, subjects were shown a screen with the three icons and asked to write down the numbers of the icons in order according to the tones from lowest to highest. They were instructed that they could hear (feel) the tones by moving their mouse over the icons. When they were done, they were to say "Finished!" in a loud voice. During the experimental session, they were presented with ten icons and asked to rank the tones they represented from loudest to highest. Again, they could activate the tone by moving their mouse over the appropriate icon.

Once they finished the learning sessions, they were immediately asked to do the experimental sessions. Completion times for the experimental sessions were recorded. The task was to arrange the icons in numerical order according to the icon's assigned pitch or the magnitude of its assigned force. The ordered responses were written down on the prepared answer sheet. After the main experiment, subjects were asked to fill out a posttest questionnaire. On the questionnaire, each subject was asked to select the easiest and hardest tasks, and to state whether or not they felt any interference between the two modes in the combined auditory and haptic display. All the experiments were videotaped with the participants' consent.

Subjects

There were a total of 23 undergraduate students from Florida State University whose major was information studies. All participated in the experiments voluntarily. Seven were female and 16 were male. Twenty of the subjects were in their 20s, two were in their 30s, and one was in his late 40s.

Variables

There were three independent variables: 1) musical competency; 2) musical performance; and 3) experience of haptic devices. Musical competency was measured by the item "Do you know how to play any musical instrument?" while musical performance was measured by the item "Have you ever participated in any band or orchestra performance?" Subjects were also asked about experience with haptics, "Have you ever used a force-feedback mouse or joystick for gaming such as Nintendo, with which you can feel some feedback to your action?"

There were two dependent measures. One was accuracy and the other was adjusted completion time. Accuracy was determined by dividing the number of correct answers by the number of levels (10). Since many responses had multiple errors, the mere comparison of the original completion times is not meaningful; therefore we decided to use the adjusted completion times instead. The adjusted completion times were calculated by adding an additional 10% of the initial time per error. For example, if there were three errors, the resulting time was 130% of the original time.

Results

Accuracy

As seen in Figure 11-1, auditory display had the lowest accuracy throughout the tests. Among the independent variables, musical performance was observed to affect the accuracy of auditory display significantly ($F = 7.371, p = .013$). The experience of haptic devices also seemed to affect the accuracy of haptic display significantly ($F = 4.786, p = .040$) and the accuracy of the combination display as well ($F = 4.363, p = .049$).

Completion Time for Perfect Subjects

Only six participants accomplished 100% accuracy in all three modes. As seen in Figure 11-2, the auditory display generally took more time to finish, and the haptic display took less.

Adjusted Completion Time

After the calculation of adjusted completion time, we found that the auditory display took the longest time, while the haptic display took the shortest time (Figure 11-3). Musical competency appears likely to affect the adjusted completion time for the combination display ($F = 4.610, p = .044$) and for the auditory display as well ($F = 4.217, p = .053$).

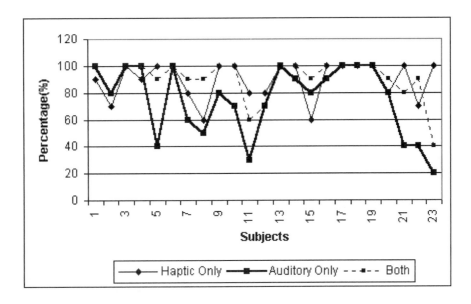

Figure 11-1: Accuracy comparison.

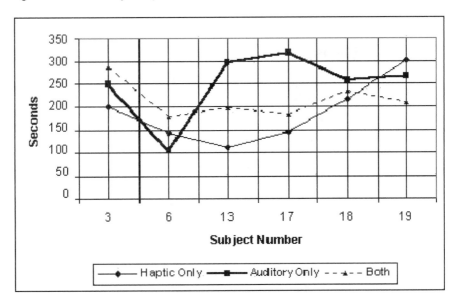

Figure 11-2: Completion time for perfect subjects.

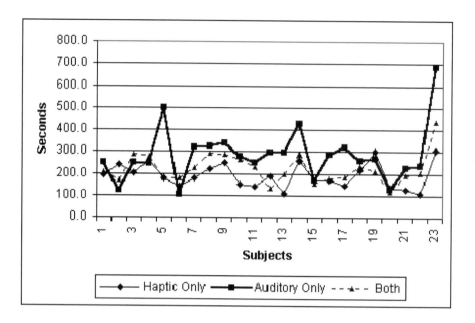

Figure 11-3: Adjusted completion time.

User Perceptions

From the post-test questionnaire, we found that a majority of the participants believed the auditory display was the most difficult task (16 participants) and the haptic display was the easiest one (15 participants). This confirms the other results above.

Discussion

Training Effect

As seen above, musical experience and haptic device experience affect the performance of the auditory tasks and the haptic tasks respectively. In terms of auditory display, it confirms Mikumo's (1997) finding that musically trained subjects had different strategies from those without musical training.

Interference

Interference occurred when a participant tried to depend on one mode, but the other mode tended to block the effort. Even though the number of respondents is equally split (12 responded that there was interference, and 11 responded that there was no interference), there is more interference, rather than mutual complementation, between auditory and haptic displays in the combination mode. Performance in the combination mode is always between that of the haptic display and that of the auditory display (Figures 11-1, 11-2, and 11-3). If the combination mode were more beneficial, it should exceed that of the haptic or the auditory mode alone.

Psychophysics

This pretest was not based on psychophysics, which emphasizes that the mere mechanical magnitude of the stimulus does not necessarily correspond to the magnitude of human perceptual response. Rather this study showed the possibility that a haptic display with ordinal data will give better performance than relatively common auditory displays. In fact, in this case it is sufficient if participants can detect all of the different stimuli because the study was not about the just-noticeable-difference in psychophysics.

Learning Effect

All the experiments were done in the same order: haptic; auditory; and combined. There could be some learning effect during the series of experiments. However, even without consideration of a learning effect, the results indicated that the haptic display is better than the auditory display. The difference will be greater if we calculate the learning effect, if any.

EXPERIMENT II

Experimental Design

Another pretest was conducted with geographic tasks in which subjects were asked to identify the right state for each question. The interfaces had nine U.S. states and each state had different tones and forces of vibration as described for Experiment I, above. For the auditory display nine tones, from middle C to D above one octave, were used, and for the haptic display each step had a 1111–unit gap (i.e., 1111, 2222, 3333, ..., 8888, 9999). The interface was built with Immersion Studio and Immersion Web Designer.

Experimental Procedure

As a learning session, subjects were asked to complete the learning session as in Experiment I. The main experimental session consisted of six different geographic tasks, such as determining the rank-ordering of juvenile crime rate among a group of states. Of the six tasks, three were to identify either the highest value or the lowest value, while the other three were to identify a middle value (the fifth). Among the tasks, two were auditory-only interfaces, two were haptic-only interfaces, and the other two were combined interfaces.

A mouse-over event triggered an auditory, haptic, or combined display. In other words, when a subject moved the mouse over a state, the system produced a tone, a force of vibration, or both, so that the subject could hear and feel the stimulus. The mouse-over event also triggered the display of the corresponding name of the state.

Subjects

The subjects were 10 undergraduate students in the School of Information Studies at Florida State University.

Results

Table 11-1 summarizes the results. For each task, completion time was measured in seconds, and the number of errors was counted when an answer from a subject was wrong. This exploratory test confirmed that the haptic display is more powerful than the auditory display with a large effect size (1.16), even though the mentally demanding tasks (i.e., identifying the middle value) required more time.

Table 11-1: Results of Experiment II.

	Tasks										
	1		2		3		4		5		6	
	Auditory Lowest		Haptic Highest		Both Highest		Auditory 5th		Haptic 5th		Both 5th	
	T	E	T	E	T	E	T	E	T	E	T	E
M	72	0.5	31	0	43	0.67	124	1.4	60	0.75	72	0.67
SD	35.8	1	14.8	0	29.8	1.32	46.8	1.6	26.6	1.49	45.4	0.58

(*M*: Mean, T: Completion Time, E: Number of Errors)

FUTURE RESEARCH

The two experiments showed that the haptic display could deliver information more effectively than the auditory display in a certain environment. However, since the effect size is quite large, a suspicion was raised that the musical tone itself may not represent the auditory display well. If the musical tone is the worst property in the auditory display and the vibration is the best property in the haptic display, it is not reasonable to claim that the haptic display is better than the auditory display. Considering the technical availability, it is decided that volume and tempo variables will be examined as well in the ongoing project.

REFERENCES

Baddeley, A. (1992). Working memory. *Science, 255,* 556–559.

Edwards, A. D. N. (1992). Redundancy and adaptability. In A. D. N. Edwards & S. Holland (Eds.), *Multimedia interface design in education* (pp. 145–155). Berlin: Springer-Verlag.

Gluck, M., Yu, L., Ju, B., Jeong, W., & Chang, C. (1999). Augmented seriation: Usability of a visual and auditory tool for geographic pattern discovery with risk perception data. *Proceedings of the 4th International Conference on GeoComputation.*

Jacobson, R. D. (1998). Cognitive mapping without sight: Four preliminary studies of spatial learning. *Journal of Environmental Psychology, 18*(3), 289–305.

Krygier, J. B. (1994). Sound and geographic visualization. In A. M. MacEachren & D. R. F. Taylor (Eds.), *Visualization in modern cartography* (pp. 149–166). Oxford, UK: Pergamon.

Mayer, R. E., & Moreno, R. (1998). A split-attention effect in multimedia learning: Evidence for dual processing systems in working memory. *Journal of Educational Psychology, 90*(2), 312–320.

Mikumo, M. (1997). Multi-encoding for pitch information of tone sequences. *Japanese Psychological Research, 39*(4), 300–311.

Mousavi, S. Y., Low, R., & Sweller, J. (1995). Reducing cognitive load by mixing auditory and visual presentation modes. *Journal of Educational Psychology, 87*(2), 319–334.

Oviatt, S. (1997). Multimodal interactive maps: Designing for human performance. *Human-Computer Interaction, 12*(1–2), 93–129.

Paivio, A. (1990). *Mental representations: A dual coding approach.* New York: Oxford University Press.

Stevens, S. S. (1957). On the psychophysical law. *Psychological Review, 64,* 153–181.

Sweller, J. (1993). Some cognitive processes and their consequences for the organisation and presentation of information. *Australian Journal of Psychology, 45,* 1–8.

Sweller, J. (1994). Cognitive load theory, learning difficulty and instructional design. *Learning and Instruction, 4,* 295–312.

Weber, C. R. (1994). *Sonic enhancement of map information: Experiments using harmonic intervals.* Unpublished doctoral dissertation, State University of New York.

Detection Thresholds for Small Haptic Effects

Jesse Dosher, Greg Lee, and Blake Hannaford

The engineering of haptic interfaces is a new and rapidly evolving field that generates many technical challenges and research issues. Control of a haptic device has a unique complexity: interaction with a human operator. This interaction is difficult to model, highly nonlinear in nature, and has demanding computational requirements. In addition to these constraints, the haptic device itself needs high bandwidth, high stiffness, low friction, and low inertia. Achieving all these properties simultaneously in a single realized design proves quite difficult.

A new and interesting direction of haptics research is that of small-scale haptic devices. Such a haptic device could provide a better mouse substitute for laptop computers or augment the ability to utilize advanced personal digital assistants (PDAs) and cell phone features fully. These applications, however, severely restrict the weight, power, and volume consumption of the device.

This chapter is part of a larger project that aims to answer the question: Can haptics be effective in low power and hand-held applications? Inevitably a haptic device that meets the strict weight, power, and volume requirements of a hand-held device will be capable of only very small forces and displacements compared to existing desktop devices. This leads to two aspects of the question. What are the weakest haptic effects that can be effectively used by humans? And how can haptic devices be designed to operate at or just above these low levels while maintaining their weight, power, and volume constraints and effective outputs?

Our project seeks to quantify the weakest haptic effects that a subject can detect with a practical haptic device and then find the threshold at which these effects become useful. Many psychophysical experiments have been conducted on the sensitivity of human touch. Studies on perceptive acuity and Braille have contributed well-designed techniques and adaptive thresholding algorithms to the study of human sensory perception (Stevens et al., 1996). Other psychophysical experiments have quantified the acuity of human spatial perception (Moy et al., 2000). However, these studies measure the threshold of human perception, which differs from the useful haptic threshold.

A successful haptic interaction involves a haptic device in contact with the human operator in a bidirectional exchange of information. In contrast to the elegant experiments of pure psychophysics, in a haptic interaction the stimulus is not independent of the user inputs. Force, displacement, velocity, and mechanical impedance all vary during this interaction. Work is being done by the human on the device as well as by the device on the human. Thus, perception through a haptic device cannot be predicted solely from pure psychophysical thresholds. Our research complements psychophysics by aiming to find the point at which a human can perceive meaningful information from a realistic haptic device, as opposed to the perceptive limit of human touch (as measured by a highly specialized apparatus and experiments). Our measurement depends on the specific haptic device as well as on the user and is not a threshold in the classical psychophysical sense. Instead we measure a data point by which we evaluate technology possibilities in an important new application area.

Other more psychological experiments show us that properly exploiting multimodel interactions and haptic illusions can enhance or attenuate haptic effects (Srinivasan et al., 1996). Increasing the effect of a small haptic device without raising its output (i.e., power cost) may also aid in the development of low power haptic devices.

The first mass produced desktop haptic device is the PHANToM (Salisbury & Srinivasan, 1997), which allows users to interact with virtual environments using a stylus-like end effector. The PHANToM opened up the area of haptics to study by a wide group of non-specialists. Our small haptic device designs have achieved higher bandwidth and greater ability to control smaller forces accurately in exchange for motion and force ranges smaller than that of the PHANToM. By advancing the technology of small haptic devices, we may enable the integration of haptics into portable and hand-held devices.

The Fingertip Haptic Display (FHD) is a 2 DOF planar haptic device, designed in the BioRobotics Laboratory, with extensive kinematic optimization that couples a lightweight and rigid haptic display with direct-drive, flat-coil actuators (Hannaford et al., 1996) (Table 12-1). Its design encompasses the index finger flexion/extension workspace of 95% of the human population (Venema & Hannaford, 2000). About 2.5 cm thick, the FHD is designed to be stacked into a four-fingered device that, when completed, will allow the four fingers to be independently curled or stroked over a virtual surface.

Table 12-1: FHD specifications.

Joint Torque	220 Nmm continuous, 450 Nmm peak
Torque Output Resolution	0.25 Nmm
Position Resolution	0.0027 degrees
Workspace	Approximately 120×120 mm
Kinematic Isotropy	≥ 0.75

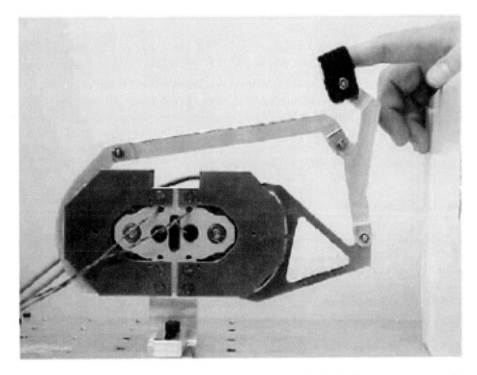

Figure 12-1: The FHD planar mechanism was optimized to fit the finger workspace of 95% of the population.

In prior research, the FHD was used to explore human perception of first and second order surface discontinuities in CAD models (Venema & Hannaford, 2000). In this chapter, we report experiments to measure the smallest haptic effects the FHD can meaningfully communicate to an operator.

In the experiments described below we study a basic attractive icon—a region of space accompanied by a local attractive force-field. We use a forced-choice protocol with an adaptive threshold-finding algorithm to determine the minimum amplitude for the haptic effect that is detectable 71% of the time. This threshold is a combined human-machine property. To estimate the effect of the device on the results we also compare this threshold with selected mechanical properties of the device.

METHODS

We checked FHD force calibration with an external gauge (Mitutoyo Digimatic Force Gauge) and verified accuracy of Cartesian end point forces commanded at the software API level.

Part of this paper reports measurements of friction in the FHD. To measure friction, we created a PD control loop ($K_p = 0.5$ N/mm, $K_d = 3.0$ N·sec/mm) and drove the loop with constant ramp position signals $(x(t) = Vt)$ at several selected velocities representative of the observed haptic interaction. The measured velocity signal (first difference algorithm) was somewhat noisy, but averaging during a 2 mm position window in the middle of the trajectory, and analysis of measured position data, confirmed that the system tracked commanded velocity within $\pm 1\%$. Force recordings were averaged during the same position window to create an estimate of force as a function of velocity.

Haptic Effects

In these experiments, haptic targets (or icons) consisted of a pair of force profiles centered on a 5 cm wide region that attracted the fingertip towards the center. The force was a linear function of the end effector's distance from the center of the target.

The peak value of the force profile was varied from one trial to the next, using an adaptive force algorithm, and recorded as the force value descriptive of that field (Figure 12-2). A set of five LEDs provided a crude position indication to the user. In the force-field detection experiment, the third and fourth LEDs were illuminated when the subject was over either icon "A" or icon "B," respectively.

Adaptive Thresholding

The adaptive thresholding method used in both experiments is designed to converge the force output such that a 71% correct response is observed from the subject (Stevens et al., 1996). Two or more correct responses decrease the force by 5%, while a single incorrect response increases the force back to its previous value.

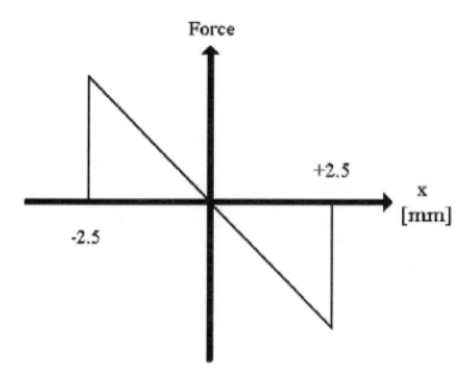

Figure 12-2: Profile of icon force-field.

Each deviation from the current trend in force was termed a "force reversal." As subjects progressed through the experiment, they might have, for example, produced five consecutive correct responses, followed by an incorrect response. This sequence would result in a reversal of the current trend, or "path." The experiment continued until 12 such path reversals occurred.

In the first experiment a "correct" response was given by properly indicating which icon had a force-field. In the second experiment a "correct" response resulted from properly indicating the presence—or absence—of force.

Experimental Procedure

In the first experiment, icons were 5 mm long and were placed 10 mm apart. One randomly selected icon had a force-field in each trial; the other icon had no force. The subject's fingertip was supported by a virtual plane approximately midworkspace, $y \geq 100$ mm. The subject's wrist rested on a platform coincident with the virtual plane. LEDs indicated when the user was inside either of the two icons.

Subjects were allowed to sample both targets indefinitely before indicating which target they perceived to contain a force. Subjects indicated their choice by moving into the target and pressing a button held in their opposite hand. This was repeated until completion of the adaptive thresholding procedure.

In another experiment, we applied pulses of force to the finger while the subjects held their finger motionless at a specified location. The wrist rested in the same position, and the fingertip was supported by the same virtual plane as in the first experiment. After a random delay of between 1 and 3 seconds, a force pulse of 125 milliseconds duration was applied. LEDs were illuminated after each stimulus, and subjects pressed a button if they detected the force pulse. Subjects were informed that no force would be applied during randomly selected trials.

In both experiments, subjects wore noise-reducing ear protection to eliminate possible sound cues. The experiments started at 500 mN of force and continued until the conclusion of the adaptive thresholding algorithm.

A threshold value representative of the subjects as a group was computed by averaging all subjects' data during their last three force path reversals.

RESULTS

Experiment 1: Active Exportation

Figure 12-3 shows the force paths taken for several test subjects. Each line represents the peak magnitude of force present for each trial during one run of the experiment. Subjects took 75 to 85 trials per experiment before incurring the necessary 12 force path reversals. All subjects started the experiment at a level of 500 mN of force. It can be noted that early "mistakes" in icon choice do not necessarily affect the final value for a particular force path; each experiment ends when 12 force reversals have occurred, rather than at a fixed number of trials. Figure 12-4 shows a magnification of the area of convergence from Figure 12-3, a region showing the last approximately forty trials for most subjects. The mean of all converged values was 30 mN.

Experiment 2: Static Force Pulses

The same adaptive force algorithm and initial starting force was used in Experiment 2, where the subject held his or her finger in one spot and a 125 millisecond pulse was applied. Subjects required a comparable number of trials as in Experiment 1 before incurring 12 force-reversals. The mean value was 41 mN (Figure 12-5).

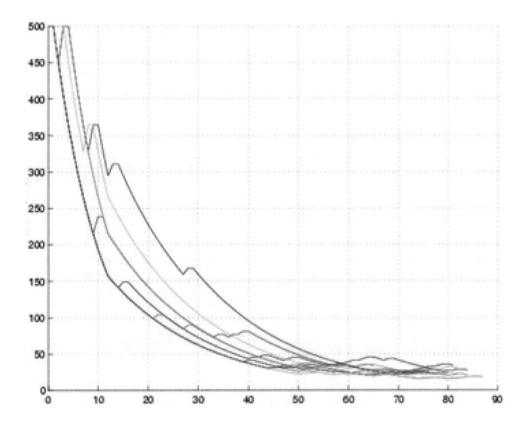

Figure 12-3: Force paths taken for two-target experiment.

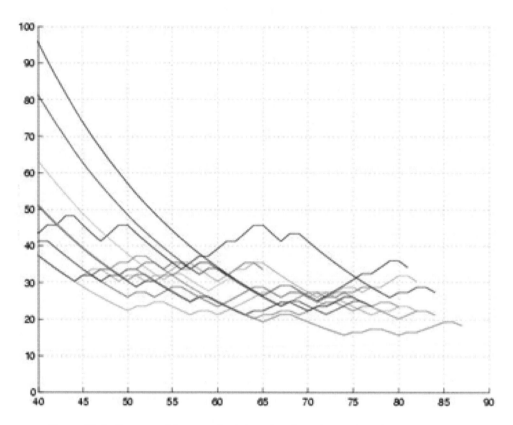

Figure 12-4: Converged force paths taken, two-target experiment.

Experiment 3: Device Friction

We measured the forces required to move the FHD at five discrete velocities $(5 + 20n$ mm/s) without contact by the human operator (Figure 12-6). Noise in the first difference velocity measurement caused some scatter in data, visible in Figure 12-6. The slope of the five data groupings is the derivative gain chosen for the PD controller used in this experiment, $K_d = 3$ N·sec/mm. Small circles represent the average observed velocity vs. average observed force for each data set. Each circle encloses a small dot representing the desired velocity plotted against the average force. Measured velocity is within 1% of desired velocity.

A straight line fit to the data points gives a coefficient of viscous friction of approximately 0.2 N·sec/m and intersects the force axis at 65 mN when the desired velocity approaches 0 mm/s. We also measured static friction or "stiction" of the device by slowly increasing force with the device at rest and recording the force at which a sustained velocity occurred. The static friction of the FHD measured by this procedure is 100 mN.

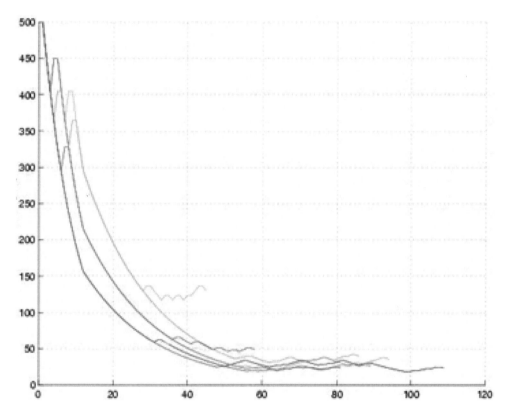

Figure 12-5: Force paths taken for static force experiment.

DISCUSSION

In this paper we reported experiments aimed at discerning the weakest haptic effects that are detectable by users of a state-of-the-art haptic device. The adaptive threshold detection method, long applied in psychophysics and clinical testing instruments, was quite practical for testing haptic devices and effects.

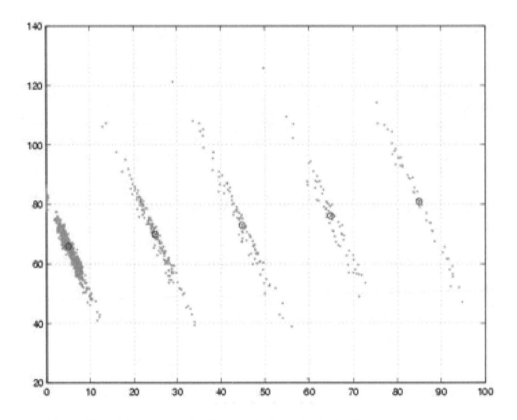

Figure 12-6: Actuator force for five selected constant velocities.

When actively exploring for a 5 mm attractive icon with our FHD, we measured an average detection threshold of 30 mN for a population of subjects. The average threshold was about 30% higher when the subjects did not move but held the finger steady and detected the presence or absence of 125 millisecond force pulses (41 mN). An interesting subjective observation was that as the magnitude of these force pulses was reduced, subjects became aware of the circulatory pulse in their fingertips; the heartbeat was sometimes hard to distinguish from the stimulus.

These results do not indicate fundamental thresholds for the human operator, but rather what is achievable with a particular haptic device. We expect that the particular type of haptic effect may change the threshold. Besides the haptic device, there are other variables that may also affect the threshold. In these experiments, the force as a function of position was a discontinuous sawtooth shape (Figure 12-2) that created an energy minimum at the center of the icon. The force values we report are the peaks of the triangles. Other shapes such as sinusoids, rectangles, trapezoids, or Gaussians can also create attractive icons and may be detectable with different peak forces. The size of the icon could also be a factor, but was not varied in these experiments. Icon size, local stiffness, and peak force are three parameters, of which two may be varied independently. Future experiments will characterize response thresholds while varying these factors and using more devices.

It is well known that touch is highly sensitive to vibration and frequencies up to 1000 Hz or more (Shimoga, 1993a, 1993b). Increasing the spatiotemporal frequency content of the haptic effects could lower the thresholds. Conversely, reducing frequency content of the haptic effects by, for example, changing the force profile to a smoother one could result in higher thresholds.

There is still no consensus on which engineering specifications predict the subjective performance of a haptic device. However, the static friction level is often taken to indicate the minimum forces that the device can represent. Friction is difficult to model but is typically thought to contain three components, static friction (stiction), Coulomb friction (a term depending only on the sign of velocity), and viscous friction. We measured friction at several constant velocities typical of haptic interaction. The force varied linearly with velocity ($B = 0.2$ N·sec/m) and extrapolated to zero velocity to estimate the Coulomb component (65 mN). Static friction (stiction) was 100 mN.

Our results show that users can reliably detect haptic effects whose maximum force is about one-half the measured Coulomb friction level of the device and about one-third the measured static friction level. We plan to repeat this set of tests on other haptic devices to determine if this rule can be generalized.

We have made these measurements to aid in understanding whether or not haptic devices can be useful and capable of being implemented in very small systems. That an effect is detectable is probably necessary but not sufficient for it to be actually useful. We plan future experiments to measure whether or not weak haptic effects at or near the threshold measured here can help a person accomplish a task more effectively. These experiments will create tasks such as selection of icons or menu items and evaluate performance through such measures as completion time and error rate in the presence or absence of weak haptic effects.

ACKNOWLEDGMENT

We are pleased to acknowledge support for this project from Ford Motor Company.

REFERENCES

Hannaford, B., Marbot, P. H., Buttolo, P., Moreyra, M., & Venema, S. (1996). Scaling properties of direct drive serial arms. *International Journal of Robotics Research, 15*, 459–472.

Moy, G., Singh, U., Tan, E., & Fearing, R. S. (2000). Human psychophysics for teletaction system design. *Haptics-e, The Electronic Journal of Haptics Research* [Online], *1*(3). Retrieved from http://www.haptics-e.org.

Salisbury, J. K., & Srinivasan, M. A. (1997). Phantom-based interaction with virtual objects. *IEEE-Computer-Graphics-and-Applications, 17*(5), 6–10.

Shimoga, K. B. (1993a). A survey of perceptual feedback issues in dexterous telemanipulation: Part I. Finger force feedback. In *VRAIS '93*, Vol. 1(pp. 263–270).

Shimoga, K. B. (1993b). A survey of perceptual feedback issues in dexterous telemanipulation: Part II. Finger touch feedback. In *VRAIS '93*, Vol. 1(pp. 271–279).

Srinivasan, M. A., Beauregard, G. L., & Brock, L. D. (1996). The impact of visual information on the haptic perception of stiffness in virtual environments. *Proceedings of the ASME Dynamic Systems and Control Division*.

Stevens, J. C., Foulke, E., & Patterson, M. Q. (1996). Tactile acuity, aging, and Braille readings in long-term blindness. *Journal of Experimental Psychology: Applied, 2*(2), 91–106.

Venema, S. C. (1999). *Experiments in surface perception using a haptic display*. Unpublished Ph.D. Thesis, University of Washington.

Venema, S. C., & Hannaford, B. (2000). Experiments in fingertip perception of surface discontinuities. *International Journal of Robotics Research, 19*, 684–696.

CHAPTER 13

Haptic Interfaces to Real and Virtual Surgical Environments

M. Cenk Çavuşoğlu, Frank Tendick, and S. Shankar Sastry

Medical robotics and computer-assisted surgery (MRCAS) is an emerging area of research on the application of computers and robotic technology to surgery, in planning and execution of surgical operations and in training of surgeons.

Telesurgery and surgical simulation are the two areas of MRCAS on which this paper focuses. With robotic telesurgery, the goal is to develop robotic tools to augment or replace hand instruments used in surgery. In robotic telesurgery, the robotic tools are not automated robots but teleoperated systems under direct control of the surgeon, hence the name *tele-*surgery. Surgical simulation aims to develop an alternate training medium for surgery in the form of a virtual environments-based surgical training simulator. This is similar to using flight simulators to train pilots. In this paper, both telesurgery and surgical simulation are discussed in the context of minimally invasive surgery (MIS), particularly laparoscopic surgery (minimally invasive surgery of the abdomen).

MIS is a revolutionary technique in surgery (Way, Bhoyrul, & Mori, 1995), where the operation is performed with instruments and viewing equipment inserted through small incisions (typically less than 10 mm in diameter) rather than by making a large incision to expose and provide access to the operation site. The main advantage of this technique is the reduced trauma to healthy tissue, which is the leading cause of patients' postoperative pain and long hospital stays. The hospital stay and rest periods, and therefore the procedure costs, can be significantly reduced with MIS, but MIS procedures are more demanding on the surgeon, requiring more difficult surgical techniques.

The first major laparoscopic surgery (MIS in the abdominal cavity), for cholecystectomy (removal of the gall bladder), was performed in 1985 by Mühe in (West) Germany. In less than a decade, there was a quick shift from open surgery to laparoscopic surgery for relatively simple procedures, with 67% of cholecystectomies performed laparoscopically in the United States in 1993 (Graves, 1993). Adoption of laparoscopic techniques has been slower for more complex procedures, largely because of the greater difficulty due to the surgeon's reduced dexterity and perception. The next frontier in MIS is thoracoscopy (MIS in the chest cavity), in particular minimally invasive coronary artery bypass grafting surgery, which has been recently getting a lot of attention in the research and commercial medical equipment development communities.

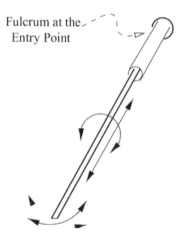

Fulcrum at the
Entry Point

Figure 13-1: 4 DOF available in conventional laparoscopic instruments.

Typical laparoscopic and thoracoscopic instruments have only four degrees of freedom (DOF) (see Figure 13-1), preventing the ability to orient the instrument tip arbitrarily at a given location in space (Tendick, Jennings, Tharp, & Stark, 1993). Dexterity is significantly reduced because of the lost DOFs and motion reversal due to the fulcrum at the entry point. Force feedback is reduced due to the friction at the airtight trocar and the stiffness of the inflated abdominal wall. There is no tactile sensing, on which surgeons are highly dependent in open surgery to locate arteries and tumors hidden in tissue.

MIS also has problems related to spatial perception. In MIS, the surgeons look at and interact with the anatomy from a completely different perspective than they are used to. In open surgery, the operation site is at arm's length, and the visual and motor spaces are consistent. However, in MIS, the surgeon literally views the anatomy from the inside through a camera, and the camera is controlled by an assistant who acts as the eyes of the surgeon. Visual and motor spaces are no longer consistent, since the surgeon watches the operation site on a CRT screen placed at a geometrically unrelated location, and the display covers a considerably smaller field of view relative to the eyes of the surgeon than the field of view of the camera. These conditions, in addition to the complications of a typical surgical scene, result in difficulties in spatial perception, particularly in identifying anatomical landmarks, navigating in the anatomy, planning for proper exposure, and handling the camera and instruments.

HAPTIC INTERFACING TO REAL AND VIRTUAL SURGICAL ENVIRONMENTS

At first, the development of a robotic telesurgical system and a virtual environments-based surgical simulator may seem to be unrelated areas. But, in fact, they are two parallel problems as illustrated in Figure 13-2.

Surgery is inherently a form of haptic interaction. During surgery the surgeon is in physical interaction with the patient either with his or her hands or through the instruments used. In the telesurgical system, the operator interacts with the master manipulator, which controls the slave robot through a teleoperation algorithm, to interact with the real surgical environment on the remote site. In the surgical training simulator, the operator again uses the master haptic interface, this time to interact with a simulated virtual environment. Therefore, telesurgery and surgical simulation are both problems of developing haptic interfaces, respectively, to real and virtual surgical environments.

From a systems engineering point of view, the development of a telesurgical system and a surgical training simulator are parallel problems. They require similar design and analysis methodologies, and there are similar or overlapping problems. The tools and results of one can be applied to the other. We can see these corresponding aspects of the two applications more clearly in Figure 13-2.

Psychophysics: It is important to identify the relevant psychophysical parameters of the human operator. The telesurgical system is augmenting the human operator; therefore, it is necessary to know the engineering specification of the underlying system (i.e., the human), such as the frequency-dependent force and impedance sensitivities. The same psychophysical quantities are also important for the surgical simulator, since they determine the level of accuracy necessary in the simulation to achieve the desired level of realism.

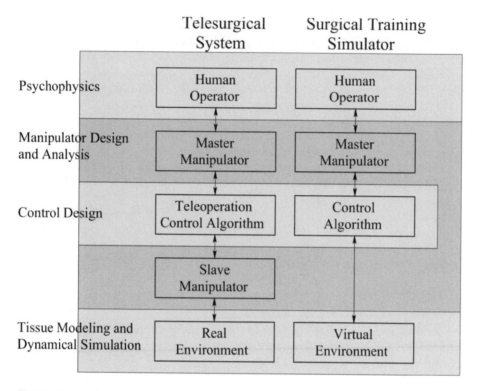

Figure 13-2: Telesurgery and surgical simulation are parallel research problems.

Manipulator Design and Analysis: The same requirements apply for the master manipulator of the telesurgical system and the haptic interface of the surgical simulator. Both need to display interaction forces of the same magnitude and bandwidth, and require similar fidelity and workspace. Essentially, they will be interfaces for interaction to similar environments, apart from the fact that the former will be used for interacting with a real surgical environment, whereas the latter will be used for interacting with a virtual surgical environment. This parallelism extends to the design of the slave manipulator of the telesurgical system as well.

Control Design: Teleoperation controller design for the telesurgical system and the control of the haptic interface of the surgical simulator are essentially two aspects of the same problem. The only difference is that in telesurgery, the remote environment is real, resulting in an unstructured system with uncertainties, and in surgical simulation, the remote environment is simulated, resulting in a different set of problems due to the discrete nature of the simulation and computational requirements. The same analysis and design tools of control theory are used in addressing these problems.

Tissue Modeling and Dynamical Simulation: One of the main problems of the surgical simulator is the development of realistic physical models of the organs and soft tissue.

Construction of these models requires data from the real tissue to determine the mechanical properties. Also, knowing the physical properties of the tissue to be manipulated is important for the design and control of the telesurgical system.

THE UC BERKELEY/UC SAN FRANCISCO ROBOTIC TELESURGICAL SYSTEM

Telesurgical System Concept

MIS is fundamentally a form of telemanipulation, as the surgeon is physically separated from the workspace. Therefore, telerobotics is a natural tool to extend capabilities in MIS by replacing the surgical tools with robotic instruments that are under direct control of the surgeon through teleoperation (Figure 13-3).

Use of a robotic telesurgical system (RTS) has been proposed as a way to improve dexterity, hand-eye coordination, and sensation in MIS. With the telesurgical workstation, the goal is to restore the manipulation and sensation capabilities of the surgeon that were lost due to MIS. A 6 DOF slave manipulator, controlled through a spatially consistent and intuitive master, will restore the dexterity, while the force feedback to the master will increase the fidelity of the manipulation, and the tactile feedback will restore the lost tactile sensation.

There are several RTSs developed by university and commercial companies, including the telesurgical system for open surgery with 4 DOF manipulators developed at SRI International (Hill, Green, Jensen, Gorfu, & Shah, 1994) (a laparoscopic version has also been developed), the telerobotic assistant for laparoscopic surgery developed by Taylor, Funda, Eldridge, Gomory, Gruben, LaRose, Talamini, Kavoussi, and Anderson (1995), the Robotic Telesurgical Workstation developed at UC Berkeley and UCSF (Çavuşoğlu, 2000; Çavuşoğlu, Tendick, Cohn, & Sastry, 1999), the Silver and Black Falcon manipulators by Madhani, Niemeyer, and Salisbury (1998), the Zeus™ system developed by Computer Motion Inc., Goleta, CA, and the daVinci™ system developed by Intuitive Surgical Inc., Palo Alto, CA.

The research problems in the development of a telesurgical system are manipulator design and achieving high fidelity teleoperation. Telesurgical manipulators need to be small—10 mm or smaller for laparoscopy, and 5 mm or smaller for cardiac and fetal surgery—yet have significant workspace and be able to apply forces in the range of several Newtons to be able to manipulate tissue. At this scale, transmission of sufficient mechanical power is the main challenge. Design of haptic interfaces, particularly 6 DOF, lightweight, high-bandwidth manipulators with workspace in the range of several liters and with at least 4 DOF (preferably 6 DOF) force feedback, which will serve as master devices, is another active research area.

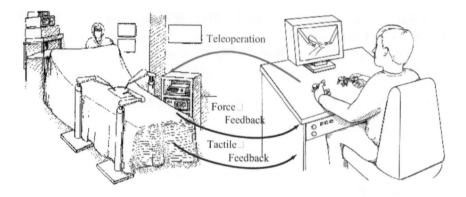

Figure 13-3: Telesurgical system concept.

Telesurgical tasks require high dexterity and fidelity during manipulation since most of the manipulation is delicate. Therefore, the design requirements for the teleoperation controllers of telesurgical systems are significantly different from classical teleoperation applications. An important component of the teleoperator design is the quantification of the human operator's sensitivity and performance. This is necessary in terms of providing the specifications of the controller as well as measures to evaluate designs.

Description of the System

In this joint project between the Robotics and Intelligent Machines Laboratory of the University of California, Berkeley (UCB) and the Department of Surgery of the University of California San Francisco (UCSF), a robotic telesurgical workstation for laparoscopy is being developed. The current design is a bimanual system with two 6 DOF manipulators instrumented with grippers, controlled by a pair of 6 DOF master manipulators.

To justify the cost and overhead of using an unconventional and complicated tool, a RTS has to either improve existing procedures or enable the surgeons to perform operations previously not possible. The target tasks chosen in the design of the UCB/UCSF RTS are suturing and knot tying, which are very difficult to perform with existing laparoscopic tools. This is mainly due to the lack of ability to orient the tip of the tools and the difficulties in hand-eye coordination. This makes performing many advanced abdominal procedures laparoscopically extremely difficult. Therefore, the design of the system is oriented explicitly towards easy suturing and knot tying.

The current second-generation system is designed for extensive operating room testing in animal experiments as well as testing with *ex vivo* tissue and in training boxes. Its goal was to show that using teleoperated 6 DOF slave manipulators, it is possible to improve dexterity and sensation in laparoscopic surgery, and therefore improve the surgeons' performance and enable them to perform previously impossible surgical operations.

Current Prototype

The slave manipulator is composed of two parts (Figure 13-4). The first part is the gross positioning stage, located outside the body. It is responsible for positioning the milli-robot, which is the second part of the slave robot. The gross stage controls the same 4 DOF as those available in conventional laparoscopic instruments. As the gross stage is located outside the body, there is not a tight space limitation. A parallel arrangement is chosen for increased rigidity and a small footprint. Three linear joints, which are connected to the base of the robot with U-joints, control the position of one end of a four-bar linkage. The tool arm and the motors actuating the gross rotation and the millirobot are connected to the opposite end of the four-bar linkage. All four actuators of the gross positioning stage are DC servo motors. In the linear joints, power is transmitted by lead screws connected to the motors. The roll axis through the entry port is tendon-driven.

The second part of the slave, the millirobot, is located inside the patient and consequently must be small yet capable of producing a wide range of motion and relatively large forces. It has a 2 DOF wrist, with yaw and roll axis rotations, and a gripper (Figure 13-4). It is 15 mm in diameter. The wrist-to-gripper length is 5 cm. The yaw and roll axes are actuated with tendons jointly by DC servo motors located on the end of the tool arm outside the body. The mechanism has 270 degrees of roll rotation, which is required for driving the needle through tissue in a single movement without regrabbing it, and 90 degrees of wrist flexion and 720 degrees of gross rotation for suturing at the desired orientations. Two full turns of gross roll rotation is chosen over a single full rotation for comfortable operation, reducing the need to readjust the instrument. The speed and bandwidth of the system are sufficient to accommodate the bandwidth of intentional hand movements.

Figure 13-5 illustrates the positioning of the bimanual system in the operating room. The two slave manipulators are located on opposite sides of the operating table. Figure 13-5 also shows the close-up view of the millirobotic section while tying a knot. Here, it is possible to see the advantage of having the 2 DOF wrist on the slave, which makes it possible to have the nice approach angle and the opposing configuration of the two tools.

The master workstation (Figure 13-6) is composed of a pair of 6 DOF haptic interfaces, each controlling one of the slave manipulators. Commercial 6 DOF force-reflecting haptic interfaces (PHANToM v1.5, SensAble Technologies Inc., Cambridge, MA) with three actuated DOF are modified to be kinematically similar to the wrist configuration of the slave manipulators. This is to avoid control problems that would arise because of the wrist singularity and also relieve the operator of the burden of dealing with nonintuitive behavior of the manipulators around the singularity. The master interfaces are also equipped with a stylus handle to give a more dextrous interface for precise manipulation.

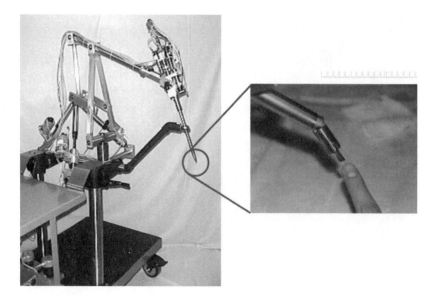

Figure 13-4: Slave manipulator of the UCB/UCSF laparoscopic telesurgical workstation. Close-up view of the millirobotic wrist is shown on the right.

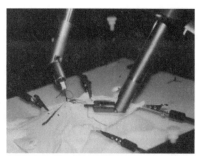

Figure 13-5(a)(b): Left: Setup of the bimanual system around the operating table.
Right: Close-up of the bimanual system tying a knot in the training box.

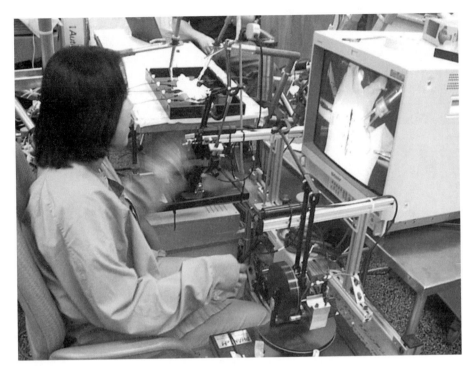

Figure 13-6: Master workstation of the UC Berkeley/UC San Francisco RTS.

The system has been successfully tested with suturing and knot tying experiments on *in vivo* and *ex vivo* tissue at the Experimental Surgery Laboratory of UC San Francisco. Details of the experimental evaluation of the system can be found in Çavuşoğlu (2000).

Bilateral Teleoperation Controller Design for Telesurgical Systems

As it was discussed earlier, the bilateral controller of the RTS is a critical part of the overall system because it is directly related to the performance and fidelity of interaction.

Previous research on teleoperation has focused on manipulation of hard objects. However, the design constraints are different in an application that involves manipulation of deformable objects. The stability-fidelity trade-off is the main determinant of the control design for teleoperation systems, as it is in many other control design problems. Both fidelity and stability are inherently dependent on the task for which the system is designed. In the design of a teleoperation system controller, there are three considerations we believe to be important. First, it is important to have task-based performance goals rather than trying to achieve a marginally stable, physically unachievable ideal teleoperator response. Second, teleoperator controller design should be expressed explicitly as an optimization problem to accommodate task-based performance goals. Third, design of the teleoperation system must be oriented towards improving performance with respect to human perceptual capabilities. It is necessary to quantify human perceptual capabilities experimentally and to develop control design methodologies that will provide the means to include this in the control design.

Teleoperation Controller Design via Optimization of a Task-Based Performance Objective

The controller to be used for the teleoperation system needs to satisfy some basic requirements, such as stability under specified environment and operator variations. Once these are satisfied, the remaining freedom in the controller can be used to optimize a task dependent performance measure, in this case fidelity.

$$\frac{\text{Controller}}{\text{Gains}} = \underset{\substack{\text{All stable controllers} \\ \text{satisfying tracking} \\ \text{condition}}}{\text{arg sup}} \left[\text{fidelity} \,\middle|\, \substack{\text{at nominal} \\ \text{environment} \\ \text{and human operator} \\ \text{operating point}} \right]$$

Any teleoperation system must maintain stability under operator and environmental variations. Robust stability of the closed loop system under unstructured uncertainty can be used to check this by properly modeling the operator and environment variations as uncertainty in the system.

The tracking requirement is necessary to prevent the final controller parameter optimization from yielding trivial solutions. To illustrate this complication, consider the case of optimizing a controller for transparency at a given environment stiffness as operating point. The trivial solution to this optimization is to have a master controller that gives the master manipulator an apparent stiffness equal to the nominal environment stiffness and have no feedback from slave to master, or even not actuate the slave at all. The most natural constraint to prevent this kind of behavior is to require the teleoperation system to have sufficient tracking performance in free space.

Fidelity Measure: Sensitivity of the Transmitted Impedance to Environment Impedance

In robotic telesurgery one would like to improve the ability to detect compliance changes in the environment, in addition to the basic requirement of "good" tracking in free space and while in contact with tissue. This compliance detection is critical in a surgical application in two ways. First, the interaction of the needle with tissue during suturing, such as feeling when the needle punctures or leaves tissue, can be detected through the change in the compliance. Second, the structures hidden inside the tissue, such as blood vessels, major nerves, or tumors, can be located by noninvasively probing the tissue. In these cases, it is more desirable to have the ability to detect the changes in the environment impedance than simple position or force tracking between the master and slave manipulators. Therefore, it is necessary to introduce a fidelity measure that quantifies this ability.

Sensitivity of the impedance transmitted through the teleoperator to the changes in the environmental impedance has been proposed as a measure of fidelity by Çavuşoğlu, Sherman, and Tendick (2001). This fidelity measure is defined as

$$\left\| W_s \frac{dZ_t}{dZ_e} \right|_{Z_e = \hat{Z}_e} \right\|_2$$

where Z_t is the impedance transmitted by the teleoperator, Z_e is the impedance of the environment, $\hat{Z}_e$ is the nominal environment impedance, and W_s is a frequency dependent weighting function that quantifies the human operator's frequency-dependant sensitivity to stiffness stimuli. A low pass filter with cutoff frequency of 40 Hz is used as the weighting function. This particular weighting function was chosen based on the results of psychophysics experiments for determining human compliance discrimination thresholds (Dhruv & Tendick, 2000).

THE TRAINING SIMULATOR FOR MINIMALLY INVASIVE SURGERY

Surgical Simulator Concept

Surgeons are trained through apprenticeship. The basic techniques are taught with simple training equipment, but the rest of the training is either with books describing surgical procedures and techniques, or in the operating room by watching and participating in actual operations (and rarely in the animal laboratories). Although actual operating room training is essential and invaluable, it does not provide the optimal environment to try or practice new techniques and procedures due to the risks to the patient. This method of training also limits the diffusion of knowledge, since only a limited number of people can be trained by one experienced surgeon.

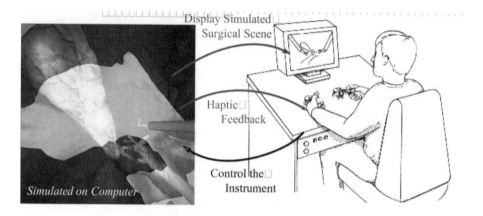

Figure 13-7: Surgical training simulator concept.

Virtual environments present an alternative to this training scheme. With virtual environments it is possible to create an interactive 3D simulation environment, where the surgeons, using a haptic interface, can manipulate, cut, or suture dynamically and geometrically correct models of organs and tissues simulated on a computer (Figure 13-7). The idea is similar to using flight simulators to train pilots. Virtual environments present no risk to a patient, and they are therefore less stressful. They are interactive and 3D in contrast to books, and they are relatively inexpensive compared to training in the operating room or animal labs. Virtual environments also give a unique advantage, as it is possible to generate arbitrary anatomies and pathologies with which the surgeons can be trained for cases that they will encounter only a few times during their whole career but nonetheless must be prepared for. This way, it is also possible to standardize the training and accreditation in surgery.

There are many research groups working on virtual environments for surgical training. These studies include surgical training simulators for laparoscopic surgery (Kuhnapfel, Kuhn, Hubner, Krumm, Maass, & Neisius, 1997; Szekely, Bajka, Brechbuhler, Dual, Enzler, Haller, et al., 1999), endoscopy of the colon (Baillie, Jowell, Evangelou, Bickel, & Cotton, 1991; Ikuta, Takeichi, & Namiki, 1998) and sinus (Weit, Yagel, Stredney, Schmalbrock, Sessanna, Kurzion, et al., 1997), arthroscopy (Gibson, Samosky, Mor, Fyock, Grimson, & Kanade, 1997; McCarthy, Harley, & Smallwood, 1999; Smith, Wan, Taffinder, Read, Emery, & Darzi, 1999), bronchoscopy (Bro-Nielsen, 1999), endoscopic retrograde cholangiopancreatography (ERCP) (Peifer, Curtis, & Sinclair, 1996), and spinal biopsy and nerve blocks (Blezek, Robb, Camp, Nauss, & Martin., 1998; Cleary, Lathan, & Carignan, 1998).

The existing successful training simulators are for applications where there are not large deformations, and mostly manipulation of hard objects. But, for other applications, deformable models are required, and the state of the art for interactive deformable object simulation is not sufficiently advanced to build realistic real-time simulations. Constructing realistic and efficient deformable models for soft tissue behavior is the main challenge in achieving realism in surgical training simulators. The deformable tissue models have to be interactive, efficient enough to be simulated in real time, visually and haptically realistic, and able to be cut and sutured.

The surgical training simulators in the literature are mostly for MIS applications. This is not a coincidence. In addition to the need for better training tools for MIS, the constraints that make MIS difficult are the same ones that make building simulators for MIS more manageable with existing technology. It is significantly easier to imitate the user interface for MIS as limited and well-constrained haptic interaction and limited amount and quality of feedback (visual and otherwise) are available.

It is also necessary to determine what to teach in the simulator. It is possible to train basic motor skills, such as using surgical instruments, suturing, and knot tying. It is also possible to train spatial skills, including navigation, exposure, and camera-handling skills. Finally, it is also possible to teach surgical tasks and complete procedures.

Verification of the transfer of skills from virtual surgery (i.e., simulator) to real surgery is an important piece of the puzzle. It is obviously important that the skills learned from the simulator are not skills in a new computer game, but rather skills transferable to actual surgery. However, there are only a few studies in the literature that have actually considered the transfer of skills from a surgical simulator to real surgery.

Laparoscopic Simulation Testbed

This paper describes an integrated effort of the Virtual Environments for Surgical Training and Augmentation (VESTA) project between the San Francisco, Berkeley, and Santa Barbara campuses of the University of California to develop a testbed for research in understanding, assessing, and training surgical skills. The testbed includes virtual environments for training perceptual motor skills, spatial skills, and critical steps of surgical procedures. It supports research into both the technical aspects of simulation and the application of virtual environments to surgical training (Tendick et al., 2000). The simulations run on a dual-processor Silicon Graphics Octane workstation with MXE graphics. They are implemented in C and OpenGL. Novel technical elements of the testbed include a four degrees-of-freedom haptic interface, a fast collision detection algorithm for contact between rigid and deformable objects, and parallel processing of physical modeling and rendering.

Interface

Motion of a laparoscopic instrument is constrained to 4 DOF by the fulcrum at the incision through the abdominal wall. To produce a 4 DOF interface with proper kinematics and force feedback, we modified a PHANToM 3 DOF haptic interface from SensAble Technologies (Cambridge, MA). The fulcrum was added with a gimbal arrangement (Figure 13-8). For torque about the instrument axis, we achieved high torque, stiffness, minimal friction, and smooth power transmission from a DC motor through a wire-rope capstan drive and a linear ball spline. The spline made it possible to transfer torque to the tool shaft smoothly while allowing it to translate. Low inertia was guaranteed by concentrating the mass of the system near the pivot.

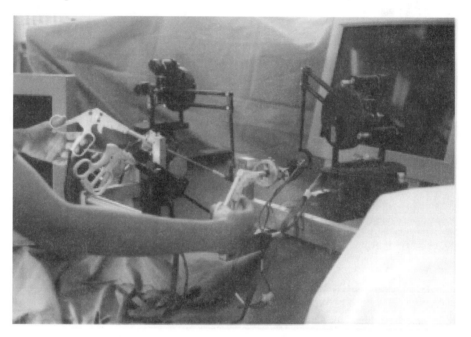

Figure 13-8: Surgical Training Simulator Interface.

The entire laparoscopic workstation comprises a pair of 4 DOF interfaces to control two simulated instruments, a 4 DOF interface with encoders but no force feedback to command motion of the simulated laparoscope (modified from a Virtual Laparoscopic Interface from Immersion Corporation, Santa Clara, CA), and a supporting adjustable frame to allow different laparoscope and instrument configurations (Figure 13-8).

To imbue the anatomical models with the characteristics of deformable objects, simple lumped parameter models are used, composed of mass-spring-damper meshes. A voxel-based collision detection algorithm is used for instrument-deformable body collisions.

We currently have several simulations implemented within the framework of the simulation testbed. The first one is a laparoscopic cholecystectomy simulation that teaches the critical steps of this procedure, determined from clinical experience and analysis of 139 bile duct injuries. This simulation uses a physical model with 2,800 deformable nodes. Because the liver model does not deform, there are many more triangles displayed (12,371). This simulation runs at an interactive speed, roughly 13 updates per second. Other simulations implemented include a virtual environment designed specifically to train the use of the angled laparoscope, which is a very fundamental skill in laparoscopic surgery that requires spatial cognition, and a simulation implemented to study visually guided point-to-point movements, which is one of the simplest perceptual motor skills (Tendick et al., 2000).

Multirate Simulation for High Fidelity Haptic Interaction with Deformable Objects in Virtual Environments

In a VE simulation of interaction with deformable bodies, for example in a surgical simulator, the physical model typically is updated at the visual update rates of 10 Hz order of magnitude, but haptic interfaces require much higher update rates, typically on the order of 1 kHz. It is not possible to increase the update rate of the physical model to the haptic rate with its full complexity due to computational limitations. The most common practice is to apply the same force between the model updates, or to low-pass filter this generated force to the bandwidth of the model update rate. These effectively reduce the haptic update rate to the visual update rate and therefore impair the fidelity of the haptic interaction. This is especially significant when the high frequency interaction forces are significant, as in nonlinear phenomena like contact.

Astley and Hayward proposed to use a multiscale multirate finite element model to address this problem. In their method, a coarse linear finite element mesh models the behavior of the overall object and a finer finite element mesh running at a higher update rate is used locally where there is an interaction (1998). Their work was based on decoupling the coarse mesh and the fine mesh by using the Norton equivalents as interfaces and is only applicable to the linear finite element case, which is not suitable for modeling the typical large deformations present during soft tissue manipulation. Also, the update rates reported were still significantly below 1 kHz required by the haptics.

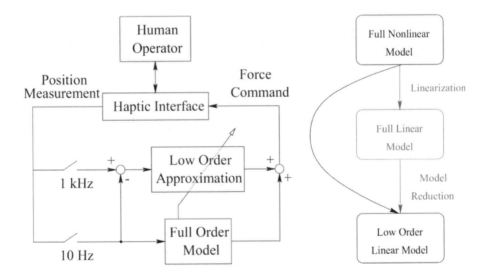

Figure 13-9(a)(b): (a) Proposed simulation paradigm. (b) Construction of the low order model.

In this chapter we introduce a multirate simulation approach to handle the difference between the update rate requirements for the haptics and the physical model during haptic interaction in VE simulations. The method, which was first proposed by Çavuşoğlu and Tendick (2000), is justified by model reduction techniques from system theory, and the approach is applied to nonlinear physical models.

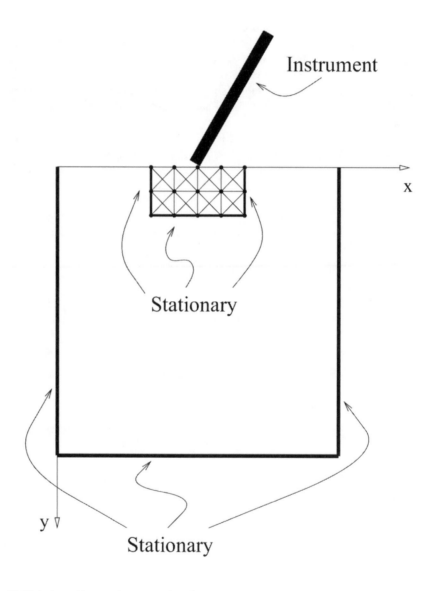

Figure 13-9(c): Local low order approximation.

When the instrument interacts with the deformable model in a VE simulator, the haptic interface will displace the node(s) it is touching and display the reaction force. Therefore, from the haptic interfaces point of view, it will be interacting with a three-input three-output nonlinear dynamical system, considering the three components of translation and force respectively. However, the underlying dynamical system has a very high order as it includes the deformation of the whole body. For example, when interacting with a 10×10 deformable cube, a midsized deformable model, the deformation will have 6000th-order dynamics. This very high-order dynamical system, which cannot be simulated in real time, needs to be replaced with a low-order approximation for real time haptic performance.

Instead of calculating the interaction force from the full nonlinear model, a low-order approximation, running at the haptic update rate, can be used on top of the full-order model to estimate the intersample behavior (Figure 13-9(a)). The low-order approximation is updated by the full model after each step.

Linearization is a basic step in the construction of the low-order approximation. The linearized model gives the tangential behavior of the full model. As we want to capture the behavior in between the model updates, the deformation will be small; therefore the tangential behavior is sufficient. However, the improvement by just using a linear model is limited, since the linearized system will have the same order as the full model (i.e., it will still be difficult if not impossible to simulate in real time). Therefore, model reduction is the critical step of the approach, as it is the means of getting a temporally local haptic model that can be simulated in real time.

To illustrate the effectiveness of model reduction, consider a two-dimensional 12×12 lumped element mesh being indented by an instrument. Linearization of such a system gives a two-input two-output 524th-order linear dynamical system. However, when we perform balanced model reduction (Zhou, Doyle, & Glover, 1996) on this model, we can approximate the system's input-output response with a 10th-order system, with the infinity norm of the error resulting from the approximation being less than 1% of the full-order model. This is a significant reduction in computational complexity while virtually maintaining the accuracy of the model.

It is important to note that balanced model reduction requires costly calculations as well, which prevents the use of this algorithm as a part of the online computation. However, analysis following model reduction, by looking at the spatial dependence of the states of the reduced order model, reveals that the approximation given by the balanced model reduction algorithm in a homogeneous medium is a local model (i.e., the force response depends mostly on the states spatially close to the interaction location). So, a natural way to construct a low order approximation with significantly less computation is to construct a local linear model directly from the full-order model (Figure 13-9(b)). One such local linear approximation is shown in Figure 13-9(c). It models the local behavior of the mesh with the nodes, springs, and dampers near the instrument.

This local model approximates the behavior of the full-order model well in the high frequency range, whereas its DC gain is significantly off. However, it is important to note that the local model is used only to estimate the intersample behavior of the full model, and therefore only needs to be close to the full model in the frequency range of around 10–1000

Hz, which is the case here. If necessary, it is possible to improve the low frequency accuracy by increasing the number of layers of nodes included around the instrument.

It is important to note that the size of the full-order nonlinear object model can be scaled without affecting the performance of the haptic interaction. Therefore the computational requirements of the construction of the local model and the haptic loop are fixed and independent of the size of the full-order model.

Stability of haptic interaction with VEs is an important consideration for design of haptic interfaces and virtual objects. The update rate of the simulation is one of the critical determinants of the stability of interaction, where increasing the update rate of the model improves stability (Colgate, Stanley, & Brown, 1995; Minsky, Ouh-young, Steele, Jr., Brooks, & Behensky, 1990). In the method discussed here, having the low order linear model running at a faster update rate improves the stability of the haptic interaction as the VE model runs at 1 kHz instead of 10 Hz.

The major limitation of this method is that the local states must be the dominant ones. This could be violated if the material was nonhomogeneous, for example if the deep tissue were significantly more compliant than at the surface so that most of the deformation occurred in states far from the interaction. Another case that would violate the dominance of local modes occurs when a relatively stiff object undergoes rigid motions, in which case the instrument forces are dominated by the inertial forces of the body, not the local stress. However, the locality of the dominant modes can always be checked by performing offline model reduction.

CONCLUSION

In this paper, telesurgery and surgical simulation are introduced as parallel research problems of haptic interfacing to real and virtual surgical environments. The discussion on telesurgery is centered around the UC Berkeley/UC San Francisco Laparoscopic Telesurgical Workstation, focusing on the design of the system and high fidelity teleoperation controller design. The discussion on surgical simulation describes a testbed developed at the San Francisco, Berkeley, and Santa Barbara campuses of the University of California for research in understanding, assessing, and training perceptual motor skills and spatial skills in surgery, and critical steps of surgical procedures. Within this context, a novel method to interface with deformable objects addressing the issues resulting from the difference between the haptic and deformable model simulation update rates is presented.

ACKNOWLEDGMENTS

This research was supported in part by NSF under grants IRI-95-31837, CISE CDA-9726362, KDI BCS-9980122, and IIS-0083472, ONR under MURI grant N14-96-1-1200, ARO under MURI grant DaaH04-96-1-0341, and NASA under STTR grant NAS1-20288.

REFERENCES

Astley, O. R., & Hayward, V. (1998). Multirate haptic simulation achieved by coupling finite element meshes through Norton equivalents. *Proceedings of the IEEE International Conference on Robotics and Automation (ICRA'98)* (pp. 989–994).

Baillie, J., Jowell, P., Evangelou, H., Bickel, W., & Cotton, P. (1991). Use of computer graphics simulation for teaching of exible sigmoidoscopy. *Endoscopy, 23*, 126–129.

Blezek, D. J., Robb, R. A., Camp, J. J., Nauss, L. A., & Martin, D. P. (1998). Simulation of spinal nerve blocks for training anesthesiology residents. *SPIE Conference 3262 on Surgical-Assist Systems*, 45–53.

Bro-Nielsen, M. (1997). Fast finite elements for surgery simulation. In J. D. Westwood et al. (Eds.), *Medicine Meets Virtual Reality: 5*. Amsterdam: IOS Press.

Çavuşoğlu, M. C., Tendick, F., Cohn, M., & Sastry, S. S. (1999). A laparoscopic telesurgical workstation. *IEEE Transactions on Robotics and Automation, 15*(4), 728–739.

Çavuşoğlu, M. C. (2000). *Telesurgery and surgical simulation: Design, modeling, and evaluation of haptic interfaces to real and virtual surgical environments*. Unpublished Ph.D. dissertation, University of California, Berkeley.

Çavuşoğlu, M. C., & Tendick, F. (2000). Multirate simulation for high fidelity haptic interaction with deformable objects in virtual environments. *Proceedings of the IEEE International Conference on Robotics and Automation (ICRA 2000)* (pp. 2458–2465).

Çavuşoğlu, M. C., Sherman, A., & Tendick, F. (2001). Bilateral controller design for telemanipulation in soft environments. *Proceedings of the IEEE International Conference on Robotics and Automation (ICRA 2001)*.

Cleary, K. R., Lathan, C. E., & Carignan, C. (1998). Simulator/planner for CT-directed needle biopsy of the spine. *SPIE Conference 3262 on Surgical-Assist Systems*, 218–224.

Colgate, J. E., Stanley, M. C., & Brown, J. M. (1995). Issues in the haptic display of tool use. *Proceedings of the IEEE/RSJ International Conference on Intelligent Robotics and Systems (IROS'95)* (pp. 140–145).

Dhruv, N., & Tendick, F. (2000). Frequency dependence of compliance contrast detection. *Proceedings of the ASME Dynamic Systems and Control Division, ASME International Mechanical Engineering Congress and Exposition (IMECE 2000).*

Gibson, S., Samosky, J., Mor, A., Fyock, C., Grimson, E., & Kanade, T. (1997). Simulating arthroscopic knee surgery using volumetric object representations, real-time volume rendering and haptic feedback. In J. Troccaz, E. Grimson, & R. Mosges (Eds.), *Proceedings of the. First Joint Conference on Computer Vision, Virtual Reality and Robotics in Medicine and Medical Robotics and Computer-Assisted Surgery (CVRMed-MRCAS)* (pp. 368–378). Berlin: Springer.

Graves, E. (1993). *Vital and health statistics.* Data from the National Health Survey No. 122. U.S. Department of Health and Human Services, Hyattsville, MD.

Hill, J. W., Green, P. S, Jensen, J. F., Gorfu, Y., & Shah, A. S. (1994). Telepresence surgery demonstration system. *Proceedings of the IEEE International Conference on Robotics and Automation* (pp. 2302–2307).

Ikuta, K., Takeichi, M., & Namiki, T. (1998). Virtual endoscope system with force sensation. In W. M. Wells, A. Colchester, & S. Delp (Eds.), *Proceedings of the International Conferences on Medical Image Computing and Computer-Assisted Intervention (MICCAI)* (pp. 293–304). Berlin: Springer-Verlag.

Kuhnapfel, U. G., Kuhn, C., Hubner, M., Krumm, H.-G., Maass, H., & Neisius, B. (1997). The Karlsruhe endoscopic surgery trainer as an example for virtual reality in medical education. *Minimally Invasive Therapy and Allied Technologies, 6,* 122–125.

Madhani, A. J., Niemeyer, G., & Salisbury, J. K. (1998). The Black Falcon: A teleoperated surgical instrument for minimally invasive surgery. *Proceedings of the IEEE/RSJ International Conference on Intelligent Robots and Systems (IROS'98)*, Vol. 2 (pp. 936–944).

McCarthy, A., Harley, P., & Smallwood, R. (1999). Virtual arthroscopy training: Do the virtual skills developed match the real skills required? In J. D. Westwood et al. (Eds.), *Medicine meets virtual reality: 7* (pp. 221–227). Amsterdam: IOS Press.

Minsky, M., Ouh-young, M., Steele, Jr., O., Brooks, F. P., & Behensky, M. (1990). Feeling and seeing: Issues in force display. *Computer Graphics, 24,* 235–243. ACM Symposium on Interactive 3D Graphics.

Peifer, J. W., Curtis, W. D., & Sinclair, M. J. (1996). Applied virtual reality for simulation of endoscopic retrograde cholangio-pancreatography (ERCP). In S. J. Weghorst et al. (Eds.), *Medicine meets virtual reality: 4* (pp. 36–42). Amsterdam: IOS Press.

Smith, S., Wan, A., Taffinder, N., Read, S., Emery, R., & Darzi, A. (1999). Early experience and validation work with Procedicus VA: the Prosolvia virtual reality shoulder arthroscopy trainer. In J. D. Westwood et al. (Eds.), *Medicine Meets Virtual Reality: 7* (pp. 337–343). Amsterdam: IOS Press.

Szekely, G., Bajka, M., Brechbuhler, C., Dual, J., Enzler, R., Haller, U., et al. (1999). Virtual reality based surgery simulation for endoscopic gynaecology. In J. D. Westwood et al. (Eds.), *Medicine meets virtual reality: 7* (pp. 351–357). Amsterdam: IOS Press.

Taylor, R. H., Funda, J., Eldridge, B., Gomory, S., Gruben, K., LaRose, D., Talamini, M., Kavoussi, L., & Anderson, J. (1995). A telerobotics assistant for laparoscopic surgery. *IEEE Engineering in Medicine and Biology Magazine, 14*(3), 279–288.

Tendick, F., Downes, M., Goktekin, T., Çavuşoğlu, M. C., Feygin, D., Wu, X., Eyal, R., Hegarty, M., & Way, L. W. (2000). A virtual environment testbed for training laparoscopic surgical skills. *Presence, 9*(3), 236–255.

Tendick, F., Jennings, R. W., Tharp, G., & Stark, L. (1993). Sensing and manipulation problems in endoscopic surgery: Experiment, analysis and observation. *Presence, 2*(1), 66–81.

Way, L. W., Bhoyrul, S., & Mori, T. (Eds.). (1995). *Fundamentals of laparoscopic surgery.* Churchill Livingstone.

Wiet, G. J., Yagel, R., Stredney, D., Schmalbrock, P., Sessanna, D. J., Kurzion, Y., et al. (1997). A volumetric approach to virtual simulation of functional endoscopic sinus surgery. In K. S. Morgan et al. (Eds.), *Medicine meets virtual reality: 5* (pp. 167–179). Amsterdam: IOS Press.

Zhou, K., Doyle, J. C., & Glover, K. (1996). *Robust and optimal control.* New Jersey: Prentice Hall, Inc.

Understanding of User Behavior in Immersive Environments

Cyrus Shahabi, Leila Kaghazian, Soham Mehta, Amol Ghoting, Gautam Shanbhag, and Margaret L. McLaughlin

Immersive evironments can facilitate the virtual interaction between people, objects, places, and databases. Immersion has several varied practical applications. It can serve as an aid to engineering applications. Immersion can also be used to understand and aid the disabled. These environments result in the production of large amounts of data for transmission and storage. Data types such as images, audio, video, and text are an integral part of immersive environments and many researchers in the past have addressed their management. However, we have identified a set of less familiar data types, collectively termed *immersidata* (Shahabi, Barish, Ellenberger, Jiang, Kolahdouzan, Nam, & Zimmermann, 1999) that are specific to immersive environments. Immersidata are produced as a result of the user's interactions with an immersive environment.

Haptic data is a kind of immersidata that is used to describe the movement, rotation, and force associated with user-directed objects in an immersive environment. We use the CyberGlove as a haptic user interface to an immersive environment. The CyberGlove consists of several sensory devices that generate data at a continuous rate. The acquired data can be stored, queried, and analyzed for several applications.

In this chapter, we focus our attention on the analysis of haptic data with the objective of modeling these data in a database. A large number of diverse applications use haptic data. Each such application may need haptic data stored and modeled at different levels of abstraction. For now, we consider three levels of abstraction. First, in Shahabi, Barish, Kolahdouzan, Yao, Zimmermann, and Zhang (2001), we made our first attempt to model haptic data at the lowest level of abstraction. There, we dealt with raw haptic data conceptualized as time-series data sets. Such a modeling approach can be used for training applications such as comparing a teacher's and a student's session with the CyberGlove, to measure the student's proficiency at following the teacher. Second, in this chapter we move a level up from our previous work in using raw haptic data by trying to understand the *semantics* of hand actions, and we employ several learning techniques to develop this understanding. The application that we focus on is *limited vocabulary American Sign Language recognition* that involves the translation of American Sign Language (ASL) to spoken words. Finally, for the third level of abstraction, there exists a class of applications that need to analyze *preprocessed* data, as opposed to analyzing raw haptic data. An example would be the application of detecting the grasping behavior of the hand. This application might need the speed of the hand in space at a certain instant of time. We intend to study this final level of abstraction as part of our future work.

We analyzed the raw haptic data acquired from the CyberGlove to recognize different hand signs automatically. We investigated three different analysis techniques and evaluated their accuracy over a 10-sign vocabulary. First, Decision Tree was used for the supervised classification of haptic data. This technique generates decision trees derived from a particular data set. In particular, we used C4.5 Decision Tree to classify haptic data into static signs. Our experiments show that this technique can classify haptic data with an average error of 22%. Second, we utilized Bayesian Classifier for the classification of haptic data. Bayesian Classifier is a fast-supervised classification technique that generates fine-grained probability estimates over the data set. In our experiments, this technique resulted in an average error of 15.34%. Bayesian Classifier appears to be the fastest classification technique providing the best classification accuracy for our experiments. Finally, we used Supervised Neural Networks as a classification technique for the recognition of both static and dynamic signs. We show that with Neural Networks, static signs can be recognized with an average error of 20.18%.

Our research is distinct and novel in the following three respects. To begin with, we are distinct with respect to the framework we have used for our research and experiments. The framework is based upon the environment provided by the CyberGlove from Immersion Corporation. All our analysis and experiments were performed on raw haptic data without any kind of preprocessing. The analyzed data sets were collected and recorded by us, using an application developed at our laboratory. In addition to a novel framework, we have taken a new approach to modeling haptic data, which is based upon various learning techniques. To the best of our knowledge, we are the first to use Decision Trees for the analysis of raw haptic data. Bayesian Classifier was used in the past for the analysis of preprocessed haptic data; however, as far as we know this classification technique was never used for the analysis of raw haptic data. Neural Networks have been used for the analysis of haptic data in many research efforts in the past. Our contributions to the analysis of haptic data using Neural Networks include the use of Back-Propagation Neural Networks for static sign recognition and the use of Time-Delay Neural Networks for dynamic sign recognition. The comparison of these three techniques within the same environment and experimental setup is also novel and unique. Finally, the ultimate objective of our research is to model and store haptic data at different levels of abstraction. Consequently, each kind of application can use haptic data stored at the level of abstraction that is most suited to its analytical needs.

The remainder of this chapter is organized as follows. First, we describe how we acquired haptic data using the CyberGlove. Our proposed techniques, fixed sampling, group sampling, and adaptive sampling, allow us to also take the time dimension into consideration, which can be used for the analysis of haptic data for dynamic sign recognition. Next we explain the three learning techniques that we used for sign recognition. The results of our experiments in comparing the three analysis techniques are then reported. Finally, we cover other research efforts in sign language recognition and outline our future research plans.

DATA ACQUISITION

The development of haptic devices is in its infancy. We have focused our research and experiments on the CyberGrasp exoskeletal interface and accompanying CyberGlove, which consists of 33 sensors (Table 14-1). We use the CyberGrasp SDK to write handlers to record sensor data for our experiments whenever a sampling interrupt occurs.

The rate at which these handlers are called is thus the maximum rate at which we can sample the input signal, and it is a function of the CPU speed. We developed a multi-threaded double buffering technique to sample and record data asynchronously. One thread is associated with responding to the handler call and copying sensor data into a region of system memory. A second thread asynchronously writes this data to disk. The CPU was never 100% utilized during this process. This prevents our recording process from interfering with the rendering process. There is obvious room for optimization here, as we can run our experiments on a dual processor machine and adjust the priority for the second thread. We used 10 letters (A to I and L) from ASL for our experiment. We term each of these 10 letters a *sign*. The 22 sensor values (excluding sensors 23 to 33 in Table 14-1) are recorded in a log file for each sign made by a *subject,* termed as a *session*. Each session log file contains thousands of rows of sensor values sampled at some frequency, which depends on the sampling technique used. We denote each such row as a *snapshot*. We thus have thousands of snapshots for each session.

Table 14-1: CyberGrasp sensors.

Sensor Number	Sensor Description	Sensor Number	Sensor Description
1	Thumb roll sensor	15	Ring middle abduction
2	Thumb inner joint	16, 17, 18	Pinky inner, middle, outer joint
3	Thumb outer joint	19	Pinky ring abduction
4	Thumb index abduction	20	Palm arch
5, 6, 7	Index inner, middle, outer joint	21	Wrist flexion
8, 9, 10	Middle inner, middle, outer joint	22	Wrist abduction
11	Middle index abduction	23, 24, 25	x, y, z location
12, 13, 14	Ring inner, middle, outer joint	26, 27, 28	x, y, z abduction
		29 to 33	Forces for each finger

Sampling Techniques

To record several snapshots for each static sign made within a session, we need to sample the values of sensors for each subject making a sign. Moreover, ASL is not restricted to just static signs. It has some dynamism in signs (e.g., the letter 'J' involves moving the hand) and in words (e.g., 'BOX' is represented by depicting a rectangular shape). Hence, the time dimension needs to be considered while recording the data. Thus for both static and dynamic signs, the time at which each sensor is sampled impacts the storage and the exact representation of the data. If a sensor value is recorded too frequently, then we will obviously get a very accurate representation of the sensor data, but the storage requirements and the transmission requirements increase. On the other hand, if the sensor value is recorded intermittently, we would save storage space but at the same time, we would run the risk of recording an inaccurate representation of the data. Thus sampling the sensors at the rate that would lead to lower storage space requirements and better accuracy is central to the task of data acquisition for any haptic device. We designed and implemented the following sampling techniques for our experiments (see Shahabi et al., 2001, for details):

1. **Fixed Sampling**: Fixed sampling can be approached in two ways. One approach is to use the maximum sampling rate *rmax* allowed by the Software Development Kit. While this technique is easy to implement, it is wasteful since it records data for each sensor at each possible opportunity regardless of the sensor type or the semantics of the session. A more efficient method in-

volves finding the minimum sampling rate $r0$ required for the entire sensor set and then using that as the sampling rate. The disadvantage to this approach is that we need to identify $r0$ before we start sampling at that rate. In our experiments, $rmax$ was 80 Hz and $r0$ was found to be 67 Hz.

2. **Group Sampling**: The intuition for group sampling is that devices such as the CyberGrasp have different sensors that can be mapped to groups (e.g., all joints of a finger). We can isolate a sampling rate for each group and acquire data at different rates, based upon the group membership for each sensor. The advantage of this technique is its improvement over the fixed sampling technique by further reducing storage space and transmission requirements while maintaining accuracy. The difficulty in pursuing the grouped sampling strategy is in identifying the groups. Our intuition about natural groups may not be correct all the time.

3. **Adaptive Sampling**: This is a dynamic form of sampling where we try to find an optimum rate r_{ij} for each sensor i during a given window j of the session. The obvious advantage is the optimality of this approach. Adaptive sampling reduces bandwidth and storage requirements to far lower levels as compared to fixed or group sampling techniques. An additional benefit is that the sampling rate changes with the nature of the sessions. This makes the adaptive approach more efficient than the fixed or group sampling approach. The drawback is that it requires a complex implementation. We used a double buffering approach where a recording thread samples at the maximum rate possible and a storage thread performs the basic sampling methodology to identify the Nyquist sampling rates. This buffering approach means that some degree of real time acquisition is sacrificed.

The adaptive sampling approach looks particularly attractive because of its efficiency and robustness. In Shahabi et al. (2001), we provide details on these sampling techniques and the various tradeoffs among factors like bandwidth, storage, and computational complexity.

CLASSIFICATION METHODS

In this chapter we explore three different classification techniques and evaluate the accuracy of each technique to detect 10 different hand signs. The employed techniques are C4.5 Decision Tree, Bayesian Classifier, and Neural Networks. Each classification technique is implemented in two different stages, the training phase and the recognition phase. We base our experiments on the data obtained from the first 22 sensors, as we believe that these sensor values are the most important and they hold all the information required in detecting a sign.

C4.5 Decision Tree

Tree induction methods are considered to be supervised classification methods that generate decision trees derived from a particular data set. C4.5 uses the concept of information gain to construct a tree of classificatory decisions with respect to a previously chosen target classification (Quinlan, 1993). The information gain can be described as the effective decrease in entropy resulting from making a choice as to which attribute to use and at what level. In addition, the output of the system is available as a symbolic rule base, which allows the system developer to determine the factors that have an impact on the selection strategy for a given application domain. C4.5 starts with large sets of cases belonging to known classes of data. The cases, described by any mixture of nominal and numeric properties, are scrutinized for patterns that allow the classes to be reliably discriminated. These patterns are then expressed as models, in the form of decision trees or sets of *if-then* rules, which can be used to classify new cases, with an emphasis on making the models understandable as well as accurate (Quinlan, 1993).

C4.5 consists of two major modules: decision tree maker and rule generator. At first the entire data set gets partitioned to a smaller subplace to construct a decision tree. However, for real world databases the decision trees become huge in practice. Large decision trees are always difficult to understand and interpret. In general, it is often possible to prune a decision tree to obtain a simpler and more accurate tree. However, a tree may not provide any significant insight into data. Figure 14-1 illustrates a rule generated by C4.5 in our experiment for the letter H.

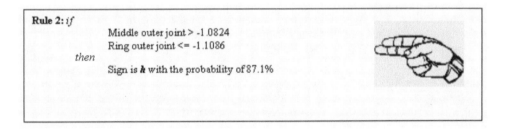

Rule 2: *if*

Middle outer joint > -1.0824
Ring outer joint <= -1.1086

then

Sign is *h* with the probability of 87.1%

Figure 14-1: Sample rule for the letter "H."

We employed C4.5 Decision Tree because it provides a model to build a sign recognition language. In addition, decision trees in general and C4.5 in particular provide results as a set of understandable and interpretable rules. Finally, C4.5 has been used as a benchmark in several other papers on machine learning, artificial intelligence, and data mining.

C4.5 complexity is $O(nt)$ where t is the number of tree nodes, and the number of tree nodes often grows as $O(n)$ where n is the number of sessions. The complexity for non-numeric data would be $O(n^2)$, for numeric data $O(n^2 \log n)$, and for mixed-type data, somewhere in between.

Bayesian Classification

Bayesian Classifier is a fast-supervised classification technique. This method is able to reduce the risk of various hypotheses about the patterns of missing data. Furthermore, it results in both an accurate analysis of an incomplete database and decisions about the predictions from the data. Naïve Bayesian Classification performs well if the values of the attributes for the sessions are independent. Although this assumption is almost always violated in practice, recent work (Domingos & Pazzani, 1996) has shown that naïve Bayesian learning is remarkably effective in practice and difficult to improve upon systematically. Bayesian Classifier is suitable for large-scale prediction and classification tasks on complex and incomplete datasets. We have decided to use the naïve Bayesian Classifier in our application, for the following reasons. First, it is efficient for both the training phase and the recognition phase. Second, its training time is linear in the number of examples and its recognition time is independent of the number of examples. Finally, it provides relatively fine-grained probability estimates that can be used to classify the new session (Elkan, 1997).

The computational complexity of Bayesian Classification is fairly low as compared to other classification techniques. Consider a session with f attributes, each with v values. Then with the naïve Bayesian classifier with e sessions, the training time is $O(ef)$ and hence independent of v.

Neural Networks

We use Neural Networks for the recognition of both static and dynamic signs with a limited vocabulary. Supervised learning is being used for the classification. In this section, we first explain the basics of the Neural Network architecture that we used and then discuss the setting of its parameters for our experiments. An artificial neuron receives its inputs from a number of other neurons or from an external stimulus. A weighted sum of these inputs constitutes the argument to an activation function. This activation function is generally nonlinear (e.g., hard-limiting, sigmoid, or threshold logic). The resulting value of the activation function is the output of the Artificial Neural Network (ANN). This output gets distributed along weighted connections to other neurons. The actual manner in which the connections are made defines the flow of information in the network and is called the architecture of the network. Useful architectural configurations include single-layer, multilayer, feed-forward, feedback, and lateral connectivity. The method used to adjust weights in the process of training the network is called the learning rule. Artificial neural systems are not programmed, they are taught. The learning can be supervised (e.g., back-propagation) or unsupervised (e.g., self-organizing maps).

A Multilayer Perceptron (MLP) is trained using the supervised-learning rule. The most commonly used algorithm for such training is the error-back-propagation-algorithm. MLPs are feed-forward networks with one or more layers of nodes between the input and output layers of nodes. These additional layers contain hidden nodes that are not directly connected to both the input and the output nodes. The capabilities of the multilayer perceptrons stem from the nonlinearity used in these nodes. The number of nodes in the hidden layer must be large enough to form a decision region that can be as complex as required by a given problem. A three-layer perceptron can form arbitrarily complex decision regions. Hence, usually, most problems can be solved by three-layer (one hidden layer) perceptrons.

A vital attribute of any trained neural network is the ability to extract the discriminant information from a large number of examples. Hence, Neural Networks are ideal for complex pattern-recognition problems whose solution requires knowledge that is difficult to specify but which is available in the form of examples. They have been studied within a variety of applications.

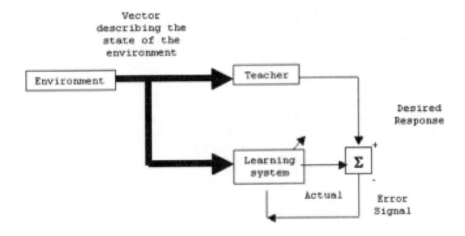

Figure 14-2: Supervised learning diagram with NN.

Supervised Learning Rules

Supervised learning is based upon the availability of an external teacher, as illustrated in Figure 14-2. The desired response represents the optimum action to be performed by the neural network. The network parameters are adjusted under the combined influence of the training vector and the error signal. This adjustment is carried out iteratively in a step-by-step fashion with the aim of eventually making the network emulate the teacher. When this condition is reached, we may remove the teacher and let the neural network deal with the environment thereafter entirely by itself. Figure 14-2 shows the supervised learning diagram. Examples of supervised learning algorithms include the back-propagation algorithm.

The Multilayer Perceptron Error BP Learning Algorithm

The back-propagation algorithm is an iterative algorithm designed to minimize the mean-squared error between the actual output of a feed-forward perceptron and the desired output. It requires continuous differentiable nonlinearity. The following equation assumes that a *sigmoid* logistic nonlinearity is used where the function $f(\beta)$ is:

$$f(\beta) = \frac{1}{(1 + e^{(\varphi - \beta)})} \tag{14.1}$$

The MLP back-propagation algorithm can be described as follows (Lippmann, 1987). First, we initialize the weights and the offsets of the neural network to *small* random values. The next step involves presenting the neural network with the input and the desired outputs. We present a *continuous value input-vector* x (0), x (1), ... x (n-1) and specify the desired outputs d (0), d (1), ... d (m-1). Since we use the net as a classifier, all the outputs are set to 0, except for the output that corresponds to the class to which the input belongs, which is set to 1. The input could be new on each trial or samples from the training set could be presented cyclically until the weights stabilize. The complete set of training inputs is called an *epoch*. Next, we compute the actual outputs. We use the sigmoid nonlinearity from Equation 14.1 and use the following equation to compute the output:

$$Y[y(0), y(1), ... y(m-1)]:$$

$$X'(j) = f\left(\sum_{i=0}^{N-1} \left(w(i)(j) \ast x(j) - \phi(j) \right) \right) \text{ where } 0 \le j \le (N_1 - 1) \tag{14.2}$$

The output for the subsequent hidden layer and the final layer is then computed using a similar equation. We recursively adjust the weights, starting from the output node, working back towards the hidden layer. We use the following formula to adjust the weights:

$$w(i)(j)(t+1) = w(i)(j)(t) + (\mu \ast \S(j) \ast x'(i)) \tag{14.3}$$

In this equation $w(i)(j)(t)$ is the weight from a hidden node i or from an input node j at time t, $x'(i)$ is either the output from node i or is an input, μ is a gain term, called the Learning Rate, and $\S(j)$ is an error term for node j. We then compute the error using the following equation. Mean Square Error: $E = 1/2 \left(\sum (d(j) - y(j))^2 \right)$

If the error is sufficiently small, we stop with the learning process; otherwise, we iterate through the above processes until the error is sufficiently small.

While the algorithm works its way forward to the output layer, the error gradient is actually computed from the output layer, backwards. Hence, it is historically being called the *back-propagation* algorithm. The Neural Network convergence is sensitive to the number, type, and sequence of inputs during training and the initialization of random weights.

Implementation of Neural Network Classification over Static Signs

We used the following parameters throughout our experimentation. These parameters were chosen to be optimal in given conditions and given data, over multiple runs.

Number of Nodes:

1. Input Layer: 22 nodes (one per sensor), plus one threshold value node for the next layer.

2. Hidden Layer: The MLP used one hidden layer with 10 nodes.

3. Output Layer: 10 nodes, each corresponding to one posture.

Training Data:

With each of the 23 inputs (22 haptic glove values + 1 threshold) connected to each of the 11 hidden layer neurons (10 neurons + 1 threshold), and again each of these hidden layer neurons being connected to each of the 10 output neurons, the total number of weights in the network is $(23 \times 10) + (11 \times 10) = 340$ weights.

For our experiment on static signs with 340 weights, we establish the cardinality of the training set to achieve a good generalization as propounded in Vapnik and Chervonenkis (1971), approximately 10 times more, to cross the "*VCDim*" threshold. We analyzed the recorded log file for every subject-sign pair session and extracted 40 snapshots from each of these 10 subjects. Hence, we have a training data set of 10 subjects, each making 10 signs, and for each sign-subject pair we have 40 snapshots, resulting in 4000 sets of sensor values. We train the network for 500 epochs. The error rate stabilizes to two places after the decimal. We generate pseudorandom weights, the range of which is −1.0 to +1.0. The data is affected by noise but was input to the neural network without any preprocessing except for normalization. It was normalized to the range of −1 to +1. We strove to make the neural network learn on raw haptic data so that it learns to handle noisy data. This can be useful when we try to use the classifier in real-time immersive applications.

Similar work has been done in Salomon and Weissmann (1999), wherein they use all possible groupings of two fingers as input. This yields very good results on the training set, but the ability of this approach to be generalized needs to be ascertained. Our approach provides a good promise for an overall generalization.

Theoretical Setup for Classification of Dynamic Signs

We were preparing to classify a restricted vocabulary of dynamic signs. Each subject might perform the same sign with different speeds. With a fixed sampling rate (Shahabi et al., 2001) for each session, the chances were high that we would have the same sign represented by a different number of samples in different sessions. This called for a way to incorporate the *temporal* dimension into the haptic data. We proposed to use the Time-Delay Neural Network (TDNN) approach towards this end.

Time-Delay Neural Network

TDNN (Waibel, 1989) is a multilayer feed-forward network and it is trained with the back-propagation algorithm. We used TDNN for haptic data because it can learn and represent relationships between events in time and it can learn complex nonlinear decision surfaces, especially with high-dimensional input data. TDNN can learn inherent features in a manner that is invariant under translation in time. This can be achieved by feeding the input sequence into a tapped delay line, and then feeding the taps from the delay line into an MLP.

Input and its Preprocessing

Taking the time dimension into consideration results in a major bottleneck for this architecture, since we can unfold the sequence only over a finite period of time. The delay line can only be of finite extent, requiring the same number of sensor-value-sets for every input. We decided upon this fixed typical number 'N' as follows:

N = (typical length of a gesture in seconds × sampling rate)

With different subjects performing the signs with different speeds, it is not possible to have constant N for every sign at a fixed sampling rate. Hence we plan to implement standard signal processing reparameterization techniques such as Dynamic Time Warping (DTW), which has been implemented earlier in the speech recognition literature (Rabiner & Juang, 1993) or similar techniques on glove-based inputs, discussed in Sandberg (1997).

After expanding the temporal dimension of a gesture spatially, we decided on the length of the input *window* as 2 seconds. With a fixed sampling rate of q sessions/second, we shall have *2q* as the length of delay line, giving $(2 \times q \times 22)$ input nodes.

Architecture

We planned to use two hidden layers and one output layer apart from the input layer. The number of units (nodes) in the output layer as well as the second hidden layer is V, where V is the size of the vocabulary. We planned to experiment with the exact number for the first hidden layer, though intuitively it seems that seven nodes to extract apparent features of a palm should be appropriate. Learning proceeds analogous to the back-propagation algorithm discussed earlier, although the optimal parameter settings will be different.

PERFORMANCE EVALUATION

We conducted several experiments to evaluate and compare our three different analysis techniques for ASL recognition: C4.5 Decision Tree, Bayesian Classifier, and Neural Networks. Below we explain our experimental setup, the results for each method and a comparison among these different techniques.

Experimental Setup

Fifteen subjects were selected to generate ASL signs from a given vocabulary. The subjects were asked to generate the following signs: A, B, C, D, E, F, G, H, I, and L, and data were stored in a database. The signs J and K are complicated and, taking the novice subjects into consideration, the signs were skipped for simplicity. We then determined the result of using each classification technique for ASL recognition. To evaluate each algorithm we used the cross-validation technique. We split the data into three sets, trained the system using two of the sets and conducted the tests using the third set. We implemented the test procedure in a round robin fashion and computed the average error (i.e., precision and recall). For example, if we split the data set into three different sets, denoted as *set-1*, *set-2* and *set-3*, we go through the following steps to perform the experiments in round robin and to compute the average error:

1. Train the data with *set-1* and *set-2* and test on *set-3*.
2. Train the data with *set-2* and *set-3* and test on *set-1*.
3. Train the data with *set-1* and *set-3* and test on *set-2*.

Storage of the Input

The Neural Network was trained using 4000 snapshots, as described earlier. This data was extracted from 100 session log files (10 subjects, 10 signs each, 40 different snapshots). The log files were produced as a result of recording the sessions.

For our experiments on static signs, we analyzed the recorded log files stored in a database and extracted the snapshot that has the sensor values consistent over a substantial period of time. To find such a snapshot, we used an SQL query similar to the one stated below. The following is an example of a simple SQL query when the database has only one snapshot and the generalization to more than one snapshot is straightforward. We assume the following table with attributes: CyberGlove (time, snapshot)

The following is a sample query:

```
SELECT snapshot FROM CyberGlove c1, CyberGlove c2
WHERE c2.snapshot IN(
SELECT max(time),snapshot FROM CyberGlove c3
WHERE c3.time < c2.time
ORDER by c3.time) AND
c1.snapshot - c2.snapshot < DELTA
ORDER BY (c1.snapshot - c2.snapshot)
```

Classification algorithms can be developed using incremental learning. The *learner* updates the rules, trees, and weights using the new session. The details of incremental learning are beyond the scope of this chapter and have been addressed in the machine learning literature. The details of the data acquisition techniques have been addressed earlier.

Results

Tables 14-5, 14-6, and 14-7 depict the precision and recall values for each of the classifiers. Figures 14-3 and 14-4 summarize the tables by comparing the average recognition error for each sign using the three different classification techniques.

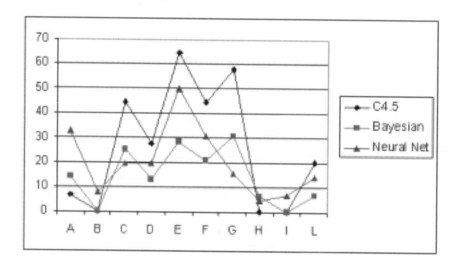

Figure 14-3: Sign recognition error.

	A	B	C	D	E	F	G	H	I	L
C4.5	6.6	0.0	44.4	27.7	64.4	44.4	57.7	0.0	0.0	20.0
Bayes-ian	14	0.0	25	13.06	28.4	20.83	30.52	6.4	0.0	6.4
Neural Net	32.8	7.87	19.6	19.5	50.04	30.55	15.73	4.9	6.67	14.24

Figure 14-4: Sign recognition error comparison.

The naïve Bayesian Classifier has the highest average accuracy with 50 training examples: 84.66% (with a standard deviation of 2.94). In contrast, C4.5 has an average of 78% ($SD = 8$) and Back-Propagation Neural Network has an average accuracy of 79.82% ($SD = 7.92$). Table 14-2 illustrates a comparison among the techniques.

Table 14-2: Overall classification error.

	Error	Standard Derivation
C4.5	22	8
Bayesian	15.34	2.94
Neural Net	20.18	7.92

Analysis

The Bayesian Classifier gives a very efficient and accurate result as compared to other classification techniques. The results of our experiments illustrate that C4.5 Decision Tree may not be suited to the task of sign recognition. Both Neural Networks and C4.5 have a large amount of variation in their performance. However, most often, C4.5 results are more interpretable and understandable. In contrast, the Neural Network architecture and procedure are not interpretable, and it is similar to a black box, in which case we only have access to input and output. Our experiments indicate that all of the classifiers performed relatively well on signs "B," "H," "I," and "L." Inspecting the signs, it appears that it was intuitive for subjects to perform these signs most consciously. Considering all the signs as points in a 22-dimension hyperspace, and computing the Euclidian distance among them, we realized that on the average, these four signs are quite apart from the rest of the signs, which justifies our observation. On the other hand, the letter "E" was quite close in distance to all the other signs and hence all classifiers were confused one way or the other with the recognition of letter "E."

The performance variation of individual classifiers over the signs can be traced back to the performance characteristics of each classifier. A neural network inherently tries to draw crisp distinguishing boundaries between groups of signs in the 22-dimensional hyperspace. Hence, it distinguished all the signs made when the hand is in the horizontal position (i.e., "C," "G," and "H") quite well (see Table 14-3). Note that although C4.5 was the best classifier for the letter "H," it had the minimum recognition error among the other letters with the neural net. With C4.5 and Bayesian Classifiers, the main assumption is that all features in a given space are independent. In general any strong dependency increases the level of error for both methods, while a low degree of dependency among features might have a negligible effect. Further, since C4.5 produces decisions based on a set of "if-then" rules, it tends to be relatively rigid, resulting in a high standard deviation as well as a high overall error. Since

Bayesian Classifier decides based on probability distribution of the input samples, it tends to perform quite well overall despite intuitive variations in performance of signs by different subjects.

Table 14-3: Best recognition technique for each sign.

A	B	C	D	E	F	G	H	I	L
C4.5	C4.5, B	NN	B	B	B	NN	C4.5	C4.5, B	C4.5

Table 14-4: Nearest neighbors for each sign in multidimensional space.

	Nearest				Farthest				Avg. Euclidean Distance
A	E	G	L	D	I	H	C	F	B	2.284044
B	F	C	D	H	E	I	A	G	L	3.308474
C	D	F	E	I	A	B	H	L	G	2.192405
D	C	E	G	L	A	F	H	I	B	2.031382
E	A	D	C	I	G	F	L	H	B	2.179982
F	C	B	D	E	I	A	H	G	L	2.578171
G	L	A	H	D	E	I	C	F	B	2.441150
H	G	D	A	L	E	C	F	I	B	2.627276
I	A	E	C	D	F	G	L	H	B	2.693604
L	G	D	A	E	H	C	I	F	B	2.697530

As illustrated in Table 14-8,[1] we see that the best classifier for a sign is not necessarily the one that confuses the sign with fewer other signs. The decision to choose a classifier from given classifiers becomes very much application-dependent. To illustrate this observation consider an example: C4.5 gives the highest average accuracy for sign L, but the other two techniques confuse L with fewer signs (one each) compared to that of C4.5 (three signs). In sum, we show that even with a small pool of snapshots, with a fast learner such as Naïve

---

[1]This table has been created using the previous tables. The percentage error > 0.00 for each sign is taken as confusion of that sign for the classifier. For Neural Networks, this threshold is fixed at 3.00.

Bayesian Classifier and an appropriate I/O design we can achieve an acceptable perform-ance.

Table 14-5: C4.5 Precision and recall.

	A	B	C	D	E	F	G	H	I	L
A	93.33	0.00	0.00	6.66	00.00	0.00	00.00	0.00	00.00	0.00
B	0.00	100.00	0.00	0.00	0.00	0.00	0.00	0.00	0.00	0.00
C	6.66	0.00	66.66	6.66	6.66	6.66	6.66	0.00	0.00	0.00
D	0.00	0.00	20.00	73.33	0.00	0.00	0.00	0.00	0.00	6.66
E	6.66	6.66	0.00	13.33	46.66	13.33	13.33	0.00	00.00	0.00
F	0.00	0.00	6.66	0.00	20.00	66.66	6.66	0.00	0.00	0.00
G	0.00	0.00	0.00	26.66	6.66	0.00	53.33	00.00	0.00	13.33
H	0.00	0.00	0.00	0.00	0.00	0.00	0.00	100.00	0.00	0.00
I	0.00	0.00	0.00	0.00	0.00	0.00	0.00	0.00	100.00	0.00
L	0.00	0.00	0.00	6.66	6.66	0.00	6.66	0.00	0.00	80.00

Table 14-6: Bayesian precision and recall.

	A	B	C	D	E	F	G	H	I	L
A	86.00	0.00	0.00	0.00	14.00	0.00	00.0	0.00	00.00	0.00
B	0.00	100.00	0.00	0.00	0.00	0.00	0.00	0.00	0.00	0.00
C	0.00	0.00	75.00	20.00	0.00	5.00	0.00	0.00	0.00	0.00
D	0.00	0.00	10.70	86.04	3.28	0.00	0.00	0.00	0.00	0.00
E	0.00	0.00	0.00	7.10	71.60	21.30	0.00	0.00	00.00	0.00
F	0.00	0.00	0.00	0.00	14.0	86.00	0.00	0.00	0.00	0.00
G	18.3	0.00	0.00	0.00	0.00	6.11	69.50	6.11	0.00	0.00
H	0.00	0.00	0.00	0.00	0.00	0.00	6.40	93.6	0.00	0.00
I	0.00	0.00	0.00	0.00	0.00	0.00	0.00	0.00	100.00	0.00
L	0.00	0.00	0.00	0.00	0.00	0.00	6.40	0.00	0.00	93.60

Table 14-7: Neural network precision (standard deviation) and recall.

	A	B	C	D	E	F	G	H	I	L
A	71.08, 15.78	1.65, 5.36	2.59, 5.62	3.90, 8.59	4.12, 10.56	3.92, 7.77	3.22, 4.67	3.00, 4.27	3.49, 7.20	2.10, 2.84
B	1.86, 4.20	93.49, 8.46	1.67, 3.02	0.57, 1.83	1.24, 2.74	0.53, 1.14	0.00, 0.00	0.12, 0.51	0.00, 0.00	0.00, 0.00
C	1.02, 3.44	9.00, 10.38	80.49, 10.17	7.12, 9.57	0.39, 2.77	0.92, 2.60	0.00, 0.00	0.41, 1.36	0.16, 1.11	0.04, 0.28
D	1.14, 5.54	1.25, 4.15	8.00, 10.66	82.08, 16.65	4.04, 8.50	2.98, 7.09	0.00, 0.00	0.25, 1.03	0.00, 0.00	0.00, 0.00
E	3.80, 8.16	0.20, 0.84	4.53, 10.62	11.63, 13.18	48.80, 21.13	11.49, 18.20	2.63, 6.84	2.45, 7.19	13.63, 21.59	0.22, 1.27
F	6.98, 11.13	0.96, 3.97	7.10, 12.74	1.18, 3.80	6.14, 9.57	75.14, 23.88	0.00, 0.00	0.80, 2.52	1.22, 3.97	0.06, 0.24
G	0.82, 3.72	1.49, 3.46	1.67, 3.56	3.61, 7.27	1.57, 5.38	0.00, 0.00	81.00, 17.87	1.65, 4.31	0.00, 0.00	7.94, 12.94
H	1.20, 4.14	1.06, 3.05	0.55, 1.83	1.29, 4.09	0.02, 0.14	0.12, 0.70	0.00, 0.00	95.51, 7.60	0.00, 0.00	0.00, 0.00
I	0.57, 2.72	0.67, 1.88	2.35, 4.67	1.43, 4.64	0.00, 0.00	0.29, 1.00	0.00, 0.00	0.35, 1.86	94.12, 9.11	0.00, 0.00
L	1.55, 4.46	0.78, 2.12	1.53, 3.33	0.88, 2.87	0.51, 2.55	0.24, 1.41	4.39, 8.20	0.86, 2.46	0.33, 1.42	88.57, 9.32

Table 14-8: Number of other signs with which each sign is confused for different classifiers.

Sign	Bayesian	C4.5	Neural Networks
A	1	1	5
B	0	0	0
C	2	5	2
D	2	2	2
E	2	5	5
F	1	3	3
G	3	3	2
H	1	0	0
I	0	0	0
L	1	3	1

RELATED WORK

Various research groups worldwide have been investigating the problem of sign recognition. We are aware of the two main approaches. The machine-vision-based approaches analyze the video and image data of a hand in motion. This includes both the 2D and 3D position and the orientation of one or two hands. The haptics-based approaches analyze the haptic data from a glove. Quantified values of the various degrees of freedom for the hand constitute the data. These efforts have resulted in the development of devices such as the CyberGlove.

We categorize the first approach based on the techniques employed. Darrell and Pentland (1993) discuss vision-based recognition with "Template Matching." Heap and Samaria (1995) employ Active Shape models. Several studies such as Martin and Crowley (1997) and Birk, Moeslund, and Madsen (1997) propose to use Principal Components Analysis. Yet another method of recognition using linear fingertips is described in Davis and Shah (1993). Banarase (1993) uses a neocognitron network. Like our group, various researchers have tried to recognize various sign languages all over the world using different methods. These include the American (ASL), Australian (AUSLAN), Japanese (JSL), and Taiwanese (TWL) Sign Languages, to name a few. As for the most relevant, the task of ASL recognition has been pursued by numerous research groups (Starner, 1995; Starner & Pentland, 1996; Vogler & Metaxas, 1997, to cite a few who use the Hidden Markov Models). An excellent survey of vision-based sign-recognition methods is provided in Wu and Huang (1999).

Using gloves and haptic data, Fels and Hinton (1995) employed a VPL Glove to carry out sign recognition. Takahashi and Kishino (1991) also investigated the understanding of the Japanese Kana manual alphabet (consisting of 46 signs) using a VPL DataGlove. They constructed a table that designated the positions of individual fingers and joints that would indicate a particular hand shape. They reported that they could successfully interpret 30 of the 46 signs, while the remaining 16 could not be reliably identified, due to a variety of constraints, such as the fact that they were moving gestures and that sufficient distinction could not be made in situations where fingertips touched. Sandberg (1997) provides an extensive coverage and employs a combination of Radial Basis Function Network and Bayesian Classifier to classify a hybrid vocabulary of static and dynamic hand signs. One more variant exists, Recurrent Neural Networks, used by Murakami and Taguchi (1991) for classifying Japanese sign language. We believe that the work by Salomon and Weissmann (1999) is the most relevant to our own, since it attempts to recognize signs using the same CyberGlove and back-propagation algorithm that we use. Hidden Markov Models are popular here too, which is reflected in Nam and Wohn (1996) and Lee and Yangsheng (1996). The latter is particularly relevant because it presents an application for learning signs through Hidden Markov Models, taking the data input from the CyberGlove. Wu, Wen, Yibo, Wei, and Bo (1998) use a combination of MLP-BP and HMM. Kadous (1995) used instance-based learning to classify Australian Sign Language. Newby (1993) studied glove-based template matching using a simple sum-of-squares approach. Rubine (1991) proposed feature extraction, while Charaphayan and Marble (1994) compared the approaches of Dynamic Programming, HMM, and Recurrent Neural Networks. Dorner and Hagen (1994) are unique in that they have taken a holistic approach to the question of ASL interpretation. Hagen's work involved building a deductive database that successfully translates from a standardized form of ASL into spoken English. Other neural network algorithms—Radial Basis Function Network (RBFN), Orthogonal Least Squares and Self-Organizing Maps—have also been tested on various kinds of data-glove inputs, in Lin (1998) and Ishikawa & Matsumura (1999). Salomon and Weissmann (2000) go further to show that RBFN is better than MLP-BP for classifying dynamic signs in an evolutionary manner.

Our work is distinct from all of the above-mentioned works because we provide a complete system including I/O unit, data acquisition module, database structure, and classification methods for ASL recognition. All our analysis is carried out on raw haptic data. We are the first to use Decision Tree for the analysis of haptic data. We are also the first to use Bayesian Classifier for *raw* (i.e., not preprocessed) haptic data analysis. Taking our framework into consideration, we are also the first to use Back-Propagation Neural Networks for the recognition of static signs. We propose to use Time-Delay Neural Networks for the recognition of dynamic signs.

CONCLUSION AND FUTURE WORK

In this chapter, we analyzed three different classification techniques for sign language recognition. We showed that Decision Tree, Bayesian Classifier, and Neural Networks could be used for ASL recognition. Bayesian Classifier proved to be the fastest classification technique among the three we evaluated. It also proved to have the best classification accuracy for static sign recognition. We carried out several preliminary experiments and the results of our experiments suggest that Bayesian Classifier can be used to develop a real-time sign language recognition system. However, more work needs to be carried out in order to establish the validity of our results, which are very encouraging in the early stages of experimentation. There are many open questions, obstacles, and problems that need to be dealt with before we achieve an efficient, reliable, and applicable ASL recognition system.

We intend to extend our work in several ways. First, in addition to Time-Delay Neural Networks, we also intend to investigate Evolving Fuzzy Neural Networks for the recognition of dynamic signs. It would be interesting to compare the effectiveness of these two techniques. Second, we want to use the analysis of haptic data that we pursued for the modeling of haptic data in a database. Our analysis would tell us what data we need to store at which level of abstraction for a given application. Third, we would like to analyze haptic data at the third level of abstraction, which requires us to analyze preprocessed haptic data. Finally, we propose to use shape recognition techniques for the recognition of dynamic signs based upon a fixed sign language vocabulary. Here, each dynamic sign would be considered to have a static part and an associated dynamic part. Using a shape to represent the dynamic part would let us view the dynamic sign in a time-independent manner. Such an approach would need an efficient technique for tracking the haptic device.

ACKNOWLEDGMENTS

This research has been funded in part by NSF grants EEC-9529152 (IMSC ERC) and ITR-0082826, NASA/JPL contract number 961518, DARPA and USAF under agreement number F30602-99-1-0524, and unrestricted cash/equipment gifts from NCR, IBM, Intel and SUN.

REFERENCES

Banarase, D. (1993). *Hand posture recognition with the neocognitron network*. Technical report, School of Electronic Engineering and Computer Systems, University College of North Wales.

Birk, H., Moeslund, T., & Madsen, C. (1997). Real-time recognition of hand alphabet gestures using Principal Component Analysis. In *Proceedings of The 10th Scandinavian Conference on Image Analysis*. Lappeenranta, Finland.

Cracknell, J., Cairns, A., Gregor, P., Ramsay, C., & Ricketts, I. (1994). Gesture recognition: An assessment of the performance of recurrent neural networks versus competing techniques. *IEE Colloquium on Applications of Neural Networks to Signal Processing*, Digest No. 1994/248, 8/1–8/3.

Darrell, T., & Pentland, A. (1993). *Recognition of space-time gestures using a distributed representation*. Technical Report No.197, MIT Media Laboratory Vision and Modeling Group.

Davis, J., & Shah, M. (1993). *Visual gesture recognition*. Technical report, University of Central Florida.

Domingos, P., & Pazzani, M. (1996). Beyond independence: Conditions for the optimality of the simple Bayesian classifier. In *Proceedings of the Thirteenth International Conference on Machine Learning* (pp. 105–112). Bari, Italy.

Dorner, B., & Hagen, E. (1994). Towards an American Sign Language interface. *Artificial Intelligence Review, 8*, 235–253.

Elkan, C. (1997). Boosting and naive Bayesian learning. In *Proceedings of International Conference on Knowledge Discovery in Databases*. Newport Beach, CA.

Fels, S., & Hinton, G. (1995). Glove-talk II: An adaptive gesture-to-format interface. In *Proceedings of Conference on Human Factors in Computing Systems*. Denver, CO.

Heap, A., & Samaria, F. (1995). Real-time hand tracking and gesture recognition using smart snakes. *Olivetti Research Limited Tech Report, 95*(1).

Ishikawa, M., & Matsumura, H. (1999). Recognition of a hand-gesture based on self-organization using a DataGlove. In *Proceedings of the Sixth International Conference on Neural Information Processing*, Vol. 2 (pp. 739–745). Kobe, Japan.

Kadous, W. (1995). *Grasp: Recognition of Australian Sign Language using instrumented gloves.* Bachelor's thesis, University of New South Wales, Australia.

Lee, C., & Yangsheng, X. (1996). Online interactive learning of gestures for human/robot interfaces. In *Proceedings of IEEE International Conference on Robotics and Automation*, Vol. 4 (pp. 2982–2987).

Lin, D. (1998). Spatio-temporal hand gesture recognition using neural networks. In *Proceedings of the IEEE International Joint Conference on Neural Networks*, Vol. 3 (pp. 1794–1798). Anchorage, AK.

Lippmann, R. (1987). An introduction to computing with Neural Nets. *IEEE Acoustics, Speech and Signal Processing Magazine*, 4(2), 4–22.

Martin, J., & Crowley, J. (1997). An appearance-based approach to gesture recognition. In *Lecture Notes in Computer Science*, Vol. 1311 (pp. 340–347). Springer Verlag.

Murakami, K., & Taguchi, H. (1991). Gesture recognition using recurrent neural networks. In *Proceedings of Human Factors in Computing Systems* (pp. 237–242). New Orleans, LA.

Nam, Y, & Wohn, K. (1996). Recognition of space-time hand-gestures using Hidden Markov Model. In *Proceedings of ACM Symposium on Virtual Reality Software and Technology* (pp. 51–58). Hong Kong.

Newby, G. (1993). Gesture recognition using statistical similarity. In *Proceedings of Virtual Reality and Persons with Disabilities*. Northridge, CA.

Quinlan, J. (1993). *C4.5: Programs for machine learning*. San Francisco, CA: Morgan Kaufmann.

Rabiner, L., & Juang, B. (1993). *Fundamentals of speech recognition*. Englewood Cliffs, NJ: Prentice Hall.

Rubine, D. (1991). Specifying gestures by example. *Computer Graphics*, 25(3), 329–337.

Salomon, R, & Weissmann, J. (1999). Gesture recognition for virtual reality applications using data glove and neural networks. In the *Proceedings of IEEE International Joint Conference on Neural Networks*, Washington, DC.

Salomon, R., & Weissmann, J. (2000). Evolutionary tuning of neural networks for gesture recognition. In *Proceedings of the Congress on Evolutionary Computation*, Vol. 2 (pp. 1528–1534). San Diego, CA.

Sandberg, A. (1997). *Gesture recognition using neural networks*. Master's thesis TRITA-NA-E9727, Royal Institute of Technology, Sweden.

Shahabi, C., Barish, G., Ellenberger, B. , Jiang, N., Kolahdouzan, M., Nam, A.,& Zimmermann, R. (1999). *Immersidata management: Challenges in management of data generated within an im-*

mersive environment. Paper presented at Fifth International Workshop on Multimedia Information Systems (MIS99), Palm Springs, CA.

Shahabi, C., Barish, G., Kolahdouzan, M., Yao, D., Zimmermann, R., Fu, K., & Zhang, L. (2001). Alternative techniques for the efficient acquisition of haptic data. In *Proceedings of ACM SIGMETRICS/Performance 2001.* Cambridge, MA.

Starner, T. (1995). *Visual recognition of American Sign Language using Hidden Markov Models.* Master's Thesis, Program in Media Arts & Sciences, MIT Media Laboratory.

Starner, T., & Pentland, A. (1996). *Real-time American Sign Language recognition from video using Hidden Markov Models.* Technical report, MIT, 1996.

Takahashi, T., & Kishino, F. (1991). Hand gesture coding based on experiments using a hand gesture interface device. *ACM SIGCHI Bulletin, 23*(2), 67–74.

Vapnik, V., & Chervonenkis, A. (1971). On the uniform convergence of relative frequencies of events to their probabilities. In *Theory of Probability and Its Applications*, Vol. 16 (pp. 262–280).

Vogler, C., & Metaxas, D. (1997). Adapting Hidden Markov Models for ASL recognition by using three-dimensional computer vision methods. In *Proceedings of the IEEE International Conference on Systems, Man and Cybernetics*, Orlando, FL.

Waibel, A., Hanazawa, T., Hinton, G., Shikano, K., & Lang, K. (1989). Phoneme recognition using time-delay neural networks. IEEE Transactions on Acoustics, Speech, and Signal Processing, *37*(3), 328–339.

Wu, J., Wen, G., Yibo, S., Wei, L., & Bo, P. (1998). A simple sign language recognition system based on data glove. *In Proceedings of Fourth International Conference on Signal Processing*, Vol. 2 (pp. 1257–1260). Beijing, China.

Wu, Y., & Huang, T. (1999). Vision-based gesture recognition: A review. In *Proceedings of the 3rd Gesture Workshop* (pp. 103–115). Gif-sur-Yvette, France.

A Haptic Exhibition of Daguerreotype Cases for USC's Fisher Gallery

Margaret Lazzari, Margaret L. McLaughlin, Jennifer Jaskowiak,
Wee Ling Wong, and Minoo Akbarian

Museums are the guardians of significant collections of objects and material essential to the study of the humanities. They serve the public not only through exhibitions and other programs, but also through the preservation of the primary resources of the nation's heritage. Art museums acquire and display works of art so that future generations of audiences may view and appreciate them. Without a strong commitment to collections care and the application of stringent guidelines for the preservation of objects, museums will be unable to meet their obligations to future generations. One of the most stringent of these guidelines is the "Please do not touch" policy that is standard in all museums, with only a few exceptions. This rule is both explicit (discreet placards placed about an installation bearing the words, "Please do not touch the objects.") and implied by the presence of gallery guards.

In the broadest sense, there are three primary reasons why objects are protected in museums by the "Please do not touch" policy. First of all, accidents happen. In a museum setting, touching an object on display can upset balance, causing a fragile vase to be smashed beyond repair or a delicately balanced assemblage to tumble. Deterring touching by visitors is a preventative measure to protect the longevity of the object. Secondly, objects need to be protected from theft. Smaller objects are subject to theft if left in the open to be handled by visitors. The third reason is the most complex and stems from conservation studies and practices aimed at protecting the object from damage caused by chemical reactions. These practices are generally unknown to the public, and the damage is not necessarily immediately evident, necessitating the utmost vigilance by collections care professionals.

Each medium employed by artists—marble, metals, granite, porcelain, ceramic, etc.—has different needs for care, different exposure thresholds, and reacts differently to the chemical effects of touch. Human skin produces oil that attracts dirt and harbors bacteria. These by-products deteriorate the chemical structure of the material, weakening the surface and endangering the object's stability. Over time, accumulations will alter the appearance of the object and violate the integrity of the chosen medium. (For example, a surface intended to be gritty gradually becomes smooth in the areas handled most frequently.)

Appropriate visitor behavior inside a museum is learned from a young age. As children, we are constantly reminded not to touch valuable or breakable objects so as to spare parents embarrassment and financial liability. Objects in the museum's collections—crown jewels, military equipment from important battles, Babe Ruth's uniform—represent important events in history. They are perceived by the visitor and presented by the museum as valuable, fragile, irreplaceable, and thus untouchable. Three-dimensional objects, though, can stir a different sensibility in the visitor.

Two-dimensional objects—paintings, drawings, and prints—are generally exhibited in frames and hung on walls. The experience of these works is completely visual and the nature of the installation is "hands off." On the other hand, three-dimensional objects require a different combination of senses to experience and understand them fully. They occupy a cube or sphere of space, rather than a plane, requiring the visitor to circumnavigate the piece to see all sides. As actual, rather than represented, objects, there is a desire to hold or handle them, to verify their existence by touch and weight. This desire is critical to the learning process and to how people experience art. Through the ongoing project described below, visitors will be able to "touch" selected objects, learn more about them, and have a richer museum experience without jeopardizing conservation standards.

HAPTICS FOR THE MUSEUM

Haptics involves the modality of touch and the sensation of shape and texture an observer feels when exploring a virtual object, such as a three-dimensional model of a porcelain vase from a museum, a tactile map, or a graphic designer's rendering of an imaginary object. The haptic devices used in our research at IMSC are the PHANToM and the Cyber-Grasp. The PHANToM is a desktop device that provides force feedback to the user's finger-tip. We currently employ two of these devices in our work, a 3 DOF and a 6 DOF model. The image below shows a researcher at IMSC exploring the surface of a digitized daguerreo-type case from the collection of the Seaver Center for Western Culture at the Natural History Museum of Los Angeles County. A visitor to the Haptic Museum can use these devices lo-cally at a desktop, in kiosk mode, or remotely over the network, retrieving models of the museum objects from our Web site.

Figure 15-1: User exploring a digitized daguerreotype case with the PHANToM.

In our most recent work we have addressed ourselves to haptic collaboration, in which users with the same and even different haptic devices can manipulate and explore the same virtual objects over the network, so that they can jointly examine an ancient pot or bronze figure and consider such questions as, "Why is there a hole on this side" or "Why is the sur-face so rough?" In short, haptics can be used to allow museum visitors to explore objects in ways that cannot be permitted in physical museums due to concerns about breakage and de-terioration of the object surface. (For another approach to the role of haptics in virtual mu-seums, see Baird, 2000). Although in the main our efforts have been directed toward explo-ration of art objects, we are also interested in extending our work to haptic exploration of objects in other cultural heritage domains and into visualization more generally. Further, we are currently attempting to modify our interfaces to make them accessible for the visually impaired (Hespanha, Sukhatme, McLaughlin, Akbarian, Garg, & Zhu, 2000; McLaughlin, Goldberg, Ellison, & Lucas, 1999; McLaughlin, Sukhatme, Hespanha, Shahabi, Ortega, & Medioni, 2000; Sukhatme, Hespanha, McLaughlin, Shahabi, & Ortega, 2000).

LOST AND FOUND: A HAPTIC EXHIBITION FOR USC'S FISHER GALLERY

Our current project in museum display was designed for the Fisher Gallery as part of its exhibition on early photographic processes, curated by graduate students in Museum Studies. The objects for the exhibition, some 90 daguerreotypes, ambrotypes, and tintypes, were on loan from a larger collection of 500 objects at the Seaver Center for Western Culture at the Natural History Museum of Los Angeles County. Many have never been displayed publicly. These objects, in particular the daguerreotypes, are treasured for their subtle tactile qualities. The portrait faces are striking and memorable, yet also silvery and elusive, shifting with every change of light. The images are encased in velvet, leather, glass, and metal trim, all wonderful elements to touch.

Figure 15-2: Unidentified photographer (American, active c. 1840–1850). Portrait of a Woman, c. 1846–1847, daguerreotype.

Daguerreotypes, ambrotypes, and tintypes are the earliest forms of photography. They are nonpaper processes, one-of-a-kind objects on copper, glass, or iron plates. Ambrotypes and tintypes were less expensive processes that required less sitting time for the subject. They were often the only portraits taken by Americans during the nineteenth century. They are reminiscent of miniature portraits on ivory that are experienced personally and individually. As items that were once personal remembrances, they seem to belong in one's hand. However, the fragility of these objects (they are highly sensitive to light, dust, fingerprints, and pollutants) demands that they be displayed in cases, under carefully controlled light.

We are attempting to restore some of the personal interaction to the display of daguerreotypes. Specifically, we propose:

1. To simulate the sense of touch, by means of a haptic device that allows the user to experience the variations in the shapes and surface textures of the daguerreotype cases.
2. To allow viewers to "tilt" the daguerreotype case as it is displayed on a computer monitor, so that they can see the subtle image shifts that occur with light changes.

In this report, we describe our efforts to date with respect to (1) and our preliminary research with respect to (2).

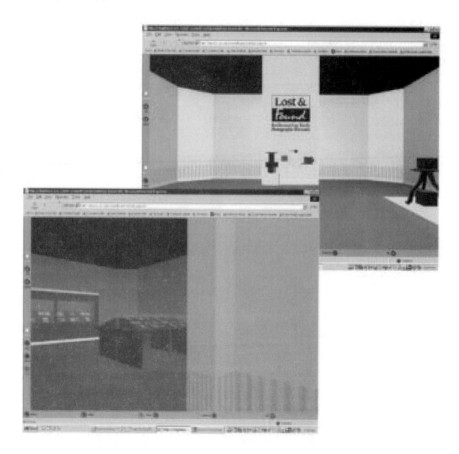

Figure 15-3: VRML model of the Fisher Gallery with cabinets housing models of daguerreotype cases.

The *Lost and Found* exhibition was made available simultaneously in kiosk mode at USC's Fisher Gallery and displayed on the Interactive Art Museum web site (*digimuse.usc.edu*); in the latter case visitors to the site with appropriate haptic devices can explore the three-dimensional models of the daguerreotype cases remotely. Objects are being housed in "cabinets" in a gallery inside a VRML model of the Fisher. The exhibition is accompanied by didactics produced by Museum Studies graduate students.

ISSUES IN THE ACQUISITION OF THREE-DIMENSIONAL OBJECTS FOR MUSEUM DISPLAY

A primary issue in haptics for museum display is the acquisition of models of art objects. Our current digitization system (LightScribe) enables us to generate fully-textured models in 3D Studio format compatible with our haptic rendering systems. The digitization system utilizes a computer-controlled turntable, which can capture images from many views and reconstruct the solid surface of objects.

Figure 15-4: Digitization system for acquisition of models of three-dimensional objects.

Our previous manual method of digitization left us with some holes on the object's surface and the bottom. The application software for our current system is equipped with decimation tools, which enables us to control the number of polygons that are created from 100 to 1,000,000. Because the system is easy to use, we can assign digitization tasks to students and concentrate our energies on some unresolved digitization problems, such as the ones we describe below.

Digitization of objects for which all or parts of the surface are porous or reflective is particularly challenging. The three-dimensional model is generated from images taken as the object rotates on a turntable. Highly reflective surfaces introduce error into the digitizing process. Consider the picture above, and think of a point on the surface of the daguerreotype case as it rotates on the turntable. If the image captured at some particular angle shows only reflection, the system considers the point as a point in the environment, not on the object. If from other angles the image has information, it will be considered a point on the object. The result is that when images are combined, an incomplete and inaccurate model results, with missing parts and/or added pieces. A further issue is that the image of a highly reflective surface depends on the angle from which the image was taken and the environment that is currently being reflected on the surface. The surface is like a mirror in that if we move it, we get a different view. Capturing the surface would require a kind of continuous real-time imaging. In short, there is no way to model the highly reflective surface of daguerreotypes and like objects.

Another challenge during the digitization process is the use of manual scanning with a hand-held laser scanner for acquiring the fine points of surface texture. Although such meticulous work is necessary for modeling the surface (as opposed to the shape) of the object, it is difficult for the operator of the hand-held scanner to hold it steady, and the sampling of points is largely unsystematic.

As noted above, the presence of reflective surfaces on three-dimensional objects can introduce error into the digitizing process, in particular creating holes in the model where images showing reflection contribute contradictory or misleading information to the algorithm for producing the solid model. The reflective surface can be masked with paper (see Figure 15-5), provided that it is comparatively flat and that the paper can be made to adhere to the surface without elements that would be harmful to it. The reflective surface can be scanned and incorporated back into the model later to produce a "quasimodel" in which the shape is faithful to the original although the representation of the angle of view on the image itself will not be.

With respect to the issue of the acquisition of surface texture with the hand-held scanner, we are currently investigating methods of automating the process to ensure smooth capture and systematic sampling of points.

To deal with the difficulties inherent in capturing the two-dimensional surface of a reflective object we are proposing the idea of a "virtual mirror" (Figure 15-6).

Daguerreotypes are the result of the earliest form of photography, a direct-positive process that creates a highly detailed image on a sheet of copper plated with a thin coat of silver without the use of a negative.   The silver-plated copper sheet had first to be cleaned and polished until the surface looked like a mirror, and the process of permanently fixing the image necessitated a complex chemical procedure that took great care. Daguerreotype images, most of which were portraits, require viewing from a certain angle. The challenge is to develop a method to capture and present the essence of looking into a mirror and seeing an image superimposed on your reflection in real time. In addition, our solution has to be practical and sturdy enough to withstand the numerous visitors who will experience the museum exhibition. Our solution is the virtual mirror, comprising a hardware, software, and digital database access system.

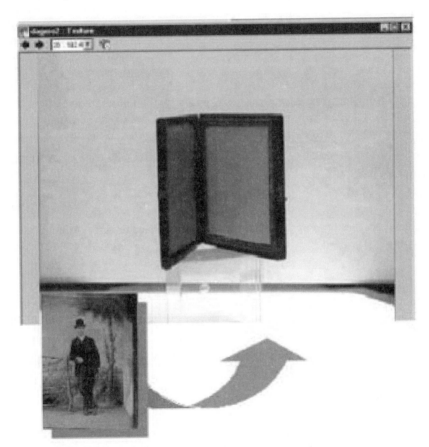

Figure 15-5: Model of daguerreotype case created with reflective surface masked.

Our approach is to create a hands-on application hardware device that consists of a video camera to capture and transmit live video, a gyrosensor to track coordinate information with respect to pan, tilt, and rotation, and a display screen to receive the processed image and coordinate information. The software will be required to perform several graphics functionalities in real time, such as a left-to-right mirror transformation, compositing, and alpha blending. There is the challenge of synchronizing multiple image streams and sensor input in real time, performing the required graphics and vision algorithms in real-time, as well as network access to the database of digitized images. The solution will require the integration of graphics, network, and software vision modules with hardware dependent parts, as depicted in Figure 15-6. IMSC's Media Immersion Environment architecture will serve as the platform to allow museum visitors an opportunity to experience the virtual daguerreotype.

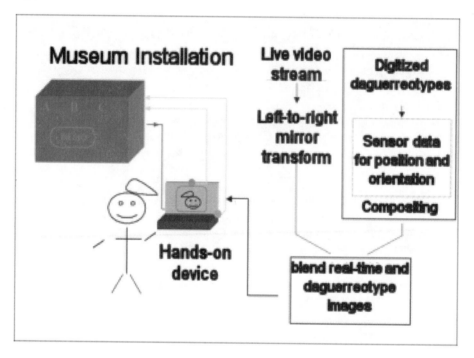

Figure 15-6: Schematic of a virtual mirror.

ACKNOWLEDGMENTS

A collaboration with the Natural History Museum of Los Angeles County, *Lost & Found: Rediscovering Early Photographic Processes* was made possible through the generous support of the USC Arts Initiative, the Graduate and Professional Student Senate, and the Department of Art History in the College of Letters, Arts and Sciences. The Lost and Found exhibition was held at the USC Fisher Gallery March 7 through April 21, 2001. This research was funded in part by the Integrated Media Systems Center, a National Science Foundation Engineering Research Center, Cooperative Agreement No. EEC-9529152.

REFERENCES

Baird, B. (2000). Using haptics and sound in a virtual gallery. *Preprints of the Fifth Annual PHANToM User's Group Workshop*, Given Institute, Aspen, CO.

Hespanha, J., Sukhatme, G., McLaughlin, M., Akbarian, M., Garg, R., & Zhu, W. (2000). Hetereogeneous haptic collaboration over the Internet. *Preprints of the Fifth Phantom User's Group Workshop*, Aspen, CO.

McLaughlin, M. L., Goldberg, S. G., Ellison, N. B., & Lucas, J. (1999). Measuring Internet audiences: Patrons of an online art museum. In S. Jones (Ed.), *Doing Internet research* (pp. 163-178). Sage Publications.

McLaughlin, M. L., Sukhatme, G., Hespanha, J., Shahabi, C., & Ortega, A. (2000). Touch in immersive environments. Proceedings of the EVA 2000 Conference on Electronic Imaging and the Visual Arts, Edinburgh, Scotland.

Sukhatme, G., Hespanha, J., McLaughlin, M., Shahabi, C., & Ortega, A, (2000). Touch in immersive environments. *Proceedings of the EVA 2000 Conference on Electronic Imaging and the Visual Arts*, Edinburgh, Scotland.

Index

J

Javascript, 8–9
Joystick, 73–74, 83, 88–89

K

Kalman Filter, 14

L

Latency, 12–14
LHX, 17
Lookup table, 77–81, 83, 88

M

Magnetic levitation, 48
MEMS arrays, 3
Military training, 7–8
Mobility training, 6
Moving objects, 97, 107, 110, 111
Museum display, 5
    Acquisition of objects for, 265–268
    Haptic collaboration in, 262
Multimodal systems, 194–204
    Comparative effects of haptics and sound
        in, 194–204
    Cognitive load theory and, 195–196
    Completion time in, 198, 200, 202
    Dual-coding theory and, 195
    Experience of haptic devices and, 197,
        198, 200
    Experimental tasks in, 196–197, 201–
        202
    Interference in, 195, 207
    Performance accuracy in, 198–202
    Redundancy and, 196
Multiuser environments, 13–14, 17, 137–168

N

Non-uniformly sampled data-sets, 111

O

One-port system, 53–55
OpenGL volumizer API, 108

P

Painting, Sculpting, and CAD, 6
Passivity Controller, 51, 53, 55–56
    See also PC
Passivity Observer, 51, 53, 56
    See also PO
PC, 51, 53–54, 56–68
    See also Passivity Controller
Perception, 194–204
Performance, task, 10, 18–19
Permanent magnet motor, 83
Pitch, 10
Plane and probe method, 13
PMDC, 83–84
PO, 51, 53–54, 56, 57, 59–62
    See also Passivity Observer
Presence, 50
Proprioception, 21
Probe, sensing with, 180–193
    Active and passive touch and, 187–191,
        193
    Effect of probe size and, 185–186
    Effect of exploration speed and, 187-190
    Effects of force and, 190-191
    Interelement spacing, effects of, 182–
        186, 189, 191
    Mechanoreceptors and, 182–183
    Perception of roughness and, 182-185
    Psychophysical roughness function and,
        186
    Vibratory coding and, 181, 183–184
Proxy, 33–34, 43
Psychophysics, 1, 7, 20, 206, 213
Puma, 43–44

The Editors

Dr. Margaret L. McLaughlin is Professor of Communication at the Annenberg School for Communication, University of Southern California, and a Key Investigator at USC's Integrated Media Systems Center, a National Science Foundation Engineering Research Center in multimedia. She is Principal Investigator for IMSC's "Haptic Museum" project. Support for the project has been provided by the Annenberg Center, the USC Arts Initiative, and Hitachi America, Inc., as well as NSF. Her current research focuses on the application of haptics (simulating the sense of touch) in immersive virtual environments. She has written or coedited a number of books, including *Touch in Virtual Environments*, *Network and Netplay: Virtual Groups on the Internet* (American Association for Artificial Intelligence/MIT Press), *Explaining One's Self to Others* (Lawrence Erlbaum), *The Psychology of Tactical Communication* (Multilingual Matters), and *Conversation: How Talk is Organized* (Sage). Since 1995 she has been co-Editor of the scholarly publication *Journal of Computer-Mediated Communication*. She also served as Editor of *Communication Monographs* and *Communication Yearbook*, Volumes 9 and 10. She is a former President of the International Communication Association, and a former Chair of the ICA Publications Committee. In addition to her work in haptics, her current research on Internet privacy issues has been supported by a grant from the Ford Foundation.

Dr. João P. Hespanha received the Licenciatura and an M.S. degree in electrical and computer engineering from Instituto Superior Técnico, Lisbon, Portugal, in 1991 and 1993, respectively, and M.S. and Ph.D. degrees in electrical engineering and applied science from Yale University, New Haven, Connecticut, in 1994 and 1998, respectively. For his Ph.D. work, Dr. Hespanha received Yale University's Henry Prentiss Becton Graduate Prize for exceptional achievement in research in engineering and applied science. Dr. Hespanha has been Assistant Professor of Electrical Engineering-Systems at the University of Southern California since 1999. Dr. Hespanha's research interests include adaptive nonlinear control, hybrid and switched systems, probabilistic games, the use of vision in feedback control, and the control of haptic devices. Dr. Hespanha is the author of over 60 technical papers, the recipient of a NSF CAREER Award (2001), and the PI and co-PI on several federally funded projects.

Dr. Gaurav S. Sukhatme is an Assistant Professor in the Computer Science Department at the University of Southern California and the associate director of the Robotics Research Laboratories. He is also affiliated with the Integrated Media Systems Center (IMSC). His research interests include embedded systems, mobile robots, multi-robot coordination, sensor fusion for robot fault tolerance, and human-robot interfaces. Dr. Sukhatme has served as PI or co-PI on several NSF, DARPA, and NASA grants and contracts. He directs the Robotic Embedded Systems Lab, which performs research in two related areas: 1) The control and coordination of large numbers of distributed embedded systems (heterogeneous information sources including embedded devices, sensors, and mobile robots), and 2) The control of systems with complex dynamics (hopping robots, robotic helicopters, and haptic interfaces). Dr. Sukhatme is a member of AAAI, IEEE, and the ACM and has served on several conference program committees. He has published more than 50 technical papers, three book chapters, and several workshop papers in the areas of mobile robot evaluation, mobile robot cooperation, embedded systems, and haptic interfaces.

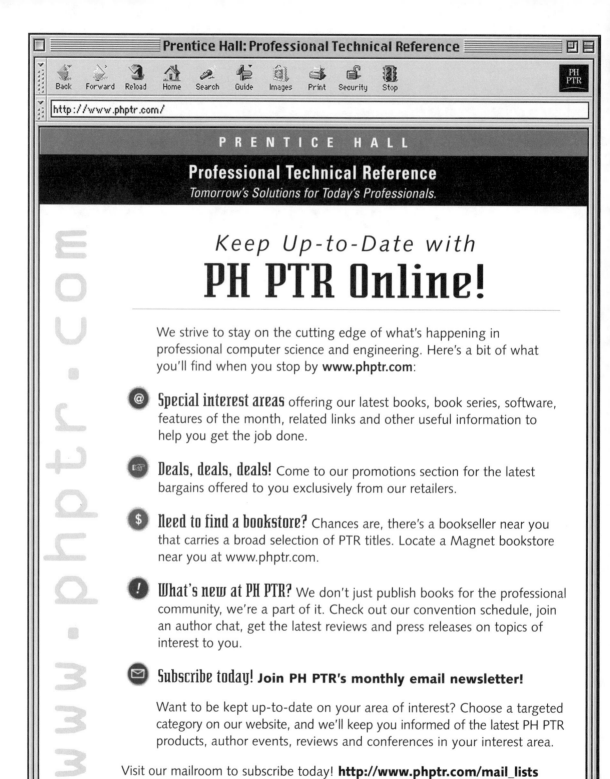